Power Grab

. . . .

Power Grab

························

How the National Education Association Is Betraying Our Children

G. GREGORY MOO, PH.D.

Since 1947
**REGNERY
PUBLISHING, INC.**
An Eagle Publishing Company • Washington, DC

Library of Congress Cataloging-in-Publication Data

Moo, G. Gregory.
    Power grab : the National Education Association's betrayal of
our children / G. Gregory Moo.
        p. cm.
    Includes bibliographical references and index.
    ISBN 0-89526-315-7 (alk. paper)
    1. National Education Association of the United States—History.
    2. National Education Association of the United States—Political
    activity. 3. Public schools—United States—History. I. Title.
LB2844.53.U6 M66 1999
370'.6'073—dc21

                                                            99-28645
                                                            CIP

Published in the United States by
Regnery Publishing, Inc.
An Eagle Publishing Company
One Massachusetts Avenue, NW
Washington, DC 20001

Distributed to the trade by
National Book Network
4720-A Boston Way
Lanham, MD 20706

Printed on acid-free paper
Manufactured in the United States of America

10 9 8 7 6 5 4 3 2 1

Books are available in quantity for promotional or premium use. Write to Director of Special Sales, Regnery Publishing, Inc., One Massachusetts Avenue, NW, Washington, DC 20001, for information on discounts and terms or call (202) 216-0600.

For
Janice Ann Moo
and the many others who
love teaching

Greg Moo can be reached at
<ggmoo@TeacherUnionWatch.com>.

Contents

Foreword

....

Peter Brimelow
Senior Editor of Forbes *Magazine*

ACTION AND REACTION are equal and opposite, at least according to Sir Isaac Newton, the famous physicist known (or, all too possibly nowadays, not known) to every high school student.

Which is a comforting thought when contemplating the seemingly irresistible rise of the teacher unions. Although the National Education Association (NEA) has been around since 1857, as Dr. Moo points out in the informative pages that follow, it was for most of that time a professional association. It only mutated into a labor union in the early 1960s. It only endorsed its first strike in 1971. The smaller American Federation of Teachers, which was founded in 1916, has always aspired to be a labor union. But it was simply unable to fully function as one until governments in the 1960s conceded the special privilege of collective bargaining to public sector union officials—yet another ill-starred innovation from that decade of notoriously ill-starred innovations. Both unions are now contemplating merger.

Thirty years or so is a very short time in the life of an institution. It is a relatively short time in the life of an individual. (At least, to me it increasingly looks like a relatively short time). The result is that many of today's politicians and pundits reached adulthood before the new reality of the teacher unions had unfolded. They haven't really noticed that it exists at all.

And the unions have helped them not to notice. Shortly after my coauthor Leslie Spencer and I published our cover stories on the NEA in *Forbes* magazine, I was contacted by a producer for a major television news show. He wanted to do a special on the NEA. Months later, I asked him what had happened. "Oh," he said, "we changed our minds—it turned out there wasn't one big teacher union, there were all these *little local unions*"

The hydra-headed nature of the NEA, and the fact that all the heads do ultimately belong to the same militant Washington, D.C.–based body, is carefully explained by Dr. Moo in his first chapter.

Power Grab is an important step in the inevitable reaction to the teacher union revolution. It contains a wealth of information on the history and current reality of the unions, written from the unusual perspective of a former high school principal who is also an expert consultant in organization and planning management. It traces the unions' power to its institutional and legal roots—this hydra did not grow spontaneously, but depends critically on legal privileges— and it concludes with specific recommendations about what to do. Because, as Dr. Moo emphasizes, in the last analysis there can be no reform of American education without reform of the teacher unions. If I have any complaint about *Power Grab*, it is that the author is too modest. We see tantalizing glimpses of his life—eighteen years in Alaska, where his sons, because they worked in the family salmon fishing business in the summer, were counted as "migrant students" by the local school district in order to claim federal grants, an example of the corrupting game of government funding. But it is clear he has more to say from personal experience. I hope he will one day say it. His voice is a welcome and valuable addition to this great debate.

Prologue

"Power Unmatched By Any Other"

"NEA will become a political power second to no other special interest group.... NEA will organize this profession from top to bottom into logical operational units that can move swiftly and effectively with power unmatched by any other organized group in the nation."[1]

—*Sam Lambert, 1967, NEA Executive Secretary*

THE NATIONAL EDUCATION ASSOCIATION'S GOALS are two: first, to create one national system of education and second, to control this national system to NEA's own ends. Its strategy is to corrupt and subvert the concept and mechanisms of local control of education in order to capture neighborhood schools and then to use public resources to build its power and promote its ultraliberal social agenda—even to the detriment of students' academic proficiency. NEA's long-standing effort to control teachers and direct public schools makes it a clear and present danger to the rights of states to conduct education, to the rights of communities to retain local control of their schools, and to the rights of parents to secure an education for their children that honors their own values and priorities.

To continue expanding its control over schools, teachers, children, and ideas, the NEA works tirelessly to extend its power. Its method of achieving this is plainly visible in the union officials' relentless push for more monopoly collective bargaining privileges and more power over teachers. The union bosses' growing control comes directly from their ability to compel teachers to pay union dues and submit to representation by NEA. In *The Constitution of Liberty*, Friedrich A. Von Hayek, noted scholar and recipient of the Nobel Prize in economics, warned about the assault of unbridled union power on the principles of freedom. He wrote:

> It cannot be stressed enough that the coercion which unions have been permitted to exercise contrary to all principles of freedom under law is primarily the coercion of fellow workers. Whatever true coercive power unions may be able to wield over employers is a consequence of this primary power of coercing other workers; the coercion of employers would lose most of its objectionable character if unions were deprived of this power to exact unwilling support.[2]

Brimelow and Spencer, in their 1993 *Forbes* article entitled, "The National Extortion Association," described NEA as a "near-monopoly supplier to a government-enforced monopoly consumer."[3] NEA, a nongovernment entity, is the largest labor union in the nation. It is unique among labor unions in that it is exempt from property taxes, not subject to National Labor Relations prohibitions on union takeover of management prerogatives, and excluded from Hatch Act restrictions on political activity.

NEA, largely because of its power to compel teachers to join, has 2.2 million members[4]; a $742 million annual income from national, state, and local membership dues[5]; millions in additional income from publishing, insurance, and credit card businesses; and a monopolistic death grip on public education. It has used its wealth and power to become the major force working against student-centered, parent-responsive changes in education.

These pages deal with NEA's accumulation and use of power—often seized outside democratic processes—to construct a national system of education that NEA controls to its own ends. This examination of NEA and its influence on education reveals that the changes many parents and taxpayers seek are not possible while NEA remains the dominant and controlling force in public education.

THE ISSUE OF CONTROL

When I was a high school principal, I often commented that NEA was out of control. But the truth is otherwise. NEA is very much in control. NEA officials have been gaining control of public schools ever since your great-grandparents' primary school days—for over fourteen decades—and their grab for unilateral power over curricula, programs, personnel, policies, budgets, and children grows daily.

We are seeing the cumulative effect of this power on the quality of education in our communities' schools. As a result, a civil war is beginning in America's cities and towns. Citizens are fighting the war in their legislative offices, state departments of education, schools, and homes. It is a war to determine who will direct the teachers, run the schools, and control the hearts and minds of our children. Right now, there is little doubt that NEA is winning on many issues.

On the issue of money for education, NEA officials maintain that every citizen must pay ever-increasing taxes to support NEA and its concept of what education should be. NEA's two-part solution to education's problems is: (1) increase taxes, and (2) give more money to public education. Since 1944 NEA bosses have actively worked against any effort to limit federal taxes.[6] Given its tax-and-spend history, NEA officials have recently, and not surprisingly, lobbied against a balanced-budget amendment.[7] To be certain that taxes, and NEA revenues, do increase, NEA bosses must control political processes at all levels and venues of government. They already do in many and are inexorably moving in on the holdouts.

Meanwhile, parents and taxpayers, who have consistently demonstrated a willingness to support public education, are learning that the singular act of adding more money to education budgets does not produce the results they want. And as this book will show, not all of the money goes to support education; much of it finds it way into NEA's coffers and favored causes.

NEA, the largest labor union in the nation, is not about education or children; NEA is about power—the aggressive, relentless pursuit of power. Most teachers are hard-working people who hold our children's and our communities' futures in their hands. But many teachers have been coerced into following NEA's false lead as the labor union extends its power over children, over teachers, over administrators, over boards of education, over the public, and over political processes.

There are differences in NEA's and the public's goals for public education. These stem from fundamental differences in worldviews and values. Consider the issue of input versus output. NEA is preoccupied with input. Public education, it holds, needs more input—more teachers, schools, computers, and money—and more power for NEA.

The paying public sees things quite differently: it is asking about output. What have children learned, good or bad? The battle is about who controls the rhetoric, frames the discussions, asks the questions, and spends the money. NEA does not take its direction from the desires of parents, the concerns of teachers, or the needs of children. NEA is about controlling teachers and the educational process to achieve its union goals and ultraliberal political ends.

CHOICES

Parents and taxpayers have three choices: (1) do nothing, accept the status quo, and thereby support NEA's continued control of public education, (2) work within the existing system to effect needed reforms, or (3) work outside the existing system to create better ways to educate, to learn, and to teach.

The first choice is unacceptable to a growing number of parents, taxpayers, and educators. The long chain of evidence strongly suggests that the second choice stands little chance of success by itself; NEA is too entrenched and too powerful. The second choice can be effective only when combined with the third choice—to introduce educational, political, and economic forces that challenge NEA's control over teachers and public education. This third choice would greatly diminish NEA's control and permit entrepreneurial ventures in education, supported by market forces, to bring a wide variety of educational services to parents.

For its part, NEA wisely understands that change is inevitable; and because compulsory unionism allows it to control almost all who would work within the existing system to effect reform, NEA nominally supports the second choice as the least bitter pill. As for choice three, NEA is currently spending huge sums of money and applying its considerable political power to defeat outside-the-system reform efforts.

For example, to stop California's 1993 Proposition 174 voucher initiative, NEA, its California State affiliate (CTA), and CTA's PACs raised an estimated $18 million, against the initiative's proponents' $2.7 million, to defeat Proposition 174. A similar fate befell choice initiatives in Oregon in 1990, Colorado in 1992, and in Washington State in 1996.[8]

We have trusted our teachers, and we must. We have trusted our teachers' labor union, and we must not.

NEA controls teachers and the venerable PTA, it limits and directs boards of education and superintendents, and it carries great weight in state and national legislation. If parents are to obtain the education they want for their children, and if communities and states are to have the educated citizenry and productive work force they must have, NEA's monopoly over teachers and education must end. To take control of their neighborhood schools, parents, teachers, and taxpayers must find ways to color outside the lines.

A NOTE OF INTEREST

During the early stages of this book, Keith Geiger was president of NEA-national. The Geiger era is now over. Geiger aggressively pursued forced unionism, monopoly collective bargaining, and NEA's ultraliberal agenda. Under Geiger's direction, NEA became recognized as the number-one obstacle to better public schools.

At the 1996 annual Representative Assembly meeting, delegates elected Bob Chase as NEA's new president. At this writing, Chase appeared to be quietly focused on the internal workings and external image of NEA and is, as a result, less visible to the general public than was Geiger.

"AN INSTITUTION AT RISK"—THE KAMBER REPORT

One of the new regime's first actions under Bob Chase was to order an outside review of NEA to assess why the union is so widely mistrusted and disliked. NEA thought only of manipulating public opinion—not of changing its mission or its methods. On February 14, 1997, after three months of interviews and study, the Kamber Group's forty-three–page report was completed. In strongly stated warnings, the outside consultants cautioned that "[w]hat NEA faces now is a crisis" and that "[t]o survive, much less to prevail over its critics, the NEA must shift to a *crisis mode of operations*"[9] (emphasis added).

As recent actions show, Bob Chase has taken to heart the Kamber Group's recommendation that NEA shore up its deteriorating image by pursuing three objectives:

- "Establish itself as *the* champion of public education through a new initiative to produce *better teachers, better students, better public schools,* and to call for all Americans to join in the challenge."[10]
- "Stake out a clear risk through a crisis strategy that seeks to win not by silencing the opposition, but by co-opting the other side's turf so the NEA can direct reform discussions rather than having them dictated to it. This will require at least two or three substantive measures the NEA should adopt, or call for, to improve schools (for example, standards for teachers, standards for students, Association accountability for teaching quality)."[11]
- "Use NEA's strongest assets—put teachers front and center—pull in allies, and work to protect public education."[12]

At the end of the report's preface, the Kamber Group again warned, "*Public education, and the NEA, are in a state of crisis. And only a focused, crisis-oriented mode of operations will suffice....*" Throughout its history, the NEA has adapted to the challenges facing it, from its founding days as a professional organization through the movement to collective bargaining. Today, the challenge requires another adaptation of its role. If NEA does so, then its best years will still lie ahead. And it will truly be the Association's finest hour.[13]

"Crisis" is a recurring theme in the Kamber Report. In a crisis, normal rules do not apply and people are often willing to give over their independence and accept the control of a strong central force. In the upcoming series of NEA-declared crises within NEA and within public education, NEA bosses will reposition themselves and NEA to be that strong central force.

Chase's apparent rush to establish an image of NEA's willingness to expel "some bad teachers" from school—"it's our job as a union to... get them out of the classroom"[14]—and NEA's push for national standards for teachers and for student learning are examples of "co-opting" the public's growing concern about public education to the ends of supporting NEA's goals and tactics. This is nothing more than a smoke screen to divert parents' and taxpayers' attention away from NEA bosses' continuing efforts unilaterally to control teachers and public education. Nothing has changed but the rhetoric.

And even the rhetoric has not changed all that much. In his introductory remarks to the *NEA Handbook 1996–1997*, Bob Chase wrote that the union has "a profound responsibility to help lead our great nation."[15] Reaffirming the high command's ultraliberal bent, Chase warned the rank-and-file that "[t]here is a tremendous paradox in America today. On the one hand, we are confronted by a cacophony of brash, extremist voices, disproportionately from the far right-wing. And on the other hand, we have a great silent mass of good, decent Americans who seem cowed by these bullying voices."[16]

FIRST PRINCIPLES

The American people have chosen freedom as a founding principle and a defining goal. I too subscribe to this belief. I support a teacher's right freely to choose to join or not join a union. I support the right of a teacher to freely negotiate with his or her employer for the best possible salary and benefits, so long as the teacher is free to use his or her own indivudual merits to justify the case for compensation. I also support a teacher's freedom to choose to have someone represent him or her in negotiations. And I support a teacher's right to back liberal or conservative political and educational agendas so long as the teacher's choice is freely made.

The problem is that many teachers do not have this freedom to choose. They are forced to support NEA. They are forced to pay dues to support an agenda that affronts their political beliefs and violates their moral code. They are forced to do so because our government grants monopoly power to NEA, requiring that teachers pay union dues—dues that NEA uses to bolster and expand its control of teachers and schools. Dues that NEA uses not to represent the best interests of teachers, but principally to preserve and expand its power to pursue its own goals.

The problem manifests itself simply and directly. In a three-step process, NEA uses its government-given and government-protected monopoly power to (1) coerce individual teachers to form and/or support a local NEA chapter, whereupon it (2) uses the local chapter's might to pressure the school board, so that (3) the school board concedes its demand—which, at its core, is that teachers be required to pay union dues as a condition of employment.

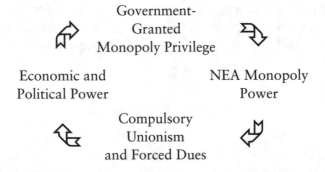

NEA'S MONOPOLY PRIVILEGE-POWER CIRCLE

It is a self-supporting circle of government-granted monopoly privilege that creates monopoly power that begets forced dues that produce economic and political power that buys government's continued protection of NEA's monopoly privilege. NEA's power is no less than a grave threat to our democratic process.

PURPOSE

The aim of this book is to inform and, through informing, better enable teachers, parents, and communities to increase their voices in shaping the education they wish for their children. It does not suggest a magic potion or single cure for the dilemmas that confront American education. But it will examine NEA and show that NEA must be forcefully and effectively challenged before any real change can come to education.

Good ideas cannot take root unless and until teachers and principals can work harmoniously in locally controlled public and private schools. As it stands now, NEA benefits from the staged turmoil, created conflict, and manufactured lack of direction that debilitate public education.

The evidence is plain. The need to act is clear. Acting on the evidence will require courage and conviction. *Power Grab* is for those of us who want to examine the evidence and give control of education back to those who put students first.

I base many of my comments on first-hand observations gained from twenty years' experience in public schools as a teacher (and NEA member), a high school principal, and a district administrator.

In the process of retaking control of our children's education, we must take great care not to harm the many good teachers and administrators who desperately want to break from under NEA's heavy hand. When they see that parents and taxpayers will no longer tolerate NEA's monopolistic control of education, good educators will join the fight to restore education to its original purpose—to teach our children.

A WORD ABOUT TEACHERS

While I am critical of NEA and its domination of public education, I have high regard and respect for teachers. Teachers are one-half of the teacher–student equation from which education, both public and private, either prospers or perishes. Through years of experience, I have observed that NEA inhibits teachers' creativity and mischannels precious time and energy that teachers could productively invest in their teaching. In truth, NEA directs teachers away from teaching and toward union activism, and rewards most highly those who commit the greatest time and energy to union causes.

Teachers are doing the best they can in an educational world awash with politics and muddied goals, a world where NEA is often the only voice they are allowed to hear. I wish to make clear that my criticism of NEA does not extend to teachers; the two are distinctly different. Yet, because teachers are fundamentally important to the process of education, they must accept a major responsibility for bringing healthy changes to education. But teachers will need the help of parents and taxpayers to put the gremlin back in the bottle.

NEA will not be as powerful, nor as radical, when teachers refuse to accept NEA's goals, antidemocratic strategies, and heavy-handed tactics. My wife, a teacher and school librarian of seventeen years, said during one of our book-in-progress conversations, "Teachers shouldn't be forced to support what they don't support."

So long as NEA can use compulsory unionism to control teachers, superintendents, school boards, and the political process, within-the-existing-system reform efforts will continue to be fruitless.

On occasion, I write about the American Federation of Teachers (AFT), an 907,000-member rival teacher union.[17] There are differences between the two unions, but their strategies and tactics are depressingly similar. While their latest two efforts to merge—December 1994 and July 1998—ended unproductively, NEA and AFT union bosses are no longer at loggerheads as once they were.[18]

In *Handbook 1996–1997* NEA told its 2,264,000 members that during 1995–1996, it had met five times with AFT to discuss unification. NEA also confided that its Board of Directors has approved a bylaw amendment that permits the NEA Executive Committee to "affiliate an NEA local association that also shall be affiliated with the American Federation of Teachers."[19] There is little doubt that NEA and AFT will meet again and again until, one day, they use forced unionism laws to become a three-million–member superunion that will have financial* and political clout like no labor union America has ever seen. In his spring 1997 *City Journal* article, Sol Stern estimated that together, the "two unions would take in about $1.3 billion each year from dues and employ 6,000 full-time staff members."[20]

I have used "NEA" throughout this book as synonymous with NEA-national, NEA-state, and NEA-local. This is appropriate for at least two reasons: (1) because NEA's own policies prescribe "unification" of its three operational levels; and (2) because this reference accurately depicts the tight link that exists between NEA-national and its state and local affiliates. In some places, I have delineated NEA-state or NEA-local to clarify a specific point.

ACKNOWLEDGMENTS

It is normal to absolve colleagues from the faults of a book. This I do, of course. And I hereby recognize that people who helped with this writing may not believe as I believe. All of this is to say that these

---

*—**NEA's income** for 1993 was **$742 million** as reported by Brimelow and Spencer in "The National Extortion Association," *Forbes* (7 June 1993), page 79.

—**AFT's income** for the period of 1 July 1991 to 30 June 1992, as reported by Haar, Lieberman, and Troy in *The NEA and AFT: Teacher Unions in Power and Politics*, was $79.5 million with assets of $42,171,670 and liabilities of $28,056,704 (pages 48–49).

—Based on these numbers, a merger of the two unions would create a superunion of over three million members with revenues in excess $821.5 million. By the time the two unions merge, and it seems they eventually will, their combined revenues might well be in excess of $1 billion annually.

writings are mine alone and do not necessarily represent the views and beliefs of any who helped.

Normally it is not difficult to thank openly the people who have helped with a writing project. In this case, however, naming people may place them and their careers in jeopardy. To these people I owe a debt of gratitude. There are several people I can, and will, acknowledge.

My wife's nudging and support were pivotal to my initial considerations of this writing project and to the project itself. I would have written nary a word had Jan not encouraged and supported the idea. As our sons grew older and experienced more of life, they both encouraged me to write about my own life experiences. Our son Cooper is a gifted writer of stories and our son Casey is a talented writer of songs.

Early in the research phase, Carolyn Kirsch, interlibrary loan librarian at Peninsula College in Port Angeles, Washington, was extremely efficient and determined in finding materials invaluable to my work. The library system of the University of Washington in Seattle granted me library privileges and made the resources of that grand institution available. When stuck on a point of history, I asked for and received the able assistance of Professor C. H. (Toby) Edson, University of Oregon, who once again helped me clarify my thinking and provided just the right example.

At the National Right to Work Legal Defense Foundation, an organization with a thirty-year history of defending teacher rights, I thank a host of people for the valuable resources and assistance they gave. Stefan Gleason, without whose commitment there would have been no book, made the Foundation's research resources available, and Jean Griffith coordinated research requests. Late in the writing, Timothy McConville, labor-law attorney and former executive at Right to Work, thoroughly reviewed a draft manuscript and offered many important suggestions. I owe him much for his ideas and clarifying questions. I also received invaluable assistance from Milton Chappell, Bruce Cameron, Mary Kate Grover, and Sandra Papandrea who do legal, research, and organizational work at Right to Work. At Concerned Educators Against Forced Unionism, Mark Mix and Cathy Jones helped me find people to interview and materials to read. With their help, I had the opportunity to talk with Dr. Robert Roesser, Jerry

Belhumeur, and Jo Seker; I heard their personal accounts and documented their resolute commitment to doing right for right reasons.

David Kendrick and the people at the National Institute for Labor Relations Research assisted in finding information on union violence, labor laws relating to union violence, and UniServ activities. Joseph Overton at the Mackinac Center for Public Policy helped me to comprehend NEA's activities in the state of Michigan. At the Evergreen Freedom Foundation in Washington State, Theresa Rudacille was instrumental in locating important information. The late Donald L. Stetson read early stages of the manuscript and shared his good ideas. And Mitchell Pearlstein of the Center of the American Experiment in Minneapolis made suggestions and connected me with valuable sources of information.

I am in debt to Don Mai, teacher, and Sam Daniel, counselor, who shared with me their deep understanding of students, teachers, and schools. To fellow high school administrator Bruce Nachtshiem, with his quiet and steady commitment to honor and duty, I owe much. I am grateful to Sharon Bodkin and Patti Ruple for proving that ethical, caring board members do, indeed, make a difference. I thank my first superintendent, Robert C. Greene, for teaching by example the importance of loyalty and support. And, because he is a person who every day demonstrates that it is possible to be a moral leader, an ethical human being, and an effective superintendent, I thank Dr. Fred Pomeroy. Since gratitude is also due to one who quietly listens, I thank Donald E. Cole, longtime family friend, for years of encouragement and support. I very much appreciate the good work of David Dortman, whose skilled editing contributed greatly. And to those I dare not mention, I thank you and wish you strength and good fortune in your commitment to teach children and lead schools.

THE TITLE

This book's title is *Power Grab: How the National Education Association Is Betraying Our Children*. Such was not always the case. During earlier stages of research and writing, the working title was *Hidden Hierarchies: The National Education Association's Reach for Power*. Although it is no longer relevant to the present title, the origins of this yet-to-be used title are still relevant to the book—since they shed light on NEA's philosophical roots and long-standing determination to control American public education.

In *Managers of Virtue*, David Tyack and Elisabeth Hansot observed how, in the early years of NEA, a self-selected group of progressive educators, concerned about growing discord in NEA, worked to "retain effective control of NEA and its component state associations" in order to assure that "a 'united profession' in education [would achieve] political power at the state and national levels."[21] This small group of progressives set out to gain control of public education in the late 1800s and early 1900s. Tyack and Hansot described the process: "Through building **hidden hierarchies** in such professional associations—in effect, powerful private governments—and in less evident ways in other groups such as the [1915 semi-secret] Cleveland Conference and their own placement networks, they gained an awesome power to define their own solutions to education problems. Their solutions, accepted as standard by a growing number of educators, helped to create a potent professional consensus despite the formal decentralization of power in American public education."[22]

The second half of the working title comes from the writings and speeches of George S. Counts, an outspoken progressive who taught at Teachers College, Columbia University. An admirer of the Soviet Union's social experiments, Counts was a critic of capitalism, competition, and private ownership of property. Counts' *Dare the School Build a New Social Order?* published in 1932 declared: "That the teachers should deliberately **reach for power** and then make the most of their conquest is my firm conviction. To the extent that they are permitted to fashion the curriculum and the procedures of the school they will definitely and positively influence the social attitudes, ideals, and behavior of the coming generation.... It is my observation that the men and women who have affected the course of human events are those who have not hesitated to use the power that has come to them."[23]

Assumptions

In writing this book, I have worked from these assumptions.

- The majority of teachers, parents, and taxpayers know little of NEA's history, intentions, strategies, and tactics.
- Once informed, teachers, parents, and taxpayers will investigate further and take actions consistent with their own and their communities' best interests.
- The absence of federal government involvement in and control over states' educational responsibilities and communities' local control of education will encourage and allow teachers, parents, and taxpayers to create more effective and efficient educational innovations that, in turn, are more responsive and responsible to mechanisms of local control.
- It is not too late to reclaim state responsibility for education, protect the principles of local control of education, and, in so doing, make it possible for educators, parents, and communities to take back control of local school districts and neighborhood schools.

Section One
NEA: Past, Present, and Future

....

Chapter One:
From Small Beginnings

Chapter Two:
NEA: Present and Future

1

....

From Small Beginnings

"Things are always at their best in their beginning."
—*Blaise Pascal,* Lettres Provinciales, 1656–1657

ON AUGUST 26, 1857, forty-three educators met in Philadelphia to create a new organization they would call the National Teachers Association.* They were grammar school teachers, school principals, and presidents of state teacher associations who, as their charter would proclaim, came together "to elevate the character and advance the interests of the profession of teaching, and to promote the cause of popular education in the United States."[1] This was to become the largest, most powerful, and arguably the most politically ambitious labor union the nation has ever known.

From its inception over 140 years ago, NEA has labored to capture and control public education in the United States. For over fourteen decades, NEA has steadily gained power over teachers, schools, and education.

One of NEA's first major victories came only ten years after its beginning. On March 2, 1867, President Andrew Johnson signed a bill that created the federal Office of Education.[2] This was the result

---

*In 1870, the National Teachers Association became the National Education Association. In this writing, I refer to this predecessor of the National Education Association as "NEA."

of a decade-long NEA effort, which began at its first meeting in Philadelphia, when Thomas W. Valentine, president of the New York Teachers Association, told those assembled, "The time will come when our government will have its education department just as it now has one for agriculture."[3] Even then, NEA envisioned a national system that would centralize education in the federal government.

NEA has labored through four eras to expand its original purpose, and its effect. During the Conference-Convention-Committee Era, from 1857 until 1920, NEA learned how to use groups of educators to develop and impose educational policy at a nationwide level. This was a time of foundation-building, a time when NEA planted its roots in big government and set its sights on centralized control of education. The Pre-Monopoly Unionism Era, 1920 through 1961, was a time for recruitment, reorganization, and redirection. The Monopoly Unionism Era, 1961 to 1976, marked a period when NEA learned from Saul Alinsky the philosophy and strategies of radicalism and the use of power politics to achieve its goals of centralizing and controlling education. NEA's Political Era began in 1976. In that year, NEA officially endorsed a presidential candidate—Jimmy Carter. During this Political Era, NEA has achieved incredible wealth and cultivated powerful connections in state legislatures and in Washington, D.C. We live in this era.

THE CONFERENCE-CONVENTION-COMMITTEE ERA (1857–1920)

In the beginning, NEA held annual conventions and worked within state and local organizations. According to Edgar B. Wesley, author of *NEA: The First Hundred Years*, NEA functioned as "a kind of super holding company that coordinated the state associations by providing an annual convention where ideas, theories, and principles were discussed."[4] At these conventions, educators from various states and communities, who were well acquainted with their unique educational programs, began learning about standardized curricula and teaching practices—NEA's one-best-way approach to education.

Explaining NEA's role in establishing its one best way, Allan West, a thirty-year NEA official and former acting NEA secretary, wrote,

"The similarity of the state school systems can be accounted for in large measure by the early influence of the national forum provided by the annual conventions of the NEA. For it was in those conventions that out of the diversity of approaches agreement was reached concerning the purposes of education and the best professional practices."[5] "By this process," West explained, "rather than by proscription* of a central government, was fashioned a *national policy of education.*"[6] (emphasis added)

Refuting the framers of the Constitution who believed each sovereign state should act as an independent laboratory of democracy and rejecting the concept of local control of education, NEA aggressively worked to give education a national policy, a singularity of purpose, and a uniform structure.

NEA's methods were effective. They created the stifling similarity of curricula and teaching methods we have today. Disallowing historical, cultural, and regional differences, NEA's "national policy of education" produced cookie-cutter programs, curricula, teaching methodology, and even school buildings across the states.

As previously explained, in its early years NEA worked through conventions and special committees to push its national educational policy. Of these efforts, two became landmarks in the history of American public education.

On July 9, 1892, NEA appointed the Committee of Ten. Composed of seven representatives from higher education and three from secondary schools, the committee worked to standardize the high school curriculum which was, at that time, differently constituted in the various schools and states across the nation. In the first portion of its December 4, 1893, report, the committee recommended "every subject which is taught at all in a secondary school

---

*West's use of the word "proscription" in this sentence seems inconsistent with his conclusion that even without "direction... from the central government," NEA conventions forged "a national policy of education." The context and West's conclusion suggest that "proscription" should have been "prescription." (For a full reading of West's thoughts on this topic, see page 5 of *The National Education Association: The Power Base for Education*, The Free Press.)

should be taught in the same way and to the same extent to every pupil as he pursues it, no matter what the probable destination of the pupil may be, or at what point his education is to cease."[7] (Ninety years later, the National Commission on Excellence in Education would recommend much the same thing in its April 26, 1983, report, *A Nation At Risk.*)

In 1905, G. Stanley Hall, then president of Clark University and author of a two-volume work on adolescence, criticized the Committee of Ten's report for its wholesale move to uniformity in subjects taught, content, and teaching method. He accused the framers of the report of believing "knowledge is no longer bullion from the mine, but is minted with a hallmark of at least some numerical committee."[8] Hall punctuated his criticism by concluding, "The evils of this dominance are now so great and manifest that they must be transient."[9] As a practical matter, the committee's report made little impact on the actual practice of education at that time. It did, however, support NEA's long-range goal for a centralized and standardized educational system. And it served a secondary function—it began to establish NEA as a force in educational policy debates.

Twenty-five years later, NEA appointed another group. In 1918 the Commission on the Reorganization of Secondary Education studied the evolving needs of society and recommended adjustments in the secondary school curriculum. This NEA-appointed commission took a different view of secondary education than had the Committee of Ten. This time, NEA's argument for a centrally controlled secondary curriculum was based on significant changes that were occurring in the United States.

The twenty-five years between 1893 and 1918 had brought a multitude of significant changes to America. It was a time of transformation and turbulence: the influx of millions of immigrants gave a new social mix to America's cities and towns, and most newcomers were not fluent in English and knew little of America's customs. The nation was embroiled in the War to End All Wars; there had been race riots in East St. Louis in 1918; and in 1919 there would be bloody race riots in Chicago. Many believed that schools should instill American values in these disparate populations so their behavior would be in keeping with American beliefs and practices. NEA's commission determined that the one-size-fits-all secondary program recommended in 1893 no longer met the needs of the new times.

The Commission on the Reorganization of Secondary Education presented its report, "The Cardinal Principles of Secondary Education," in 1918. It advocated a differentiated curriculum—one they believed better matched the needs and goals of individual students. But like its predecessor, this new commission intended that its curriculum be the only one used in every secondary school across the nation.

The commission's curriculum was not focused solely on academics. This curriculum was to give students the tools they needed to live and function in a changing society. The commission framed its recommendations in the first sentence: "Secondary education should be determined by the needs of the society to be served, the character of the individual to be educated, and the knowledge of educational theory and practice available."[10]

In a statement that is appropriate even today, the authors of the Cardinal Principles warned that secondary education, "like any other agency in society, is conservative and tends to resist modification. Failure to make adjustments when the need arises leads to the necessity for extensive reorganization at irregular intervals. The need is strong that such a comprehensive reorganization of secondary education is imperative at the present time."[11]

In the last section of the report, "Recognition of the Objectives in Organizing the School," the authors offered a succinct and clear statement that, more than they could have realized, foreshadowed a politicized future for public education. They warned, "The objectives must determine the organization, or else the organization will determine the objectives."[12] The authors, however, felt that they, not local communities, must structure and operate schools around the educational needs they considered most important.

At its 1918 convention, NEA President Mary Bradford presented the report from the Commission on the Reorganization of Secondary Education. In what was obviously another move toward a "complete national plan" for education, Bradford included "a description of the school crisis: the preparation, supply, and salaries of teachers; special problems of rural schools; a program for physical health education; problems of immigrant education and adult illiteracy; compulsory continuation schools; and the need for a National Department of Education and national cooperation with the states to strengthen the public schools."[13]

The plan was bold in its scope and clearly focused on control of teacher preparation programs and school curricula. NEA was also continuing to build a foundation for a cabinet-level Department of Education and to fashion a method for gaining sole control of teachers.

At this time, NEA's membership included administrators from schools, colleges, and universities. One such member, Joseph Swain, then president of Swarthmore College, spoke at the convention. The year was 1918, the nation was at war, and Swain declared:

> Education is a national matter. The man who denies that at this hour is not worth listening to. The man who denies that education is a national matter is capable of denying that our army and navy are national matters, of thinking that our states and towns and cities, left to themselves, could carry on the War....
>
> But suppose the nation cannot be made to see its duty. Then there is only one other way: The teachers, by concerted action and the application of the principles of *collective bargaining*, must compel the nation to wake up.[14] (emphasis added)

Never mind that national defense is an enumerated power in the constitution and its proper execution resides with the federal government. Never mind that education is *not* an enumerated power and, by virtue of the Tenth Amendment, "powers not delegated to the United States by the Constitution, nor prohibited by it to the States, are reserved to the States respectively, or to the people." Never mind that a principle of local control of education provides that parents, taxpayers, and citizens elected to boards of education will set policy for local schools. Leaders within NEA, then as now, were eager to use collective bargaining to "wake up" and "compel" the nation to march to NEA's drummer. As early as 1918 NEA wished to use "collective bargaining" as the principal weapon to gain its ends. But NEA would have to wait until 1959 before it gained legislative authority to use collective bargaining against communities and schools.[15]

THE PRE-MONOPOLY UNIONISM ERA (1920–1961)

Although America had changed in twenty-five years, NEA's push to be the controlling force in public education had not. Its continual efforts to wrest the powers of education from the states by centralizing control in Washington, D.C., were well under way.

LEGISLATION AS A TOOL

During its Pre-Monopoly Unionism Era, NEA's membership grew exponentially. Despite a setback during the Depression, its membership—increasing from 52,850 in 1920 to 765,616 in 1961—became an astonishing fifteen times larger.[16] NEA continued to work for federal control of education through lobbying and legislative efforts. By the beginning of the 1960s, this push had created great tension between those who believed NEA should be an association of professionals concerned principally with educational issues and those who were convinced NEA should impose forced unionism on teachers, collective bargaining on school boards, and social-activist educational goals on parents and communities.

The 1920s were boom years for the nation, and for NEA. In one decade, NEA's membership more than tripled—growing to 163,782 in 1929.[17] NEA continued its efforts to make education a national concern. According to Allan West, former NEA interim executive secretary, "President Hoover in 1929 appointed the National Advisory Committee on Education to study the relationship of education to the federal government. The committee report, presented two years later, recommended the establishment of a Department of Education at the cabinet level. A bill was subsequently introduced in the House of Representatives based on the committee's recommendation." [18] The bill failed.

Despite this initial failure, NEA continued to lobby for a cabinet-level Department of Education. In 1933 the newly elected U.S. president, Franklin Roosevelt, appointed an advisory Committee on the Emergency in Education. Even with shrinking resources caused by the Great Depression, "the NEA," according to Allan West, "gave both financial and staff support to the president's commission, whose work was responsible for a number of short-range emergency programs for schools."[19] From 1937 through 1954, NEA supported numerous legislative acts, including:

- 1937—a law to abolish loyalty oaths for teachers in the District of Columbia
- 1938–1942—a law to exclude teachers from the provisions of the Hatch Act
- 1944—a defeat for the "millionaires' amendment," an effort to limit federal taxes in peacetime to 25 percent
- 1954—the Mason Bill, giving tax relief to retired teachers.[20]

The Hatch Act deserves elaboration. President Franklin Roosevelt signed the Hatch Act in 1939. Because public employees work in government-protected monopolies, the Hatch Act limits the political activity of government workers; this prevents them from being forced to lobby for candidates who, in return for their support, would levy taxes to increase federal workers' incomes and power— thus increasing the income and power of public-sector unions.

After four years of lobbying, NEA gained exclusion from the provisions of the Hatch Act. In this regard, NEA members still enjoy special status among government workers. In 1993 a *Wall Street Journal* article observed, "Federal employee unions have always envied the political muscle of the [2.2] million-member National Education Association, the nation's largest union. Because it is generally not subject to Hatch Act-like curbs on its activities, it has been able to build itself into a giant lobby for its own self-interests."[21]

During the 1992 campaign, presidential candidate Bill Clinton promised union bosses that he would support legislation to water down the Hatch Act.[22] "The irony here," a *Wall Street Journal* article warned, "will be that the candidate who promised to 'reinvent government' will preside over a 'reinvigoration' of a fossilized federal bureaucracy that represents everything people dislike about Washington today."[23] Perhaps the most alarming warning in this article concerned NEA's demand that a portion of teachers' pay be "turned back to it in the form of dues, which are in turn used to further enhance its political clout. The weakening of the Hatch Act may soon create several more 800-pound political gorillas that will be able to just say no to any proposals for cutbacks in entitlement spending or the bureaucracy."[24]

In a report entitled "Monopolizing Teachers," William P. Hoar, writing for *The New American*, noted that NEA's unbridled efforts to shape laws and economic foundations to its purposes are not new. Hoar believed, "The guiding goals of the NEA have included statism and socialism."[25] To add support to his contention that NEA has long sought "social control," Hoar quoted previous NEA executive secretary Willard Givens, who in 1934 declared, "A dying laissez-faire must be completely destroyed and all of us, including the 'owners,' must be subject to a large degree of social control."[26]

REORGANIZATION AND UNIFICATION

NEA needed to reorganize its internal structure to support its growing appetite. In 1944 NEA crafted a five-year plan of unification and expansion[27] and began to combine its three-level membership into a single national-state-local membership. At that time, teachers could belong to a local classroom teachers' association while not belonging to NEA-national. Unification would require members of NEA locals to join and pay dues to their state organizations *and* to NEA-national.

By 1957 only seven states had adopted mandatory unified membership.[28] But then came NEA's Monopoly Unionism Era, and a significant change took place. In 1972 NEA revised its national bylaws to make it mandatory in all states for members to belong to all three levels. Consequently, from 1972 to 1973, membership in NEA-national increased by 211,795—an 18 percent gain.[29] Through this bold but simple mechanism, NEA gained a larger body of members, more revenue, and burgeoning political power.

In the meantime, NEA needed to find ways to put itself in a positive light. In 1941 NEA had appointed members to a group with a curious name, Commission for the Defense of Democracy Through Education. The commission's charge, according to Allan West, was "to investigate alleged cases involving the violations of teachers' rights."[30] By 1957 the commission was functioning as an investigative board that explored a teacher's complaint, wrote a report, and after reviewing the matter, according to West, made "the reports available to the press and other media."[31] Today, as then, NEA uses the media as one of its most powerful tools.

In his book *Notes from a Schoolteacher*, James Herndon, a local American Federation of Teachers (AFT) union president, explained that he and his colleagues used the media when collective bargaining did not go their way. Describing one such time, Herndon wrote, "By God. We're not putting up with it. We call the newspapers. We meet together and drive each other crazy with the question, What are we going to do?"[32]

Even before knowing what course of action they would eventually take, these union negotiators "call the newspapers." Education unions, whether AFT or NEA, understand the power of the media and know how to use the media to attack individuals and achieve their ends.

By the end of the Pre-Monopoly Unionism Era, NEA was concentrating on creating a rift between teachers and administrators and between teachers and school boards. The house of public education was dividing against itself—a new era was beginning.

THE MONOPOLY UNIONISM ERA (1961–1976)

Although NEA was acting like a monopolistic labor union, some members still believed it should primarily be an educational association. Many teachers wanted a professional organization that supported them with research on classroom-related issues such as instruction, curricular design, and student motivation. Then, in 1959, Wisconsin passed the first public-sector collective bargaining law.[33] This law, according to labor-law attorney Tim McConville, formerly of the National Right to Work Legal Defense Foundation, was a major milestone in the growth of public-sector unions in general and of the NEA teachers union specifically. It mirrored the National Labor Relations Act by providing organized labor a monopoly over the work force. Ultimately, thirty-three other states would follow suit.[34] The landscape was changing for organized labor, and it would soon change for teachers.*

---

*As this book was going to press, Governor Gary Johnson vetoed reauthorization of New Mexico's monopoly bargaining statute. In doing so, the governor struck down the statewide mandate that had previously

In 1960 the issue of collective bargaining came before teachers in New York City. Walter Reuther, then associated with AFT, resolved to organize teachers in New York City and directed AFT to capture the city's teacher membership. NEA had a lot at stake. It knew that if a majority of New York's teachers voted for collective bargaining, another vote would soon follow to determine whether AFT or NEA would gain monopoly control over the city's teachers. NEA's top officials decided to organize a local affiliate in order to win the power to represent New York's teachers. On December 15, 1961, the election took place. NEA lost by a wide margin.[35]

Losing something this significant was not acceptable. NEA beefed up and repackaged its product.

Becoming more aggressive in organizing teachers, NEA hired Saul Alinsky. Alinsky, a professional organizer and author of *Rules for Radicals*, traveled to local NEA chapters to teach them how to become activist unions. Alinsky plied his well-practiced techniques of staged conflict and managed turmoil. According to one NEA official, Alinsky "preached a rough-and-ready credo and urged confrontation over conciliation. 'You people don't know the first ?*#!* thing about organizing,' he would roar at [NEA] protégés sitting at his feet. He told us that the only way to get administrators to take us seriously was to escalate the conflict—threaten a strike, mount one if the threat didn't work, and take any other steps necessary to put pressure on the other side. Alinsky set the tone for the relations that have since evolved between teachers and the people who run the schools."[36]

NEA had now joined the ranks of hard-core labor unions. To all but the most partisan observer, it abandoned any pretense of being a professional association. Yet, from 1906[37]—when Congress

---

forced all eighty-nine of New Mexico's school districts to submit to union monopoly bargaining strategies and tactics. Having lost the battle at the state level, NEA can now be expected to focus its might on individual school board members in efforts to force them to "voluntarily" commit their school districts to the monopoly-bargaining trap from which the governor's veto just delivered them. (Gleason, Stefan and Mark Mix both of National Right to Work Legal Defense Foundation, telephone conversation with author, 10 June 1999.)

granted NEA a tax exemption it has never given to another labor union—until 1997, NEA's self-proclaimed "educational purpose" netted the union ninety years of exemption from property taxes, an estimated annual tax savings of some $2 million in recent years.[38] (In 1997, however, when it became obvious that its special tax exemption was about to be repealed, NEA upstaged the pending legislation by[39] "endors[ing] the repeal of the Association's real estate property tax exemption and committ[ing] to pay $1.1 million in property taxes on its 16th Street headquarters."[40])

In the 1960s NEA scored one victory after another. In return for union support during his successful presidential campaign, President John F. Kennedy signed Executive Order 10988 in 1962 to legalize collective bargaining for federal employees.[41] In 1963 Congress committed $3 billion to fund the Higher Educational Facilities Act, the Vocational Education Act, and legislation to extend the National Defense Education Act.[42] In 1964, with the presidential campaign between Barry Goldwater and Lyndon Johnson close at hand, NEA all but abandoned its then-official policy of withholding public support from presidential candidates and unofficially communicated its clear preference for Johnson; Johnson handily won the election. Continuing to build this partnership, NEA actively supported President Johnson's successful efforts to pass the Elementary and Secondary Education Act of 1965, then the single largest federal aid to education program ever passed by Congress.[43]

With support from both the executive and legislative branches of the federal government and with collective bargaining added to its arsenal, NEA had captured the tactical high ground, and union officials reveled in the spoils that came with victory. NEA bosses had aggressively begun their move into politics. NEA was ready for a new era.

THE POLITICAL ERA (1976–PRESENT)

NEA's Political Era really began in 1976 with the election of Jimmy Carter to the presidency of the United States. NEA had never officially endorsed a presidential candidate. But in the mid-1970s NEA decided the time had come to put its political power and formidable resources behind a candidate who was outspokenly its ally.

Jimmy Carter was such a candidate. He was little known nationally; but with NEA's help, Carter defeated Gerald Ford.

James Earl Carter was now in position to return the favor.

In 1979 President Carter and NEA created the Department of Education that Thomas W. Valentine had envisioned at NEA's first meeting in 1857. In 1980 the department reported a budget of $14.17 billion. In 1994 the department boasted a budget of $25.33 billion.[44] And, according to its "Fiscal Year 2000 Budget Request," the Department of Education intends in the year 2000 to increase its appropriation to $38.21 billion.[45]

During the 1976 elections NEA won more than a U.S. president. In *NEA: Trojan Horse in American Education*, Samuel Blumenfeld wrote that NEA's political action committee, NEA-PAC, "scored an 83 percent win record in Congress. Of the 323 House candidates it endorsed, 272 won; and of the 26 Senate candidates it endorsed, 19 won."[46] NEA bosses know how to lobby for what they want. "When the National Education Association, the nation's largest union and one of the biggest congressional campaign contributors, wanted to protect federal education programs, it used its $170 million budget and 50-person government relations staff. It also used its new interactive computer network to prod its then 2.1 million members to visit and write lawmakers,"[47] said a July 27, 1994, Associated Press News Service article.

NEA's primary weapon is political power, not economic power, asserts economist Leo Troy, a distinguished professor of economics at Rutgers University and an authority on trends in public-sector unionization. Troy maintains that NEA, like other public-sector unions, uses its political power to redistribute income, a process he calls "new socialism." Just as alarming, according to Troy, NEA uses its political muscle to insulate itself from any competition.[48]

Today, NEA's political agenda strays a long way from what the *Washington Post* called "its school-centered, reform-minded origins." In 1992 NEA was a major player in Democrat Party politics. It claimed to have sent more delegates to the presidential nomination convention than any other contingent of the Democrat Party.[49] Former Secretary of Education William Bennett said, "NEA only likes people it can control."[50] He told *Forbes* reporters that when looking at NEA, "you're looking at the absolute heart and center of the Democratic Party."[51]

But NEA does not put all its eggs in one political basket nor ply its political might only at the national level. Consider, for example, the following comments taken from periodicals across the country:

- May 1984: "Instruction and professional development have been on the back burner for [NEA], compared with political action," said NEA [past] president Mary Futrell.[52] *Reader's Digest*

- April 8, 1993: Linda Cross, a public schoolteacher, ran for Wisconsin school superintendent on a school-choice platform. The Wisconsin Education Association Council, the state's most powerful teachers' union, made certain Ms. Cross wouldn't get a chance to alter the state's educational status quo. The union poured an estimated $200,000 into an independent expenditure campaign against her (add to that inestimable "soft" contributions in the form of volunteers) and charged that "Linda Cross wants to use your tax dollars to help rich parents pay tuition at private schools."[53] *Wall Street Journal*

- June 7, 1993: The 1990 Alabama legislature was composed of 40 percent teachers, ex-teachers, or teachers' spouses. State Education Association Executive Secretary-Treasurer Paul Hubbert won the Democratic gubernatorial nomination, and his staff was asked to raise twenty dollars per member to finance his unsuccessful general election campaign.[54] *Forbes*

- November 15, 1993: The NEA spent $50,000 on a victory party to celebrate its overwhelming defeat of California's controversial Proposition 174, which would have established a statewide voucher system.[55] *Alberta Report*

- December 12, 1993: "The MEA [state-level NEA affiliate in Michigan] is the state's largest single-interest lobbying group, spending more than $1.4 million in political contributions to lawmakers and causes last year. The MEA coordinated the campaign that defeated Governor John Engler's 'Cut and Cap' tax reform package.... The MEA controls a financial empire with more than $430 million a year in revenues."[56] *Detroit News*

■ July 4, 1994: Rejecting claims that American taxpayers are being unfairly penalized, the nation's largest teacher's union came out Monday against California's proposal to deny social services to illegal immigrants.[57] *Associated Press News Service*

Throughout its Political Era, NEA has actively worked in the Democrat National Committee, state legislatures, local governments, and local school boards. During this time, NEA has accumulated incredible financial resources and made fruitful connections in Washington, D.C., and at the state and local levels.

We are living in the midst of this era. Just as surely as history continues its march through time, NEA bosses continue their march toward the creation and control of a centralized national system of education.

2

....

NEA: Present and Future

"Since 1963, the percentage of public school teachers belonging to a union has soared from less than 1% to 70%. That increase and the near-monopoly status of public education have turned teachers' unions into big political players. They elect school boards, block reforms such as school choice and intimidate legislators."

—Wall Street Journal, *June 15, 1994*

NEA TODAY

NEA'S RESOURCES ARE ENORMOUS. From its 1993 membership of 2,172,343,[1] NEA collected unified dues estimated at $742 million.[2] Its total revenues in 1995 were approximately $785 million.[3] Of the 1993 revenues, NEA collected and used $165 million (22 percent) for its own agenda, and the remaining $577 million was divided between NEA local ($72 million—10 percent) and state ($505 million—68 percent) affiliates.[4]

A major source of NEA's funds is membership dues, which, in many states, are coerced from teachers as a condition of employment. NEA reports that the average teacher salary in public education in 1995–1996 was $37,846, plus benefits.[5] Applying its dues formula,[6] this works out to a yearly $105 per teacher to NEA-national alone. Members must also pay state and local dues. The average total dues for teachers is about $400 per year. North

Carolina had the lowest state dues at $115, and Puerto Rico the highest, at $579.60.[7]

Described in 1875 as "a Gigantic Educational Ganglion—a sort of pedagogical, cerebra-spinal centre,"[8] NEA today is much larger and more complex. Its $65 million,[9] eight-story headquarters at 1201 Sixteenth Street, Washington, D.C., has an auditorium, a broadcast studio, and a cafeteria.[10] Its national organization is composed of:

- a 9-member Executive Committee that includes 3 executive officers
- a 9-member Board of Review, appointed, and with ethics oversight responsibilities
- a 164-member Board of Directors
- 54 state affiliates—including 2 affiliates in D.C., 1 in Puerto Rico, and 1 overseas
- a 9,044-member Representative Assembly, elected from local affiliates, that meets each summer to vote NEA's resolutions for the coming school year
- 1 executive office and 6 major centers with 42 subordinate offices
- 19 standing and special committees
- a 50-person government relations staff[11]
- a 550-member staff that works in Washington, D.C., and in 6 regional offices
- 1,117 separate UniServ* offices with 1,500[12] UniServ field agents[13]
- 13,000 local affiliates[14]
- 2.264 million members.

---

*NEA's 1,500 UniServ staff are "professionals, at least one in every congressional district. Their official function [is] to assist locals with collective bargaining. But they also constitute what has been called the largest field army of paid political organizers and lobbyists in the U.S., dwarfing the forces of the Republican and Democratic national committees combined." From Peter Brimelow and Leslie Spencer's 7 June 1993 *Forbes* article "The National Extortion Association."

Until July 1996, when he completed the maximum six years in office, all of this was presided over by NEA's president, Keith Geiger, a former Michigan teacher who drew $240,000 in salary, allowances, and expenses in 1993.[15] NEA's executive director, Don Cameron, also a former Michigan teacher, received $194,000.[16] In 1995 their total compensation packages were estimated at $335,000 for Geiger and $300,000 for Cameron.[17] The National Right to Work Legal Defense Foundation estimates that current NEA President Bob Chase draws a compensation package similar to Geiger's 1995 salary and benefits. Perhaps as many as two thousand NEA officials are paid over $100,000 a year,[18] and some secretaries earn $40,000 annually.[19] NEA's 1,500 UniServ agents, who act as field operatives with at least one in each congressional district, receive between $60,000 and $100,000[20] annually, plus fringe benefits in the range of 35 percent.[21]

NEA'S AGENDA

NEA presents its official agenda in its annual *Handbook*. In 1996–1997 this 474-page book contained, among other entries, its constitution, bylaws, resolutions adopted by the Representative Assembly, legislative program for the next Congress, strategic plan for the coming year, and Budget by Strategic Objectives. From this official agenda, we can learn NEA's vision for a new America.

We can also learn a great deal about NEA by studying how it uses its money. NEA spends its resources on what it holds most important. Its 1994–1995 Budget by Strategic Objective shows that, after subtracting the $1,500,000 set aside as a contingency reserve from the total $179,157,000 budget,* NEA dedicated the majority of its money, $161,258,679 (90.8 percent), to activities that increase union strength and accomplish union goals. Some of these expenditures included $63,862,696 to "strengthen its capacity to attract,

---

*In their *Forbes* article, "The National Extortion Association," Brimelow and Spencer estimated NEA-national's dues revenues at $165 million. NEA's figures, as found in *Handbook 1993–1994*, showed a $173 million budget—an additional $8 million dollars from other sources, one can assume.

represent, and serve members in all membership categories"; $39,799,333 to "advance the economic interests, protect the job security, and improve the terms and conditions of employment, and to secure the right to collective bargaining for all education employees"; and $46,320,492 to "maintain the organizational systems essential to fulfill the mission of the Association." NEA designated another $11,276,158 to "expand and protect quality public education as a basic right (pre K-G) and secure its adequate and equitable funding."[22] In its 1996–1997 strategic budget NEA officials set aside $1,691,000 for contingencies, $40,026,000 for UniServe grants, and another $16,515,000 for its Unified Services Program.[23]

In its 1994–1995 budget, NEA allocated $16,398,321 (9.2 percent) for strategic objectives that might be described as educational in nature. These included such topics as "restructuring of schools," "enhanc[ing] the preparation, practice, and professional standards of education employees to improve student learning," and "promot[ing] equity for all and the elimination of discrimination and other barriers to learning."[24] While no objective spoke directly to improving student learning, these three goals seemed the most closely—albeit ever so vaguely—related to academic education.

But even here, NEA bosses spend members' money to bolster their own agenda by tapping into the American public's traditional willingness to support good education. In his 1980 book, past-NEA Executive Secretary Allan West matter-of-factly explained, "NEA sought to advance the welfare of its members by providing resources to its affiliated state and local organizations and to schools that, in turn, would make possible economic benefits to members."[25]

To realize this and make money for itself, NEA used what West described as "a strategy based on the conviction that the American public was more concerned about quality schools for pupils than it was in the welfare of those who provided the services." "Therefore," confided the unapologetic West, "it was argued that urging citizens to provide good schools for children would bring better results than pressing for fair and adequate salaries for teachers."[26]

Through this sleight-of-hand strategy, NEA gains tax money under the pretense that the money will go to "good schools for children," and then, through forced dues, it takes a percentage of the increased teachers' salaries to pay its executives and support their political and social causes.

NEA combines this bait-and-switch tactic with politics. In *The NEA and AFT: Teacher Unions in Power and Politics*, Haar, Lieberman, and Troy quoted a 1993 *AFL-CIO News* article to explain why the unions supported President Clinton's health care plan as a way to gain increased dues for themselves. The *AFL-CIO News* article boldly stated:

> To the extent that government spends more and employers spend less on health care, more funds would be available for wages and other economic benefits. If the federal government absorbed some of the costs of health care that are currently paid by school districts, the teacher unions could negotiate for the savings to be distributed to teachers' salaries.

Of course, a portion of teachers' salaries is automatically converted into sizable sums of money that go directly into NEA's coffers and labor chieftains' high salaries. It is difficult to know which is the more disheartening: the dues NEA forces teachers to pay or the blatant abuse of taxpayers' willingness to support schools.

Along with its budget, NEA's 305 resolutions and 400 legislative targets tell something about its priorities. NEA's resolutions filled 108 pages of *Handbook 1996–1997*, and its legislative targets filled another twenty-three pages. In what must be a painful admission that a problem does in fact exist, NEA's first resolution asks its members to do what it would like to force the general public to do. "Members and Associate members are encouraged to show their support of public education by sending their children to public educational institutions."[27]

In 1993 then-NEA President Keith Geiger admitted in an interview on "This Week with David Brinkley" that "about 40 percent" of urban-area public school teachers with school-age children send their children to private schools.[28] In his analysis of 1990 U.S. census data, Denis P. Doyle, an MD from Chevy Chase, Maryland, found that on a national level 12.1 percent of public schoolteachers send their children to private schools while in Jersey City 50.3 percent send their children to private schools.[29] Controlling for income, teachers with family incomes greater than $70,000 are "three to four times as likely as the public at large to use private schools."[30]

NEA sets its policy through resolutions enacted at the annual Representative Assembly convention held each July. Among the "Resolutions Adopted by the 1996 NEA Representative Assembly" were these:

- Tax reform should "not be used to place arbitrary maximum limits on any state or local government's ability to spend or tax."[31]
- There should be "federal support for the whole of public elementary, secondary, and postsecondary education."[32]
- "The National Education Association believes that voucher plans and tuition tax credits... undermine public education.... The Association opposes all attempts to establish and/or implement such plans."[33]
- "The National Education Association believes that all visual representations using maps of the United States should depict all fifty states and Puerto Rico."[34]
- Local NEA affiliates should "seek an optimum class size of 15 students in regular programs."[35]
- All home school instructors should be "licensed by appropriate state educational licensure agency, and curriculum approved by the state department of education."[36]
- "Competency testing must not be used as a condition of employment, license retention, evaluation, placement, ranking, or promotion of licensed teachers."[37]
- There should be "implementation of community-operated, school-based family planning clinics that will provide intensive counseling by trained personnel."[38]
- "Efforts to legislate English as the official language... must be challenged."[39]

In *Handbook 1993–1994*, NEA urged local affiliates to "work toward a *teacher-controlled* educational system,"[40] but three years later, *Handbook 1996–1997* counseled locals to "work toward a *teacher-led* educational system"[41] (emphasis added). Perhaps in the intervening three years, NEA remembered that elected school boards have the responsibility for "control" of educational systems, sometimes called school districts.

NEA's legislative program is a study in how this labor union intends to control far more than teachers and the schools in which they teach.

As NEA wrote in its *Handbook*, "NEA supports federal legislation consistent with its principles."[42] NEA skillfully uses federal legislation and federal regulations to gain its long-held goals to create and control one system of education. To these ends, NEA will:

1. continue to use the federal government to standardize and centralize key elements of education
2. accelerate and strengthen its assumption of responsibility for setting public policy on education issues
3. incrementally gain legal control over American education, without acquiring legal responsibility.

NEA is well along in the first two phases of this three-step plan.* To accomplish the third step, NEA needs to extend and expand its already powerful presence in the legislative process.

NEA talks of its legislative agenda in terms of achieving a "Legislative Program [that] sets forth the federal legislative policies that facilitate accomplishment of the strategic objectives in pursuit of the Association's mission."[43] To assist the federal bureaucracy in

---

*Chapter Eight discusses NEA's active involvement in national standards boards to control student learning and teacher certification. Less obvious, but nonetheless significant, NEA has become the "official" source that media and even the Department of Education go to for information. On page 78 of his 1993 book, *Public Education: An Autopsy*, Myron Lieberman referred to the Department of Education's use of NEA-derived teacher salary data. He wrote, "The department did not conduct the research on teacher salaries; instead it relied on the estimates and interpretive comments of the nation's largest teacher union. Such reliance was neither new nor secret; the media rely almost exclusively on the NEA salary data. By doing so, they misinform the American people about teacher compensation."

enacting "federal legislation" to accomplish its mission, NEA has arranged its legislative program in three tiers, according to the level of importance NEA places on its proposed federal legislation.

The first tier, the most important, has only two programs: "increased federal funding for education" and creation of "a federal statute that would guarantee collective bargaining rights to employees of public schools, colleges, universities, and other postsecondary institutions."[44] On these NEA intends to build and expand its empire. It is clear that "nationalization" of public education is one of NEA's goals. For NEA to play this political card openly now must mean it believes that victory is close at hand.

There are eighteen major second-tier legislative categories supported by 248 goals. Among them are:

- support for a "Comprehensive National Health Care Policy" including a "tax-supported, single-payer health care plan for all residents of the United States, its territories, and the Commonwealth of Puerto Rico"[45]
- opposition to "any constitutional amendment imposing limitations on taxes or the federal budget"[46]
- support for "a progressive tax system based on individual and corporate ability to pay to yield sufficient revenues to address national needs"[47]
- opposition to "tuition tax credits at elementary, secondary, or postsecondary levels."[48]

NEA's third-tier legislative goals refer to:

- support for "continuation of the cabinet-level U.S. Department of Education"[49]
- opposition to "tax deductions to business for donation of computers to schools, unless the computers are designated solely for classroom use"[50]
- support of "provision of federal funds to school districts for the education of children of undocumented workers [and] immigrants"[51]
- opposition to "federal initiatives that mandate or promote traditionally defined merit pay schemes."[52]

NEA's annual *Handbook* is a revealing document. A copy of the *Handbook* may be obtained from a public or university library or ordered from NEA at the address listed in Chapter Eleven.

NEA's Structure

NEA is organized into four levels. The national office is in Washington, D.C. State offices are in all fifty states, the District of Columbia, and Puerto Rico. NEA also has an office in Washington, D.C., for Department of Defense schools located on seven military bases in the United States and in twenty overseas countries and their possessions.[53] NEA has 13,000 local affiliates.[54] Situated between the state and local levels are approximately 1,500 UniServ operatives[55] whose salaries come from dues paid by individual members but who serve as lobbyists and political activists for state-level NEA officials and as grievance and collective bargaining consultants for local NEA organizations.

NEA admits to a staff of 550 who work in Washington, D.C., and in six regional offices.[56] In addition to directing an organization with over $742 million annual dues revenues and 2.264 million members, NEA-national oversees six regional offices that, in turn, manage fifty-one administrative units providing direction and services in areas such as:

- "work[ing] with international organizations, including the United Nations and its specialized agencies of the U.S. government, on issues affecting international education/or foreign policy"[57] under the Office of International Relations
- "litigating important test cases to create legal precedents in the area of human and civil rights"[58] under the Office of General Counsel
- "elect[ing] pro-education candidates to federal office; influencing the executive branch in its development of legislative proposals and its regulation of programs of interest to NEA; working with organizations of educational policymakers at the state, local, and regional levels to adopt positions compatible with NEA's and advancing NEA's Legislative Program in Congress"[59] under the Office of Government Relations.

Working together, the national, state, UniServ, and local levels call school strikes, dominate contract negotiations, elect carefully picked school board members, recall school board members who do not support their agenda, negotiate school board policy, write curricula, gain labor laws favorable to NEA causes, advance chosen social issues, influence state and national legislation, and help elect presidents. NEA is organized, ambitious, and effective.

NEA OF THE FUTURE

If we learn anything from NEA's history, it is that NEA has accomplished what it set out to do. From its beginning membership of forty-three, NEA has grown to over 2.2 million; it has created a de facto "system of public schools" that look like clones; it has gained the cabinet-level Department of Education it dreamed of in 1857; and it has become the "political power second to no other special interest group" as envisioned in 1967. What remains? NEA's agenda suggests where NEA seems most likely to go from here.

NEA'S AGENDA

An examination of NEA's history, practices, and stated goals shows that NEA's agenda for take-over of education in the United States has three parts:

1. gain exclusive bargaining-agent control (monopoly representation and mandatory dues) of all public schoolteachers and achieve licensure authority over teachers in public and private schools
2. wrest policy-setting authority away from school boards and management authority away from administrators at the local level
3. dominate both the state and national legislative and regulatory processes that define and direct education in the fifty states.

To take control of education, NEA must gain ground in each of these three areas.

Gain Control of Teachers

In large measure due to forced unionism, NEA in 1997 had 2.264 million members.[60] Of these, just over 1.6 million were teachers.[61] The American Federation of Teachers (AFT) and NEA hold a combined membership of almost 70 percent of the teachers in public schools.[62] AFT, the rival teacher union, has approximately 850,000 members—of which 600,000 are teachers and the remainder are professors and university employees, public school classified employees, and public employees.[63] Together NEA and AFT have three million members, many of whom have been coerced into joining one or the other union. Together NEA and AFT annually collect dues of $1.3 billion and employ 6,000 full-time staff people.[64]

If merged, NEA and AFT would become the largest labor union in the world. The product of this merger would become a superunion monopoly within the monopoly of public education.

In *The NEA and AFT: Teacher Unions in Power and Politics*, Haar, Lieberman, and Troy warned, "The size and resources of a merged organization would be awesome, yet retain the potential for substantial growth."[65] One source for this growth is the American Association of University Professors, presently a membership group of only 33,000[66] but with potential for many more members and an expressed interest in joining the superunion.[67]

With a merger of these two labor unions, NEA bosses would gain control of America's teacher corps. But how realistic is it to expect NEA and AFT, longtime labor union rivals, to come to agreement on the philosophical and educational differences that have separated them?*

It has already happened: in 1989 in San Francisco[68] and in 1993 in Stockholm, Sweden—places where NEA's Keith Geiger and

---

*AFT, in comparison to NEA, is generally known for its willingness to try innovations. Perhaps the biggest potential conflict between the two unions is AFT's association with the AFL-CIO and the strong feeling of some NEA members that they do not want to be associated with, much less come under the umbrella of the AFL-CIO.

AFT's Al Shanker met to merge the two unions' international affil-iates[69]—and again in 1998 in Minnesota.[70] Although these merg-ers are small in relation to full merger of the two unions, they signify a strong willingness by bosses of both unions to overcome long-standing differences. Al Shanker, twenty-three–year president of AFT before his death in 1997, said, "NEA members... are not any different than our members. If anything, our members are likely to be more liberal, left."[71] NEA is making moves toward merging. After conducting a survey of its members, NEA received a recommendation from its "Board of Directors that NEA invite AFT and/or other labor organizations to enter into discussions with NEA regarding the possible establishment of a unified orga-nization." NEA also got a "yes" vote from its nine thousand-member Representative Assembly and began formal merger talks with AFT.[72]

Although the most current merger effort was not successful, it seems likely the two teacher unions will someday merge. Given the threat NEA perceives in the growing school choice movement, it may be looking for ways to shore up its membership, financial position, and political power base against possible encroachment from private-sector schools.

Gain Control of Management and Policy-Setting Authority at the Local Level

Even without a merger, the two teacher unions have made tremen-dous inroads into gaining control of management and policy-setting authority at the local level. An NEA-AFT merger will give the superunion power while decreasing the ability of principals, super-intendents, and school boards to lead and manage schools and school systems democratically. Duly elected boards of education would lose control of everything NEA controls on the policy-setting and oversight side of public education.

Some management theorists argue that when management "shares" power, it actually gains effect. True enough—in circum-stances where labor and management have a common mission and where market forces reinforce consumer-centered decisions. This, however, is not an accurate description of conditions in public education. In 1990 public education was a $213 billion enterprise.[73] It is an enterprise protected from going out of business regardless of what it does or how well it does it. Its operating revenues and employment are all but guaranteed, and there is no customer and no bottom line in the way these terms are understood in a market-driven system. As it now exists, public education breeds and supports a myopic view of doing what is best in the short term for the education producer while giving little attention to what is best for the education consumer or for the taxpayer.

Given that the whole industry does not have to produce and deliver a superior product to stay in business, union activists can play power politics and commit tremendous energies to determining who will set the agenda and make decisions. Thus the day-to-day operations of public education—as they currently exist—will always have more to do with serving producers than serving consumers.

These realities notwithstanding, management theorists argue it is management's responsibility to create a sense of common mission within the teachers' corps. In public education, school board members theoretically lead schools in the best interests of students, parents, and community. But the teachers' union is predisposed to usurp control from school boards and run schools according to its wishes. It is an environment where NEA plies its coercive might against teachers and school board members alike.

NEA does not place the best interests of students and parents anywhere near the top of its hierarchy of concerns. Long-practiced, union-created strife and union-manipulated turmoil are tools NEA actively uses to create the illusion of a common foe and keep itself center stage to ensure that teachers are beholden to it for its frequent interventions on behalf of issues it tells teachers are important. NEA is not about shared missions and service for the greater good of students and community. It is about manipulation and coercion to gain its own ends.

It is not in NEA's interests to build a professional relationship with boards of education and administrators and to help structure an educational system for students, parents, and teachers. It wants control borne of induced turmoil and constant conflict. Many boards of education and administrators bow to NEA on issues of the union's choosing. Often these boards and administrators see only the options that NEA wants them to see. Management theorists have not effectively dealt with how to lead and manage in these messy circumstances.

In its quest for control of local schools and school districts, NEA says it supports "teacher empowerment." Like others who have wrestled with this concept, I have not yet discovered just what a teacher would do, once empowered, that he or she could not do before empowerment. The reach for power is endless and connotes a view of power as the principal basis for success; if one is not successful, then it is because one does not yet have enough power.

The central issue should be "enablement." Teachers should be enabled to make decisions and act on them to teach more effectively and efficiently. The empowerment battle is a straw man NEA uses to create a gap between what it has told teachers they want and what management is able to grant. The empowerment battle is another way for NEA to champion a "teacher cause," albeit a fictitious one, to make its services seem necessary to teachers.

NEA-defined "teacher causes" become battles that consume vast quantities of time, energy, and public funds without contributing to educational goals. In the majority of cases, teachers are good at what they are hired to do—they know how to teach and how to do those things necessary to the teaching-learning process. NEA, however, has convinced generations of union activists that they should be directing the school district. Its own resolutions and my years of observation show that NEA wants teachers to set district goals, write district policy, hire personnel, allocate budgets, and choose and fire their bosses. As a consequence, too many teachers have too little time to prepare lessons and too little energy to teach. Moreover, the system is not working to the benefit of many students, parents, teachers, and taxpayers.

Concepts of shared power and practices that enable people to do their jobs better make a great deal of sense. The literature is full of strong arguments and some evidence that flat-structure, people-centered, results-driven organizations are more productive in today's competitive global market than hierarchical, top-down, multilayered organizations—the latter being a fair description of today's bureaucratic school system. Schools miss a lot of good ideas and waste a lot of valuable talent when they leave out teachers and other employees in deliberations and decisions about how the work is to be done. The problem is that union-activist teachers often take their direction from NEA rather than from their local communities through elected boards of education. "Empowerment" and "shared-power" management strategies assume greater agreement on goals and a less politicized work environment than currently exist in NEA-dominated public education.

Gain Control of Legislative and Regulatory Authority at the National Level

As earlier noted, NEA's two, top-tier goals are "increased federal funding for education" and creation of "a federal statute that would guarantee collective bargaining rights to employees of public schools, colleges, universities, and other postsecondary institutions."

With increased federal funding comes increased federal control. NEA data bases are already the font of knowledge the Department of Education frequently turns to for data and advice, and NEA's backing of political candidates has gained it a win record of 76 percent from 1973 to 1984 and 80 percent in 1986.[74] NEA bosses are gaining ground.

NEA's move to control Congress and direct legislative and regulatory processes is neither new nor accidental. At the 1978 NEA convention, then-Executive Director Terry Herndon announced,

> "The ultimate goal of the NEA is to tap the legal,
> political, and economic powers of the U.S. Congress....
> [W]e want [NEA] leaders with sufficient clout that they
> may roam the halls of Congress and collect votes to re-
> order the priorities of the United States of America."[75]

Wow! What happened to democratic process? What happened to the association of teachers who came together in Philadelphia in August of 1857 "to elevate the character and advance the interests of the profession of teaching"? Herndon's rhetoric does not reflect loyalty to the principles of democracy, commitment to the practice of public debate, or dedication to legislative proceedings conducted in an open public forum. These comments reflect an organization determined to abuse and short-circuit the democratic process as a means to get what it wants.

UNIONS

This chapter relates a history of NEA, a non-government, public-sector union. None of this is intended to suggest that unions are inherently wrong. But it is wrong for NEA to use forced unionism to coerce teachers and compulsory public-sector collective bargaining to control school boards. Its power to usurp policy-setting and oversight responsibility from local school boards and its wielding of economic and political might to wrest public policy-setting responsibilities from elected public officials are fundamentally wrong. Union membership should be voluntary. NEA should not use its government-granted monopoly to control education at all levels and, if one believes Terry Herndon, to "re-order the priorities of the United States" to NEA's liking.

From the very beginning, NEA has fought to create and control one system of education in America. It is a matter of opinion whether NEA has achieved its original goals "to elevate the character and advance the profession of teaching, and to promote the cause of popular education in the United States." Few, however, could argue that NEA has failed to become a "power unmatched by any other." The teachers' association has become a union, and the union has become a major power in the politics of public-policy formulation, in the allocation of public tax money, and in the creation and control of a monopolistic, government-sponsored system of public education.

Section Two
Taking Control of Teachers

....

Chapter Three:
Teachers: Taking Role

Chapter Four:
NEA's Control of Teachers: The Carrot and the Stick

3

···················

Teachers: Taking Role

"The typical teacher... is an idealist who genuinely wants
students to succeed, who wishes them well. Most teachers
accept unquestioningly the American conviction about the
worth of schooling."

—*Theodore R. Sizer,* Horace's Compromise

IN THE INDUSTRIAL AGE people thought of organizations as
bricks, mortar, machines, and the capital necessary to produce. In
today's world, we recognize that an organization's strength and
future are the people it takes into membership, imbues with its
beliefs, and depends on to generate new ideas, provide leadership,
and do the work. In public education, teachers are the majority of
that important human element. To understand how NEA works and
how it holds so much control over teachers and over public education, it is necessary to know something of its 2,264,000 members—
1,600,000 of whom are teachers—who represent approximately
63 percent of all public schoolteachers.

WHO ARE OUR TEACHERS?

In school year 1990–1991, American communities supported
approximately 15,000 school districts and 105,000 public and private schools.[1] Taxpayers and tuition payers hired and paid the

salaries of 2,900,000 teachers, 106,000 guidance counselors, 9,000 vocational counselors, 83,000 librarians and media specialists, 62,000 library and media aids, 454,000 teachers aids, 148,000 other professional staff, and 982,000 noninstructional staff to teach and tend to the 44.8 million students (52 million 1997) in public and private schools.[2]

Since much of the current school choice debate centers around private schooling as an alternative to public schooling, this chapter includes data for private as well as public elementary and secondary teachers. The majority of data is from three reports published through the National Center for Educational Statistics: *America's Teachers: Profile of a Profession 1993; Digest of Educational Statistics 1996;* and *Schools Staffing in the United States: A Statistical Profile, 1990–91.*

PUPIL–TEACHER RATIO

In 1993–1994, some 41,621,660 students enrolled in 80,000 K-12 public schools, and 4,970,548 students enrolled in 25,000 private schools.[3] Public schools employed 2,561,294 teachers and private schools employed 378,365 teachers.[4] In 1990–1991, approximately 811,000 public and private schoolteachers taught in central cities, about 853,000 in suburban communities and large towns, and 1,109,000 in small towns and rural communities.[5] From 1985 through 1996, public school enrollment grew by 21 percent at the elementary level (from 27.0 to 32.8 million) and by 5 percent at the high school level (from 12.4 to 13.0 million).[6] The net increase, estimated at approximately 6.7 million students, represented a 16 percent gain in public school enrollment.[7]

The number of public schoolteachers increased from 2,206,000 in 1985 to an estimated 2,679,000 in 1996, a growth of over 21 percent.[8] This increase in the number of teachers in relation to students, coupled with class-size limits negotiated into teachers' contracts, resulted in a decreased pupil–teacher ratio. In 1982 the pupil–teacher ratio in public schools was 18.6 students per teacher. In 1996 the projected ratio had fallen to 17.4.[9] The National Center for Educational Statistics attributed the declining pupil–teacher ratio to "the trend toward smaller classes and more specialized education programs."[10] In a 1994 *Anchorage Daily News* article about one effect of this shrinking pupil–teacher ratio, the writer observed that in Anchorage "in 1980, there was one teacher for every 18.5 kids. Today, there's one for every 17.25 kids. That may not seem like much, but it translates to an additional 197 teachers beyond what was required by more students. At average pay and benefits of $60,000, that's $11.8 million in expenses added to the budget base that wasn't there 15 years ago."[11]

In a 1993 *National Review* article, Chester Finn, Jr., former assistant secretary of education and Fellow at the Hudson Institute, observed that "teacher salaries rose 21 percent in real terms between 1965 and 1990, while pupil–teacher ratios fell by 30 per cent."[12] Meanwhile, the cost per public school student for school year 1992–1993, as expressed in estimated current expenditures* per student, was $5,762. Adjusted for inflation, this is an increase of 34 percent since 1982–1983.[13]

Chart 3.1

Pupil–Teacher Ratio[14] & Number of Teachers in Public Schools[15]

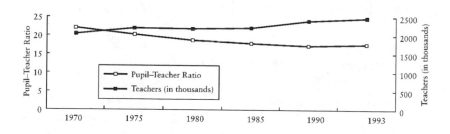

---

*The National Center for Education Statistics uses these definitions: Current expenditures include salaries for school personnel, fixed charges, student transportation, school books and materials, and energy costs. Total expenditures per pupil include all current expenditures allocable to per pupil costs including interests on school debt and capital outlay.

SEX, AGE, AND RACE

Teaching has traditionally been a female-dominated occupation. In a 1993 report on its 1987–1988 study, the National Center for Education Statistics reported that females were 71.4 percent of all teachers. At the elementary level, women were 87.6 percent of the teaching staff in public schools and 92 percent in private schools. At the secondary level, women made up 53 percent of the teaching staff in public schools and 63.2 percent in private schools. Combining elementary and secondary levels, women were 70.5 percent of the teaching staff in public schools and 78.2 percent in private schools. Women made up 70 percent of beginning teachers in public schools and 78.5 percent in private schools.[16]

Contrary to a popular notion that women are abandoning teaching in preference for occupations not previously available to them, data from the National Center for Education Statistics showed a growth in the percentage of women teachers from 1961, when women were 68.7 percent of the teaching force, to 1994, when women were 72.1 percent of all public schoolteachers.[17] Of course, an implied part of the female-flight theory is that the better-qualified women have left or are leaving teaching for other occupations. These data do not address this contention.

According to *America's Teachers: Profile of a Profession 1993*, the teachers' average age was forty.[18] Slightly over 49 percent of teachers in public school were under forty years of age, and 56 percent of teachers in private schools were under forty.

The Bureau of Census found that in 1990–1991, whites were 74.8 percent of the general population in the United States, blacks 11.9 percent, Hispanics 9.5 percent, Asians and Pacific Islanders 3.1 percent, and Native Americans 0.7 percent.[19] For public and private schools combined, 87.2 percent of teachers were white. In public schools, 86.5 percent of teachers were white. In private schools, 92.2 percent of teachers were white. Hispanic teachers were 7.6 percent of the total teacher population in public and private schools, black teachers 3.4 percent, Asian teachers 1.1 percent, and Native American teachers 0.7 percent.[20]

DEGREES AND TEACHER CERTIFICATION

Teaching is, in many respects, a matter of degrees. Only 1 percent of the teaching force teaches without at least a baccalaureate degree. Un-degreed teachers are usually "technical experts" hired to teach vocational courses, or they are hired under emergency conditions and issued provisional certificates to fill a position until the district can hire a degreed and certified teacher. In 1988, approximately 53 percent of teachers had a B.A. or B.S. as their highest degree, and 46 percent had earned an M.A., M.S., or higher degree.[21] Comparing public to private schoolteachers, 40 percent of public schoolteachers earned an M.A. or M.S. as their highest degree, and 1 percent held Ed.D. or Ph.D. degrees. Just under 30 percent of private schoolteachers earned M.A. or M.S. degrees as their highest degree, and almost 2 percent held Ed.D. or Ph.D. degrees.[22]

Every state requires public schoolteachers to hold a teaching certificate or, in unique circumstances, a special exemption that allows them to teach. Some states are changing their requirements by opening teaching certification to those with non-education degrees.

In 1991 eleven states issued teaching certificates based on such considerations as degrees earned and courses taken. In addition, some states required prospective teachers to take and pass qualifying examinations. According to a 1991 U.S. Department of Education survey:

- twenty-one states reported they required successful completion of the National Teacher Examination (NTE)
- eight states indicated the test used to certify teachers was yet "to be determined"
- eight states reported that "data [were] not available or not applicable"
- one state required the California Basic Education Skills Test
- California required the California Achievement Test
- one state required the Preprofessional Skills Test
- one state required candidates to meet state degree and course requirements and pass the NTE.[23]

Five years later, the certification landscape had changed. In 1996, the majority of states required teacher applicants to demonstrate satisfactory completion of two, three, or more assessments.[24] Thirty-nine states required satisfactory completion of basic skills tests, and forty-four required satisfactory teaching performance as evaluated by in-class observation.[25] Thirty-two states required additional examinations:

- thirteen required the NTE
- six required "specialty area exams"
- three required "Praxis"
- three required "Pedagogical" exams
- two required "State and undetermined tests"
- one required "Institution's Exit Exam"
- one required "General knowledge" tests
- one required "Tests for foreign language, bilingual, and English as a Second Language"
- seven required unspecified "other exams."[26]

In what may be a new trend, increasing numbers of professionals are turning to teaching in midcareer. Because of "fatter teacher salaries and efforts by many states to speed up the certification process,"[27] this new kind of teacher is coming to education in larger numbers. In 1987–1988, as many as 2,500 teachers in twenty-four states received training through alternative certification programs.[28]

According to *Education*, "Proponents of this trend say career changers are often more motivated and more effective than teachers who took the conventional path to the blackboard—they bring more life experience with them."[29] Yet, teachers trained through the conventional method do not always warmly welcome these newcomers. In some states, teachers' unions are actively opposing laws aimed at attracting this new kind of teacher.[30] Karen Joseph, spokesperson for NEA's New Jersey affiliate, said of this phenomenon, "Many believe if you want to be a classroom teacher, you should go through the same training that they did."[31]

Notwithstanding alternate methods for accepting a new kind of teacher, teacher certification continues to be a significant issue in the debate about how to improve public education. One report from the National Center for Educational Statistics said that "almost all public school teachers had regular or advanced certification in their main assignment field. In contrast, just over half of private school teachers held similar certification."[32] For the observer who is "process"-oriented, these data may seem significant. For those who are "results"-oriented, however, these data may be less important than the demonstrated ability to teach effectively.

How should the quality of an education system be evaluated—by the training of its teachers or by the quality of the education of its students? A focus on "results" shows that 53 percent of public school twelfth graders applied to two- or four-year colleges for admission, whereas 76 percent of private school twelfth graders applied to two- or four-year colleges.[33] Of course, many factors affect these numbers and no single measure can indicate success or failure of an endeavor as complex as public and private education. Nonetheless, one's position on the process-versus-results argument determines what statistics are considered important. Additionally, these data suggest that private schools are competent and very competitive options for students wishing to pursue a college education.

SALARIES AND COSTS

Education is a people-intensive enterprise, and the single largest cost in a school district's budget is salaries and benefits. In 1990–1991 nationwide expenditures for only the instructional part of public elementary and secondary schools amounted to $122.2 billion. Of this, salaries and benefits accounted for almost $113 billion, some 92 percent of the instructional total.[34] Between 1980 and 1993 the average overall teacher salary, after adjustment for inflation, increased by 21 percent, from $29,766 to $35,873. According to NEA, in school year 1995–1996 the average salary for public schoolteachers was $37,846.[35] The average beginning salary for the same period increased from $20,504 to $23,969, a 17 percent gain.[36]

The vast majority of teachers are locked into union-negotiated salary schedules that limit and mechanically determine salary advancement according to the number of years taught and the degrees and credits earned. In NEA's world, the union's needs—protected by union-controlled, lock-step pay schedules—are more important than rewarding excellent teaching, with a salary increase.

Tim McConville, former executive for the National Right to Work Legal Defense Foundation, recounted that one teacher union boss was so arrogant she stated in a newspaper that she didn't push for salary increases because she wanted the power to force all the teachers in the school district to pay dues.[37] She traded teachers' salaries for union power, and blatantly at that. Even on casual examination, it is clear that NEA uses the bogus appeal of lock-step salary schedules to gain forced union membership and forced dues. And year-after-year, the many all-too-compliant school boards nod their heads in passive agreement.

Many critics today mistakenly blame teachers for all that is wrong with public education. Some express their frustration by condemning teachers and asserting that their salaries and benefits are too much for too little. This is neither accurate nor appropriate. Nor is it productive to conclude that teachers are overpaid. Good teachers deserve to be well compensated. Teachers are vital to our children's learning and to their school's effectiveness. Teachers should be compensated individually for superior performance—as are people in other occupations; they should not be forced to accept what the union gets for them. On the other hand, critics do have the right to expect teachers to be part of correcting the wrongs that plague public education.

WORKING CONDITIONS

Exploring the working conditions of teachers provides an additional view of teachers and their world. Averages do not, of course, tell much about working conditions in unique teaching situations. For their safety, some inner city teachers must leave their schools almost immediately after the school day ends. In contrast, some teachers in remote Alaskan villages live in "teacherages," teacher housing attached to the school—they may seldom leave the building in which they teach, and the school and teacherage are often the day-in and day-out center of village activity for young and old alike.

Such exceptions aside, under what conditions do most teachers teach? The vast majority, 91 percent in school year 1990–1991, were employed full time—with 8 percent in public schools and 15 percent in private schools employed part time. Teachers worked an average of thirty-five hours per week at school. (There were no data on the time teachers commit to their teaching duties off school premises or after school hours.) During these thirty-five hours, public schoolteachers who taught core subjects spent 20.2 hours each week teaching their specialty: English, math, social studies/history, or science.[38] Private schoolteachers spent 17.7 hours per week teaching these same four core subjects.[39] Both public and private schoolteachers presumably spent the remainder of the thirty-five hours teaching other subjects and attending to ancillary duties.

In 1987–1988 the average elementary teacher in a self-contained classroom spent twenty-one hours teaching the four core subjects. By 1990–1991 the time devoted to teaching these core subjects had decreased to twenty hours per week.[40] The average class size for self-contained public schoolteachers (usually elementary) was 24.7 students, and 20.7 for private schoolteachers. The average class size for public schoolteachers in departments (usually secondary) was 23.1 students, and 19.6 for private schoolteachers.[41]

Satisfaction with Teaching

In a 1987–1988 study the National Center for Education Statistics found that about one-third of all teachers would become teachers again if they again were to choose a career. Among the 5.6 percent of public schoolteachers and the 12.7 percent of private schoolteachers who left teaching from 1987 to 1989,[42] nearly 18 percent of the former and 12 percent of the latter said they expected to return to teaching within one year.[43] Although the data showed that private schoolteachers increased their income by an average of 23 percent within one year of leaving teaching for another occupation, the National Center of Education Statistics cautioned that the sample was too small and the standard error too high to be statistically significant.[44] "Teachers who left the profession in 1988–1989," the center concluded, "did not increase their incomes, on average, at least not immediately."[45]

Costs and Benefits

In considering these data about teachers, it is easy to forget that education is about students and what happens to them as a result of their association with teachers. A focus on teachers is a focus on input and process; a focus on students is a focus on output and results. As a rule, teachers' pay automatically rises for each year they teach and for earning credits by taking classes related (and sometimes unrelated) to their areas of teaching. But teachers do not award grades based on years the student has spent in school or on the number of credits earned over the student's career. Teachers award grades based on how well the student has learned a subject, as measured by student performance. Grades are awarded on individual student merit.

In 1966, just five years after NEA's transformation from a professional association to a labor union (a change that has increasingly misfocused teacher's efforts and energy), the average SAT verbal score for college-bound high school students was 466. The average math score was 492. In 1992 the average SAT verbal score for college-bound high school students was 423—down forty-three points. The average math score was 476—down sixteen points.[46] No wonder NEA's legislative program opposes "use of student test scores as criterion for teacher evaluations."[47] Yet, in-class tests are a major tool teachers use to measure a student's learning and to award grades.

It is ironic that the system of paying teachers is so disconnected from teacher achievement whereas the system those same teachers use to "pay" students is determined by student achievement. NEA seems to have little faith in a teacher's ability to produce and in a school board's willingness to compensate teachers fairly for students' achievements. NEA bosses, moreover, consistently block any district's effort to allow teachers to earn better pay when they successfully improve student learning. Individual achievement—student or teacher—is not the union's goal.

Instituting a system that does not reward teachers for improving the outcome of their teaching (student learning) is out of sync with market principles. In the short run, this may be a good union strategy. In the long run and on a larger scale, it hurts good teachers, diminishes the education of students, and causes the tax-paying public to lose faith in public education. We are beginning to see the results of NEA's failed strategy.

THE TEACHER CULTURE AND NEA CONTROL

Some familiarity with these statistics is important in order to learn about teachers, but numbers and statistics cannot tell the whole story. Perhaps more important are the values and beliefs these teachers hold and transfer from each generation of teachers to the following generations. The history and norms of the teacher culture tell us more about who teachers are and what they do than the statistics that describe who teaches; the data derive from what teachers *value* and *do*, not the other way around.

To know teachers, it is necessary to learn about the teacher culture that guides and directs them. What forces shape the culture that begets the mission that directs them? What role does NEA play in determining this culture and defining this mission?

Americans react with predictable fury when told someone or some organization has control over them. So it is with teachers who, in so much of their professional lives as semiautonomous agents, go into their classrooms, shut their doors, and teach children. Yet, we are all affected by the associations we keep and the organizations to which we belong. Compulsory unionism forces teachers to allow NEA to give form and substance to their daily lives. The union's monopoly bargaining powers mean that it negotiates the contracts that define their working lives and set out:

- grievance procedures that terminate with final and binding third-party arbitration
- mandated union fees for those who do not belong to NEA
- contractually defined procedures for evaluation
- release time for association business

- contractually defined procedures for ensuring educational employee decision making
- salary schedules based on preparation and length of service that exclude any form of merit pay.[48]

These and a host of other prescriptions and proscriptions impose NEA's notions of "the one right way" to be a teacher and deny teachers the liberty to step away from the crowd and follow their own ideas and ideals. Teachers are better than NEA wants them to be. Forced unionism allows them no choice but to accept the negotiated constrictions that are virtually universal facts of life for the majority of school districts in our nation. Maybe more than most teachers know or wish to admit, NEA has a controlling impact on their thinking and actions. Through this, NEA has control of the teaching corps, the control it has long sought.

How is it possible for a labor union to have such strong control of over 2,264,000 union members, 1,600,000 of whom are classroom teachers?

4

....

NEA's Control of Teachers: The Carrot and the Stick

"You take [NEA] members that don't believe in collective bargaining, that don't believe in our political ends, but you talk to them about [insurance benefits], they'll stand in the middle of the highway to defend it. That's the tie."[1]

—*Al Short, NEA/MEA lobbyist*

NEA HAS CAREFULLY CRAFTED A RELATIONSHIP with its members that gives the illusion of a democratically run union. But the truth is that NEA forces union membership, extracts compulsory dues payments, and then uses dues money to aggressively pursue political ends in which many of its members do not believe. That 35 to 40 percent of NEA's 2.2 million members describe themselves as Republicans gives an indication of the political disagreement within NEA[2]—an organization that gives its political power and financial support almost exclusively to Democrats and ultraliberal causes.

NEA claims phenomenal success in getting salaries, benefits, working conditions, and job security for its members. Of course, it matters little for many teachers whether these claims are real, since state law requires their union membership as a condition of employment. Whereas school officials must use good leadership skills to enlist teachers' commitment to school goals, NEA bosses have only to use legislature-granted power to hold teachers captive to union goals. If it were otherwise, NEA would not prevent teachers from negotiating their own contracts based on individual merit. NEA will not allow teachers to leave the collective to act in their own best interests. (Appendix B shows which states are compulsory unionism states and which are right-to-work states.)

On the day-to-day level, it is less evident what prevents usually independent teachers from revolting against NEA's often heavy-handed control. In the past fourteen decades, NEA has fashioned many methods of control. To begin, however, it is good to understand the dual buffer function NEA's Representative Assembly plays in: (1) insulating NEA-national from members' concerns about students and teaching, and (2) translating NEA-national's goals to local NEA affiliates in ways individual teachers support—or at least tolerate.

AN UNREPRESENTATIVE REPRESENTATIVE ASSEMBLY

Annually, each local union affiliate sends teachers to NEA's summer conference. These delegates to the Representative Assembly, nine thousand in total and some 4/10 of 1 percent of the total membership, are often the most militant union activists in the school districts. In what NEA widely heralds as a democratic meeting, delegates congregate in July ostensibly to bring their local concerns to a national arena and to vote the labor union's resolutions and legislative program for the following year. Once these nine thousand delegates present their chosen causes and vote resolutions into the record, the organizational belief statements and action platforms become the marching orders NEA expects its 2.2 million members to follow. How can NEA-national effectively commit 2.2 million members to resolutions and legislative programs many do not support?

Powerful mechanisms give NEA its hold on teachers—the old carrot-and-stick strategy.

THE CARROT

To the extent that traditional labor unions are a viable concept, NEA's existence as a labor union is not questioned. Ignoring for the moment that in twenty-one states NEA has acquired the legal muscle to force teachers to join the union as a condition of employment, it helps to understand how NEA union bosses use their claims of unparalleled success in contract negotiations to control teachers. Although in actual practice NEA's various carrot strategies are inseparably woven together, these activities are examined separately here.

First, it is important to recognize that good teaching deserves reward. When considering NEA's "carrot" strategies, this analysis may seem to be critical of teachers or to argue against teachers being fairly compensated. This is not the case. To the contrary, teachers are fundamentally important to the success of the teaching–learning relationship, and they should be free to negotiate whatever salaries and benefits their individual achievements merit. The point of this examination is that NEA first restricts teachers' freedom to do for themselves and then repackages its collectivist control of teachers as a good thing for which teachers must be beholden to NEA.

NEA'S DEFENSE OF TEACHERS

While the media, parents, and taxpayers sometimes publicly criticize teachers for not meeting expectations, NEA is consistently outspoken in its defense of teachers. In its many publications and frequent informal communications, NEA tells teachers they are important, they are doing a good job under difficult circumstances, and they are valued—if not by anyone else, at least by NEA.

The point, however, is that NEA bosses skillfully use public discontent against public education to make teachers feel the need to circle their wagons in support of NEA and against their critics. This we–they tactic is a time-proven gambit to galvanize usually independent teachers into a tight group for the common defense. The result is more than a response to broad and often unfocused criticism; it is, with manipulation, a powerful force in the union bosses' efforts to gain teachers' loyalty. Teachers come to feel they must pay their dues to keep NEA defending them or face firing by hostile forces.

MONEY TALKS

NEA lives by the old axiom "money talks." The union knows that the sum of dues it collects is based on a percentage of each teacher's salary; therefore, one of the best ways to increase the money in its coffers is to increase its members' salaries. To these ends, NEA is hard-nosed, if not brutal, in its collective bargaining.

Forced to follow the union, teachers cannot negotiate individually for a salary based on their own merits. They take whatever NEA negotiators get for them—even if that turns out to be less than they could have gotten on their own—and pay their dues. It is easy to see NEA's two-part strategy: (1) force teachers to be dependent on NEA for salary negotiations, and (2) keep the dues-paying cash cow producing a steady stream of money to replenish the union's coffers.

All of this is packaged and marketed so that few teachers—or parents, taxpayers, policy makers—consider there could be other ways. Teachers are given to understand that they would be cast upon a rocky reef of economic ruin if it were not for NEA's strong hand. Teachers are also told that the only way NEA can continue to fight the good fight is if teachers give up their individualism and band together under the NEA banner of collective might—as if their membership in NEA were voluntary. The result, for the most part, is that NEA negotiations are presently viewed as normal and desirable.

THE MICHIGAN STRONGHOLD

NEA bosses also take advantage of teacher benefit packages to curry favor with teachers and, more importantly, make money for the union—at taxpayer and teacher expense. In Michigan, long a citadel of NEA activity and the home state of recent NEA president Keith

Geiger and current Executive Director Don Cameron, it appears the Michigan Education Association (MEA) has gained generous revenues for itself through manipulating teacher health insurance benefits. According to *Forbes* magazine, MEA created the two hundred–person Michigan Education Special Services Association (MESSA), and through MESSA, Blue Cross/Blue Shield offers comprehensive teacher insurance.[3]

The MESSA scheme works like this. MEA first negotiates health insurance demands into teacher contracts. Then MEA requires the district to buy the insurance through MESSA. Since MESSA insurance costs about $1,000 more per teacher per year than comparable insurance the districts could obtain from other sources,[4] there is plenty of profit. School boards, however, understand that MEA is serious about selling insurance, and any dissent could result in a strike or some other unpleasant reaction.

In 1992 the lucrative MESSA generated $360 million in revenues and $87 million in "surplus" from its insurance plan. From its earnings, MESSA paid MEA an annual fee of $1.5 million—a nice addition to MEA's financial coffers and to the war chest of an NEA subsidiary already known for its aggressive union activities.[5]

Following its nine-month investigation of MEA and MESSA, the Mackinac Center for Public Policy published a sixty-four-page report documenting two major findings: "(1) tens of millions of educational dollars are wasted each year on unusually costly teacher health insurance; and (2) the MEA's insurance subsidiary is part of a systematic plan to use money intended for education to subsidize the MEA's basic operations and political activity."[6] In its study, the Mackinac Center also found that the generous insurance benefits MEA negotiates for its members are "an effective program for controlling the loyalty and support of the union's members."[7]

Michigan is a compulsory-unionism state where teachers are forced to join a union or not be allowed to work. In Michigan in 1994 there were 80,522[8] active teachers; NEA claimed a membership of 136,507 in all membership classes—active, retired, life, student, substitute, reserve, staff, and associate.[9] From these members MEA says it enjoys unquestioned support. But how do teachers feel about the ideological bent of this organization? The Mackinac

Center's 1989 survey of MEA members revealed deep discontent with MEA's political and social stands:

- 86 percent of leaders in the union are bothered that "the MEA takes stands I do not agree with"
- 69 percent of teachers are bothered that "the MEA takes stands I do not agree with"
- 55 percent of teachers are bothered that "the MEA is too liberal"
- 64 percent of teachers are bothered that "the MEA is mainly committed to union goals, not professional goals for education"
- 75 percent of teachers are bothered that "the MEA gets involved in issues, like abortion, that have nothing to do with education."[10]

But despite their differences with MEA, Michigan teachers are forced to pay dues to support it and its political agenda. MEA chief lobbyist Al Short's machiavellian depiction of Michigan's teachers cited at the head of this chapter shows an arrogant union boss's flaunting of NEA's power over teachers. The truth is that many teachers do not believe in MEA's political ends but are forced to accept them. That NEA and MEA have long forgotten the critical connection between a principled teaching profession and the survival of a democracy is painfully obvious. That Michigan's teachers are forced to play a role in this abuse of the public trust is, at minimum, hurtful. If this is a carrot, it is a carrot with a sour taste. Yet, until NEA's iron-fisted control of teachers is broken, it will continue to force feed such schemes to a couple of million teachers.

But NEA goes well beyond the familiar salary and benefits carrots. Within the collective bargaining agreement your local school board has negotiated with the teachers' union, you will find contract language on grievance procedures and, sometimes, maintenance of standards agreements. These two contract guarantees are good examples of tools NEA uses to control school districts and the people who work in them.

GRIEVANCE AND BINDING ARBITRATION

Good grievance procedures are helpful when people who disagree over issues stand firm. They lend structure to disputes and depersonalize disagreements between teachers and administrators. These procedures keep disputes within local districts where local people resolve them. This is the theory. But in practice, NEA representatives negotiate contract language into grievance procedures that effectively extends the union's power to write changes into the master contract even when the district is not holding formal negotiations—a strategy that extends NEA's monopoly power over school boards and teachers.

Taxpayers elect fellow citizens to local school boards to, among other duties, represent them in contract negotiations with teachers. Teacher-filed grievances, however, create a separate form of negotiations that can end in compulsory arbitration where a third-party arbitrator, who is frequently not a local resident, decides the outcome. This outside arbitrator can render decisions that become school district policy and obligate local taxpayers to spend more money on education or agree to practices they otherwise would not approve. Grievance procedures that end in compulsory arbitration—sometimes called binding arbitration—usurp the authority of local school boards to set policies for school districts and circumvent local elections that establish school funding.

Consider how a grievance procedure can circumvent contract negotiations. Wise school boards will not agree to negotiated class-size limits. Nonetheless, union negotiators keep pushing until eventually a board agrees to contract language that, in some small way, mentions class size. The union knows that once an issue is mentioned in the contract, it becomes a grievable item. And, as part of its strategy to move the issue into binding arbitration, the union waits for—or encourages—the right case and then files a grievance. Once the union files its grievance and forces the issue to binding arbitration, each side must present its case before an arbitrator.

In all likelihood, the arbitrator determines a resolution somewhere between the union's demands and the district's position. Each time the union files such a grievance, the arbitrator's middle-ground finding moves the union one step closer to obtaining the class-size limit it wants. At some point in its long-term, incremental-gain strategy, the union achieves the power to insist on class-size limits. Without ever going back to the bargaining table or the school board, the union has successfully forced the school board to hire, at taxpayers' expense, additional teachers for the same number of students.

Yet, the research on class size does not support NEA's current campaign for smaller classes—at least not as a student-learning issue. Research certainly does not support NEA's Resolution B-5 Class Size that "urges its affiliates to seek an optimal class size of fifteen students in regular programs" and further declares "that class size maximums must be established, with Association involvement."[11] It is logical to assume that fewer students in a teacher's classroom correspondingly reduces that teacher's work load. But it is not sound reasoning to assume that reduced class size automatically, and by itself, increases student learning.

The class-size issue, one NEA has camouflaged as a student-learning issue, is actually a workforce-expansion, forced-dues issue. The union's ultimate goal is to increase the number of teachers needed to teach the same number of students, thereby creating more teaching jobs and funneling more compulsory dues into NEA's pockets.

A good bit of "research" on class size as it relates to student learning seems designed to support the opinions or goals of some researchers who favor class-size limits. This, of course, is not research; it is false science and academic fraud. But not all research supports NEA's contentions. To summarize previous research on class size *as it relates to student learning*, Glen E. Robinson published a 1990 study that determined:

■ The most positive effects of small classes on pupil learning occur in grades K-3 in reading and mathematics, particularly in classes of twenty-two or fewer students. However, the first year's positive effects may not be sustained in subsequent years.

- Studies examining student attitudes and behavior found the most favorable effects of smaller classes in the primary grades.
- Smaller classes can positively affect the academic achievement of economically disadvantaged and ethnic minority students.
- Within the midrange of twenty-three to thirty pupils, class size has little impact on the academic achievement of most pupils in most subjects above the primary grades.
- The positive effects of class size on student achievement decrease as grade levels increase; however, the available studies in specific subject areas in the upper grades are limited in both number and quality.
- Little if any increase in pupil achievement can be expected from reducing class size if teachers continue to use the same instructional methods and procedures in the smaller classes that they used in the larger classes.
- Reductions in class size have small positive effects on achievement in comparison to many less costly learning interventions and strategies.[12]

In a 1994 study entitled "The Relationship Between School Size, Student/Teacher Ratio and School Efficiency," John W. Alspaugh of the University of Missouri discovered that an "*increase* in school size and S/T [student/teacher] ratio are also associated with an increase in sixth grade achievement"[13] (emphasis added). In his study, Alspaugh found:

> As the student teacher ratio increases the sixth grade achievement scores also increase for all subject areas. This seems to be a little inconsistent with what one would logically expect to find.... With the increase in S/T ratio or class size there is probably a change in the class environment. The small classes may have a relaxed atmosphere with a lot of social interaction at the expense of time spent on instructional activities that lead to achievement as measured by MMAT [Missouri Mastery and Achievement Test]. Whereas the teachers in

the larger classes must be more organized and keep the students busy to maintain an orderly class so there is more time on the learning task and hence higher achievement test scores. The larger class size may be more stressful for both the teachers and students. Teaching is a personal thing so most teachers and students prefer small classes. However, small classes as reflected in a low S/T ratio do not lead to higher production efficiency as measured by test scores.[14]

NEA masks its labor union goals in campaigns ostensibly conducted to help teachers and improve student learning. Perhaps this would be acceptable if communities had unlimited resources to fund policies that, if not supported by research, at least make parents feel better.

Unfortunately, the hard realities of today's school finances demand staffing decisions based on research about how best to improve student learning.

The Minneapolis School District recently confronted such a situation. Its school board had painted the district into the class-size corner and was wrestling with the dilemma of whether to keep to the letter of its 1990 referendum promising maximum class sizes or to the spirit of the referendum by maintaining control of district resources and stepping away from its rigid class-size limits. The board could do the latter by using the $3.6 million garnered through increasing class size to balance the district's budget while continuing to find ways to improve learning for all the district's students.[15] Had Minneapolis written class-size limits into the contract it has with its teachers' union and then increased student enrollment above the contracted limits, it would likely have faced grievance and arbitration—or it would have had to concede to other union demands in an effort to negotiate itself from under the class-size agreement.

Confirming that grievance procedures are an extension of collective bargaining, NEA's *Handbook 1996–1997* combines grievance procedures and collective bargaining in the same resolution—F-6 Collective Bargaining and Grievance Procedures.[16] NEA makes it clear that it sees these two artifacts of union life as two sides of the same negotiations coin. In many local collective bargaining agreements, binding arbitration is the final step in grievance procedures. Contract language is much alike from district to district:

> The arbitrator's decision will be in writing and will set forth his/her finding of fact, reasoning, and conclusions on the issues submitted to him/her. The decision of the Arbitrator shall be final and binding upon the Employer, the Association and the grievant(s).[17]

From the perspective of the teacher who initiates a grievance, this final step promises resolution of an issue. In theory, through the grievance process the teacher's concerns receive due consideration against the arguments of an administrator, and an arbitrator resolves the grievance with a just decision drawn on the merits of the arguments. In practice, however, arbitrators—who are jointly selected by NEA and the school district and who make their living by being acceptable to both sides of what becomes a union-administrator dispute—cannot afford to antagonize one side or the other. They often work more on finding an acceptable, middle-ground, political solution than on deciding issues on their merits. Arbitrators almost never find totally in favor of one side against the other, and often the individual teacher is left out in the cold.

Milton Chappell, an attorney for the National Right to Work Legal Defense Foundation and a leading expert on NEA, pointed out that an exception to middle-ground findings sometimes occurs when a teacher takes legal action against his or her union, and that action ends in binding arbitration. The teacher, who will in all likelihood never need an arbitrator again and who has nothing to do with hiring the arbitrator, has no clout with the arbitrator. In such cases, it is not unheard-of for the arbitrator to find totally in favor of the union.[18]

The effect of any one grievance-initiated binding arbitration case on board policy is usually limited. Because it is rare that the arbitrator totally favors either the teacher or the administrator, splitting the difference is the predictable outcome. The filing of grievances, however, often stems less from an individual teacher's concerns than from the union's desire to "test contract language" or "push the interpretation of contract language." Middle-ground compromises resulting from a series of two, three, or more grievances are a sure strategy by which NEA incrementally gains ground without risking or trading anything at the negotiations table. When the United States of America celebrated its bicentennial in 1976, NEA's communications to its local affiliates invited teachers to file two hundred grievances in celebration of the nation's two hundredth anniversary. A series of carefully selected grievances over one issue all but assures the expansion of union power.

Though some grievances have little to do with individual teacher issues and a lot to do with union strategy, NEA touts the gains the union makes through binding arbitration as yet another carrot to inspire teacher loyalty.

NO-REPRISAL CLAUSE

To bolster their powers further, union negotiators expand grievance procedures with a "no-reprisal" article. Such wording is intended to prohibit a school board and its agents from taking reprisals against a teacher because he or she filed a grievance.

Because of the protections teachers have in statute law, case law, labor law, civil rights law, school board policy, administrative regulations, and negotiated agreements, these no-reprisal clauses are superfluous and unnecessary. Union negotiators add no-reprisal clauses to contracts primarily for show. Since these clauses *assume* unethical behavior on the part of the district, they are an insult to school board members and administrators. By agreeing to no-reprisal clauses, school boards give the appearance that reprisals against individual teachers are a common practice. This further supports the union's contention that teachers need NEA to protect them from unethical board members and administrators. Maybe because of this, the no-reprisal clause is a popular item in NEA-negotiated contracts.

The union can use no-reprisal clauses for another purpose. When no-reprisal clauses include protection for the person filing the grievance and for the members of the union committee that investigates the grievance, these clauses become a guarantee that no adverse district-initiated action can befall the grievant or his or her support team—even if that action is unrelated to the issue of the grievance. Under this special cloak of protection, union members who believe, for example, that they will not be given tenure or who think they may receive some disciplinary action for reasons unrelated to the grievance, rush to become active in a grievance action. They do this for the purpose of gaining protection from board of education or administrative action. Since the union decides which teachers will serve on grievance committees, the union can in this way protect anyone it chooses.[19] Another plus for the union; another loss for students, parents, and taxpayers.

MAINTENANCE OF STANDARDS

Making sure it has not missed any opportunity to strengthen its power and give teachers the impression they need NEA's protection, NEA uses a device called "maintenance of standards." A maintenance of standards contract clause extends NEA's power over school boards by allowing the union continuously to negotiate "conditions of employment and working conditions." Typical language of a maintenance of standards clause is:

> All conditions of employment and general working conditions shall be maintained at not less than the highest minimum standards in effect in the school system at the time this agreement is executed, provided that such conditions shall be improved for the benefit of teachers as required by this agreement. This agreement shall not be interpreted or applied in any manner which will in any way deprive teachers of professional and/or employment benefits and/or advantages heretofore enjoyed. Except as required by this agreement, the duties and responsibilities of teachers in any position in the negotiating unit will not be substantially altered or in any way increased without prior negotiation with the organization.[20]

In other words, unless the local NEA affiliate agrees, the board of education and its administrative staff cannot make adjustments to meet the changing challenges of education if the union construes those changes as negatively affecting conditions of employment and working conditions. So, while NEA militants often test contracts through application of grievances and consume many hours of administrators' time to see how far they can push interpretations of contract language, NEA protects itself by making certain that school boards and administration can make no changes in conditions of employment and working conditions.[21]

The conditions of employment protected by maintenance of standards clauses could preclude any number of school board decisions and administrative actions. A maintenance of standards clause could stop a school principal from changing a teacher's schedule to accommodate an increase or decrease in student enrollment; or preclude an assistant principal from changing teachers' room assignments to accommodate increases and decreases in class sizes; or prevent a school board from changing the starting time of a school because of adjustments in districtwide bus schedules brought on by an influx of new families to the district. No matter the changing conditions and finances of a school district and no matter the fate of students, these clauses can prevent school districts and administrators from having the flexibility needed to pursue school board objectives and the public good. It is another example of NEA against the taxpayers.

The maintenance of standards clause is difficult for principals to administer. Consider a district where an NEA affiliate has negotiated contract language that presents class-size limits only as recommended guidelines. Acting in good faith, a principal for a time voluntarily and carefully observes "class-size limitation guidelines," but, because of increased student enrollment, must later exceed these guidelines. The union considers the principal's actions a violation of the standards he or she earlier established when following the class-size guideline. (The principal's previous actions have become an "established past practice.") The union then objects to the principal's action under the maintenance of standards clause by arguing that the standard that earlier defined teachers' working conditions—the "guideline" the principal voluntarily observed—had "not been maintained at the highest minimum standard." The union takes the issue through binding arbitration and wins a small concession. A series of such grievances eventually results in mandated, hard-line, class-size limits. In this way, the interplay between a maintenance of standards clause and a grievance procedure that ends in binding arbitration requires a school board to hire, and taxpayers to pay, additional teachers—which feeds the union more dues and boosts its power.

With no danger of overstatement, it is accurate to say that a local NEA affiliate with monopoly bargaining, a maintenance of standards clause, and a grievance procedure that ends in binding arbitration literally runs the school district and every school in the district.

THE SOCIALIZATION OF TEACHERS

To continue to exist, every group must recruit new members and educate them into the group's purposes, norms, and traditions. New people also want to be accepted and feel welcome. Socialization of new members is the process through which both the group and new members' needs are met. NEA activists use the socialization of new teachers to make certain these teachers think they need the union to protect their jobs.

School districts are no different from other complex organizations, and socializing new employees is important. School districts and schools are made up of formal and informal groups, each with its own view of what the organization is about. To a large extent, the group that socializes new teachers into teaching and into the school district controls the attitudes and orientation of those teachers. The teacher whom the district hired can become a very different teacher one or two years into the teacher-socialization process. In *Managers of Virtue*, Tyack and Hansot recounted how "[v]eteran police told rookies to forget the police academy and to learn from peers about the real world of the beat."[22] In like fashion, the most powerful socialization for new teachers comes from fellow teachers and the teacher subculture.

The importance of teacher socialization and its potential is not lost on teacher unions. Nina Bascia described the process of socialization in *Unions in Teachers' Professional Lives*. She wrote about a longtime teacher who "considered district labor history a crucial part of new teachers' socialization." Describing her work to socialize new teachers to a union mentality, this teacher recounted how "[l]ast year when we had the [walk out], as younger teachers came in, they were quite starry-eyed and we old veterans sat down and explained this long history of things to them."[23] It was the union teachers' view of the labor dispute that new teachers heard. If the district had tried to tell new teachers its view of the issues, the union would probably have filed an unfair labor practice charge to stop the district's "unlawful" communication with union members.

Clearly, teacher unionists consider socialization important in determining whose reality, the district's or the union's, becomes the dominant influence in shaping the attitudes and directing the actions of new teachers. When push comes to shove during teacher-contract negotiations, the socialization of teachers pays off for union officials. Sometimes teachers must decide between doing what they know is best for their students and doing what the union wants them to do.

Describing the conflicting thoughts in such situations, a California teacher recalled that "the people that were in the union were really riding the people not to do any extra supervising, not to write letters for kids, and these sort of things that hurt the reasons we're here."[24] In this case, the union gained the effect it wanted. Teachers stopped directing club activities and refused to write recommendations for students. Teachers, torn by pressures to choose one of two mutually exclusive actions, followed the expectations and traditions of the union. The union frequently initiates demands that generate conflicts and put teachers in difficult circumstances. However, if the union has successfully socialized the teachers into NEA's worldview, the path through seemingly impossible choices is much more clear.

Principals, too, are socialized into the education culture. In fact, one of the transition rituals for a newly hired principal occurs after various members of the staff have formally or informally assessed the "needs" of the new leader. Then begins a process of socialization to bring the new principal more closely in line with the prevailing practices of a particular school. While this process is necessary to some degree and can be productive, it can be counterproductive to children's education and to teachers' effectiveness if NEA representatives are successful in "socializing" new principals to the extent that they cannot do the job they were hired to do. It is not uncommon for NEA building representatives to put pressure on principals during their first year to bend on this or give a little on that. If necessary, the union will send a UniServ operative to make the message more clear and to show who has the power. Unless the principal responds appropriately, union militants let the principal know they will speak for the staff in expressing their unhappiness and loss of confidence in the new principal's leadership, management style, communication style, or some other aspect of administration. Since superintendents and school boards hold principals accountable for running a happy ship, the message to principals new to a school is quite clear: Keep the union happy or bad things will happen to you and your career.

KEEPING THE ADMINISTRATIVE WOLF FROM THE DOOR

NEA representatives convince teachers they need union help for contract negotiations and for violations of teachers' "rights." NEA also wants teachers to believe the union knows best how to manage events in teachers' daily lives. With little or no freedom to break from the union and control their own professional lives, teachers are encouraged to become rule-driven rather than guided by professional standards.

Examples of work-limiting articles that litter negotiated agreements include these few taken from one district's union contract:

- Faculty-type meetings do not extend normally more than one (1) hour prior to staff arrival time at the individual building or extend normally more than one (1) hour beyond the individual building's staff dismissal time.
- No more than one (1) extended-time meeting shall be required of any individual during any given school week. Emergency-type meetings shall be called when conditions require.

- No meetings shall be held after the student day on Fridays, or days preceding holidays except in emergencies.
- No certified employee shall be required to attend more than one (1) "open house" type meeting per year unless covered by Appendix S.[25]

These "agreements" might seem superfluous—what sane building principal would call a staff meeting on a Friday afternoon? But display of these statements in a negotiated agreement is one more reminder that, if it were not for NEA, administrators would routinely mistreat teachers.

Consider these same prohibitions in the context of an enterprise that must sustain its existence in a competitive marketplace. Only in a government-protected, public-sector "professional association" could one find such an attitude. Isn't it a hallmark of professionals to work until the "job" is done and they have served the clients' best interests, even if that requires more than one meeting a week? When the Fief, Washington, NEA affiliate went on strike in October 1995, an Associated Press article reported the "talks reached an impasse two weeks ago and the union asked teachers to avoid volunteering for after-school work, such as supervising at football games or attending staff meetings."[26]

NEA's Defense of Nontenured Teachers

In many states, teachers begin teaching for a two- or three-year probationary period to demonstrate their teaching competence and/or improve their teaching skills. Because they have not yet received tenure,* they are called nontenured or probationary teachers. At the end of the probationary period, the local school board either promotes them to tenure or releases them from employment. Nontenured teachers who receive two or three years' satisfactory

---

*Defined in *The American Heritage Dictionary* as "permanence of position, often granted an employee after a specified number of years." Tenure is usually defined in each state under statute law or administrative code.

evaluations almost always gain tenure. Those few who do not are nonretained—that is, not rehired by that district.

As expected, evaluation of teachers, especially of nontenured teachers, is a high-stakes issue for NEA. Since principals are responsible for writing the performance evaluations of teachers, NEA building representatives and UniServe agents make certain that principals understand how important it is for them to write "good" evaluations. Even when he or she has worked with and tried to help an underperforming nontenured teacher, the principal who recommends nonretention is in for a painful demonstration of NEA zeal and cunning.

In many states, the principal's recommendation for nonretention will end in a hearing before a special board or before the school board. At the teacher's discretion, the hearing can be public. During this hearing, the principal will need to describe in great detail the specific problems the teacher has not rectified during the two- or three-year period of trial employment and document all remediation support provided. NEA may only marginally defend against the charges. Instead, it will aggressively attack the competence, professionalism, and motivation of the principal. People who attend these hearings, and are not aware of NEA's tactics, could only conclude that the principal is on trial and is an incompetent and loathsome beast. Even if NEA loses the case, the principal has learned a lesson—and in full view of teachers whom NEA is trying to impress. It is a painful process most principals never experience. The few who do seldom again make so bold an action.

To clarify his and NEA's position on the issue of teacher tenure, former NEA President Keith Geiger explained, "I don't ever want it to be cheap to lay off an incompetent teacher." Realizing, evidently, that this statement might sound extreme even for him, Geiger added, "I don't want it to be impossible either."[27] Even in situations where NEA's aggressive defense of a nontenured teacher is unsuccessful, its apparent willingness to defend even the most incompetent teacher, no matter the issue and weight of evidence, may impress some NEA members.

Under increasing public pressure and with a new president, NEA bosses stated in July of 1997 that the union would no longer automatically defend bad teachers. This presents at least two interesting dilemmas for NEA. First, how will NEA determine which teachers it will not defend? What criteria will NEA establish to define a "bad" teacher, and how will NEA determine if a teacher meets or falls short of the criteria? In what ways will this be the same as or different from the criteria school boards apply? Second, UniServe agents have told me on more than one occasion that they had to defend a bad teacher, or else the teacher would sue NEA for lack of representation and breach of contract. What, if anything, has changed that now allows NEA to step away from its self-described responsibility to defend all teachers?

THE COLLEGE CONNECTION

In the early 1800s teachers were often graduates of programs in arts and letters. They were not schooled in pedagogy or in what was later called the science of education. In 1880 Charles Francis Adams, grandson and great-grandson of former U.S. presidents, spoke before NEA to argue his plan for educational reform. Adams believed the only correct principle around which to organize schools was science, what he described as the study of how children learn.[28] At about this time, Thomas Bicknell—who had been Rhode Island commissioner of schools and was then editor of the *Journal of Education*—observed that universities had not taken control of education. He lamented that local school committees (precursors to today's school boards), which he believed unfit to lead schools, were the controlling agents of local schools. Bicknell, who built his ideas on the European model for central-government control of education, decided that American education needed a central policy-forming group. He appealed to his colleagues to establish such a group within NEA.[29]

The connection between NEA and college programs in teacher education grew from those early years into the close relationship NEA holds now with many teacher education programs and professors. It is not uncommon for professors of education to facilitate student membership into NEA. In 1994 approximately 48,560 university students[30] and more than 85,000 university professors were NEA members.[31] NEA's Resolution Program declares that college and university teacher education programs should "include instructional content in the areas of job contracts, salary schedules, benefit programs, and working conditions."[32]

NEA's reasons for demanding this inclusion are obvious enough, and its intent becomes even more clear when considered in the context of a 1997 resolution that states NEA "believes that its affiliates should take immediate steps to become involved in college and university committees that control teacher education programs."[33] Just as NEA President Mary Bradford's 1918 "complete national plan" for education called for NEA control of teacher preparation programs, so today NEA officials seek to control college and university teacher education programs.

Jo Seker is a veteran classroom teacher of fifteen years, co-founder of an Ohio independent teacher organization, and author of articles on teachers and forced unionism. I asked her how NEA could control all the independent people who are our schools' teachers. She replied, "I think the reason is historical for one thing. When I was coming out of school, we were taught the professional thing to do was to belong to an association, at that time it was an association.... So I think we have that among teachers in the older generation,... many [of whom] still will not take a position against the union."[34]

CONTROLLING WHO GETS CERTIFIED TO TEACH

NEA continues to lobby aggressively for what it describes as "rigorous state standards for entry into the teaching profession."[35] NEA says it wants teachers (or, as it puts it, "professional educators, the majority of whom are licensed and practicing public school-teachers"[36]) to control state teacher licensing and certification boards. Certainly licensing—where there is to be licensing—and granting of teaching certification should involve teachers; that is not the issue. The issue is whether NEA—a private labor union—should control this gateway into teaching. NEA is working to control state licensing agencies and impose adoption of the proposed and much-discussed Professional Standards Boards, as defined and advanced in NEA Resolution G-1.[37] This board would give NEA yet another government-mandated, centralized bureaucracy by which to control public education and, eventually, gain control over who can teach in private schools.

In the same set of resolutions that demands "rigorous state standards for entry into the teaching profession," NEA declared, "[t]he Association urges the elimination of state statutes/regulations that require teachers to renew their licenses. Where such renewal continues to be required, standardized literacy and basic skills tests to determine competency should not be used."[38]

This is most curious: NEA wants rigorous standards for those who wish to enter teaching and it also wants lifetime teaching licenses or no renewal standards for those already in teaching. Does NEA's desire to control who enters the teaching profession reflect a concern for licensing only qualified and capable people or does NEA have other purposes in mind?

Revealing its real concern, NEA proclaimed, "A teaching license must be recognized as the primary requirement for employment in every public *and private school* (pre-K through 12). No license should be issued unless an individual possesses the entry-level knowledge and skills required for teaching"[39] (emphasis added). NEA clearly wants to control who enters both public and private teaching.

But strangely, NEA believes that once a person gains entrance into teaching, some reasonable level of demonstrated "literary and basic skills" is no longer relevant to quality teaching. Could it be that NEA is: (1) concerned with retaining union members who are already paying dues and who may not be able to pass current or future "literacy and basic skills" tests, (2) maneuvering to gain control of and authority over boards that determine who can teach, even in private schools, and (3) erecting road blocks to stop, or at least control, all efforts to bring higher standards to the teaching ranks?

If NEA controls access to teaching in public and private schools and, through compulsory unionism, can force all teachers to join the union, NEA bosses assure themselves a constant flow of dues dollars. That money will then buy the power to effect the changes they want in education, and in American communities across the land.

TEACHER CERTIFICATION—TEACHER COMPETENCE

The loose connection between teacher certification and assumed teacher competence deserves examination. NEA is on record regarding its views of teacher competency testing. It has stated, "The National Education Association believes that competency testing must not be used as a condition of employment, license retention, evaluation, placement, ranking, or promotion of licensed teachers. The Association also opposes the use of pupil progress, standardized achievement tests, or student assessment tests for purposes of teacher evaluations."[40]

Closing another door to accountability, NEA's 1993–1994 resolutions declared that "evaluation by private, profit-making groups" is a "deleterious" practice that is "detrimental to public education" and "must be eliminated."[41] NEA's *process* actively resists all attempts to use *output* (student learning) as a means of accountability.

Parents and taxpayers are less satisfied with the old "process" charade. In the January 3, 1995, edition of the *Minneapolis Star Tribune*, a reporter on the education beat observed, "Just as many students have been rewarded for merely showing up, so have teachers and administrators. Without a fair mechanism to assess and reward quality teaching, the time clock and other mechanical indicators—such as time in service and number of post-graduate credits or degrees—[will continue] to suffice." The reporter warned, "The public is demanding better services from the [public school system] it is paying for now, before it will even consider paying more."[42]

Despite public sentiment on this issue, NEA, with the help of the United States Department of Education, is moving to take control of who gets certified to teach.*

---

*In his 27 July 1993 memorandum, "Analysis of S.1150 for Compulsory Union Power," Milton Chappell, staff attorney for the National Right To Work Legal Defense Foundation, examined S.1150, the *Goals 2000: Educate America Act*, and warned that "S.1150 gives these various boards and panels [created by the *Goals 2000: Educate America*

THE STICK

NEA is a self-serving labor union, and it aggressively pursues its goals even when these goals work against students, parents, school boards, and taxpayers. NEA is also heavy-handed, even ruthless, with teachers who are not sufficiently attracted to NEA's goals to think and act the way NEA would have them think and act.

FIRING TEACHERS WHO DO NOT PAY UNION DUES

To assure power and prosperity, labor union officials maintain that their unions must have the membership of a strong majority of employees and the exclusive right to represent the whole employee group in negotiating agreements with management. In states where NEA does not gain this majority by using state-granted compulsory unionism laws to force teachers to join, NEA is aggressive in recruit-

---

Act] the authority to work with such broad-based entities, that it is certain that labor organizations, especially the NEA, will be supplying these panels with the criteria, goals and standards which the panels will eventually adopt and impose on the Nation." Mr. Chappell also observed "that membership on each of the 52 state panels must include "school teachers" and "representatives of teachers' organizations... and labor leaders," to be appointed by the Governor and the chief State school officer. Eight of the 28 members of the National Skill Standards Board must be "representatives of organized labor selected from among individuals recommended by recognized national labor federations." ("State" includes the District of Columbia and Puerto Rico.)

Further, Title III of S.1150 "requires each State improvement plan to 'involve broad-based and ongoing classroom teacher input in... the State's system of teacher... preparation and licensure, and of continuing professional development programs.'" Teachers should be involved in these various panels and boards, if these panels and boards are to exist at all. But, in these and similar situations, the term "teacher" is synonymous with "NEA union activist" and represents further NEA encroachment on states' rights to certify teachers.

ing teachers and exacting from local school boards the exclusive right to represent teachers. NEA often gains its majority membership by negotiating a contract provision that requires all teachers who work in a district to join NEA, or at least to pay union dues—what is variously called agency shop fees, service fees, or, in the twisted rhetoric of NEA, fair share fees.* When a teacher refuses to join NEA or pay dues, the terms of the negotiated agreement may require the local school board to fire the dissident teacher—even if he or she has an excellent teaching record.

Samuel Blumenfeld cited well-known cases in his 1984 book, *NEA: Trojan Horse in American Education.* Blumenfeld wrote:

> Tenured teachers have been fired because they refused to
> join the union or pay its fees. This is what happened to

---

*In *The NEA and AFT: Teacher Unions in Power and Politics*, Haar, Lieberman, and Troy discussed service fees. They wrote: "The union rationale for service fees is that members of the bargaining unit should not receive the benefits of representation without paying their 'fair share' of its costs. This rationale is based on the fact that when a union becomes the exclusive representative, it must represent everyone in the bargaining unit, whether or not the individuals are members of the union. Thus the interests of the employees are to be 'free riders,' that is, to receive the benefits of representation without paying for the union services that supposedly were responsible for them.

"There are several objections to this rationale. Obviously, if a union did not seek exclusive representation, it would have no right to force nonmembers to pay for the union's services. In practice, the unions demanded the right to represent everyone, and then, having achieved this right, cited it as a reason to force nonmembers to pay the service fee. It is as if someone painted your house against your wishes, and then demanded that you pay for the services so that you would not be a 'free rider.'

"The most basic objection to service fees is that they violate the rights of individuals to contract for their labor. In effect, collective bargaining forces individuals to accept representation they may not want and terms and conditions of employment that may not be as good as those that could be negotiated individually." (page 37)

Kathryn Jackson of Swartz Circle, Michigan, with
19 years of classroom experience; Anne Parks of Detroit
with 40 years['] experience; and Susan LaVine of Lyons
Township, Illinois. In Fremont, California, 11 teachers
were fired in April of 1982 because they preferred to pay
their forced union dues in monthly installments instead
of by payroll deductions or in a lump sum as insisted
upon by the union. Nine of the teachers caved in and
agreed to pay as dictated by the union rather than lose
their jobs. However, one teacher resigned rather than
work under such conditions. She is Charleen Sciambi, a
13-year veteran of the Fremont school system who had
been voted the best foreign language teacher in the state
of California by the Foreign Language Teachers
Association. Apparently the payment of union dues is
more important to the Fremont school board than the
quality of teaching.[43]

In the case of Ms. Jackson, the Swartz Circle, Michigan, teacher,
actions against her were quite violent. Recently recounting events
that took place two decades earlier, Jackson recalled the litigation,
social ostracism, and personal trauma that accompanied her refusal
to join the teacher union. She believes the tactics used to convince
her to join included dead cats thrown at her home and the killing of
her pet German shepherd.[44]

In a 1984 case a church-affiliated university fired a professor who
refused, on religious grounds, to pay dues to an NEA affiliate. The
University of Detroit, a Catholic university under the Jesuit Order,
fired Professor Robert Roesser for his refusal to allow the university to deduct union dues from his pay. The university routinely
deducted union dues from its teaching staff's paychecks and subsequently transferred the money to the coffers of MEA, the Michigan
Education Association.

A professor in the university's Department of Electrical
Engineering with a Ph.D. in electrical engineering, Dr. Roesser had
for two years paid dues to the union. Then he learned of MEA's
aggressive efforts to remove a Michigan state probate judge from the

bench because of the judge's anti-abortion ruling in a case involving the pregnancy of an underage girl. Dr. Roesser also "became aware of the NEA's position through its statement of December 16, 1981, before the Subcommittee on the Constitution of the Senate Judiciary Committee, in which it expressed strong opposition to 'all proposals that would constrict the availability of abortions and other reproductive health care.'"[45] A Roman Catholic who follows the teachings of his church, Dr. Roesser could not reconcile NEA and MEA's strident position on abortion with his own religious and moral beliefs. Therefore, he directed the University of Detroit to discontinue deducting union dues from his pay. After five years of teaching service, Dr. Roesser (at the age of forty-one, with a family of three children) was fired from the university because of its agreement with MEA to deduct union dues from all teachers and fire those who did not allow the deduction. It is unmistakably clear that the welfare of individual teachers is secondary to MEA and NEA's concern for the unions' financial security and their desire to further their ultraliberal political agenda.

The story ends happily. As Dr. Roesser put it, "God was kind to me." In 1991 the case was settled in Roesser's favor. Rejecting union president Mary-Jo Nichols' offer to "reduce the agency service fee by an amount proportional to the percentage of the MEA budget which is even remotely connected with the alleged support of issues to which you take exception,"[46] the Court of Appeals "held that proposal to reduce union dues did not make any effort to accommodate employee's religious beliefs which prevented him from associating in any way with the union."[47] Roesser received a settlement from MEA. By then he had taken a position with General Motors. Like other teachers who have come under NEA's wrath, Roesser benefited from the legal counsel of Bruce Cameron, a staff attorney with the National Right to Work Legal Defense Foundation.[48]

For some teachers who have fought NEA, the outcome has not been so positive—at least not yet. For James Belhumeur, Massachusetts computer teacher and past AFT local president, a reluctant early retirement from teaching and legal expenses of almost $10,000 were just the initial costs in a case still pending. In 1985 his school district suspended Belhumeur from his teaching job because of the district's fair share agreement with NEA. As he put it, "I wouldn't join the association because I disagreed with them politically."[49]

His conflict with NEA, and the pending litigation, began after teachers voted NEA as the union to represent them. Belhumeur said that NEA "passed this agency fee thing on the basis of fair share. Well, it turned out it was financial rape. It wasn't fair share at all."[50] Although Belhumeur frequently reminds his listener that he is pro-union, he strongly disagrees with NEA's requiring teachers to join and pay dues to NEA-state and NEA-national when they join the local NEA affiliate. "This thing started not because I don't believe in unions," he says, "but because I don't believe in blackmail."[51]

Reflecting on his years of teaching and union leadership, Belhumeur believes "unionism was one of the greatest things that ever happened to teachers. Agency fees is the worst. It was the destruction of unionism. Because now they do what they want to do and you have to pay the dues anyway.... Your one right to quit a union that's not doing what you want it to do is gone."[52]

For Belhumeur, his multiyear trudge through Massachusetts Labor Relations Commission hearings was more educational than legally productive. In recounting the events of the past decade, Belhumeur recalls, "We went through the Labor Relations and... they stalled the case off for ten years. And I've been through the courts with [NEA] a couple times; I've spent many thousands of my own dollars, and they've always managed to beat me through trickery. All the way through the labor relations cases, I thought that there was a record being accumulated. And when we finally got to court, there was no record. Nothing. Absolutely nothing. It all disappeared! And they used one stall after another.... Finally we get to court and then the lawyers pull[ed] the last trick out of their bag— which had never been mentioned in any of these hearings—and that was the time [limit]. You know, we have to do it in six months or it's not legal."[53]

Like Professor Roesser, who at first stood his ground alone to take on the combined NEA/education bureaucracy, James Belhumeur eventually found his way to the National Right to Work Legal Defense Foundation. As of September 1997 Belhumeur has won two hearing board rulings and his case is still wending its way through the legal system.

In 1994 Indiana provided yet another "NEA vs. Teacher" case. Despite NEA's recent resolution on "Freedom of Speech" that stated "[t]he NEA shall educate its members on the importance of vigilantly guarding all our constitutional rights,"[54] the Indiana NEA filed a lawsuit to stop Dennis J. Norman, Portage High School English teacher and regional National Honor Society Advisor of the Year, from "tell[ing] his colleagues about the union bosses' forcing teachers to underwrite the activities of organizations they philosophically oppose."[55]

Because he objected to his school district agreeing to changes in the contract that forced him to pay union dues, Norman set out to challenge the union by investigating its activities. He found a multitude of reasons why he and his colleagues should object to supporting NEA and its affiliates, and he communicated them to fellow teachers in a six-page letter. Among the items he described was that "[i]n direct violation of [Right to Work Legal Defense] Foundation-won Supreme Court precedents, the teacher union chiefs forced teachers to pay for all weeks of [the union chiefs'] vacation time, in addition to all the [Indiana State Teachers Association] top union boss's $140,000 annual salary, $14,700 housing allowance, and free luxury car."[56] After Norman exercised his right of free speech and shared this information, the union bosses filed a $100,000 lawsuit against him for defamation of character. The National Right to Work Legal Defense Foundation took up Norman's cause and agreed to represent him against the union. In 1995 Norman settled the defamation suit out of court by paying $1.00 each to NEA's state and local affiliates and the union insurance trust and agreeing to write another letter to teachers clarifying his first letter.[57] Norman was happy to do just that.

The defamation suit was a smokescreen for a much bigger issue— NEA's power to force teachers to pay union dues. On this very important point, Norman's cause has been winning big for him and teachers throughout Indiana. First the appeal court ruled that the forced-dues wording the union had negotiated into contracts across the state, including Norman's contract, was a violation of the

Indiana constitution. The union appealed the appeal court's ruling all the way to the Indiana Supreme Court, which let the appeal court's ruling stand. To make matters worse for NEA's affiliates, the Indiana legislature has now passed legislation making forced dues illegal.[58] In retrospect, NEA bosses would likely be pleased to refund Norman his three dollars and return to the pre-Norman world.

A NEW STRATEGY

As the practice of firing independent-thinking educators became more visible to teachers and more repugnant to the public, NEA and school boards began to rethink the negative image they were painting of themselves. Perhaps because they knew the American people hold teachers in high regard, NEA bosses developed a new strategy to get the dues money they need to attain their goals.

Avoiding the negative publicity and the bully image it gained by forcing teachers to resign or coercing school boards to fire them, NEA now quietly enforces a different dues deduction scheme— under authority of state law and contract agreement with school boards. As Milton Chappell, attorney for the National Right to Work Legal Defense Foundation, explained, the new system NEA uses is as simple as it is direct: Now the school district just takes the money. School districts are routinely deducting dues from teachers' paychecks and transferring the accumulated dues deductions to the NEA affiliate.[59] In the past, school boards held public hearings to decide what fate would befall the dissident teacher who refused to join the union or allow the district to deduct dues. School boards and NEA now avoid public condemnation, because dues money is "automatically" deducted from pay checks, and that is less visible than firing a teacher.

School boards do not appear to have a choice in matters of dues deductions. Ostensibly state law or contractual agreements between school boards and NEA require districts to deduct union dues from teachers' pay. Over the past ten years, NEA has successfully cajoled state legislatures to pass laws and coerced school boards to write agreements that give school districts authority automatically to deduct NEA dues from teachers' paychecks. Many school district personnel directors routinely advise newly hired teachers to sign documents giving the district this authorization. In this symbiotic relationship between the district and NEA, districts find it beneficial to represent NEA membership to new teachers, not as a choice, but as a fact of district employment. School districts assume responsibility for deducting compulsory dues and for transferring collected dues to NEA's affiliates without any charge to the union. Thus, taxpayer money intended for the support of students' education underwrites the process of putting dues money in NEA bank accounts and union bosses' pockets.

Through this automated arrangement, NEA compulsory dues deductions become an established fact, and few teachers give the issue much thought. Some teachers, however, are rethinking this practice and balking at the union's automatic dues deductions and its use of their money to further political and social agendas in which these teachers do not believe.

In the spring of 1995, a group of one hundred Washington State teachers retained two attorneys to represent them as they pursued a case against WEA, the Washington Education Association state affiliate of NEA. The teachers agreed to pay to the union those "chargeable" costs associated with collective bargaining, grievance resolution, and contract administration; but they refused to pay the costs NEA incurs lobbying for social and political ends—known as non-bargaining activities—the teachers do not wish to support.[60] According to legal counsel from the National Right to Work Legal Defense Foundation, NEA is less and less eager to litigate against such teachers.

And no wonder, for on October 8, 1998, the Foundation issued a news release outlining a proposed settlement of the major class-action lawsuit it filed against NEA and WEA affecting some nine thousand Washington teachers—more than triple the number previously reported by the media. In part, the news release read:

> A group of Washington state teachers filed the class-action suit after the NEA union and its affiliates illegally seized and spent compulsory union dues on political, ideological, and other non-bargaining activities. If a

federal judge approves the settlement terms at a fairness hearing scheduled for December 3[, 1998], WEA officials would return tens of thousands of dollars in illegally seized forced union dues and account for their spending.

Part of the proposed settlement covers all teachers who were victims of the unions' illegal activities in refusing to provide teachers with audits showing how all of their forced union dues were spent. Another part of the settlement—which results in a lump-sum payment of $40,000—covers about 250 teachers who objected to the outright illegal seizures of compulsory dues for politics and other non-bargaining activities.

"Teacher unions are running a political spending scam," said Stefan Gleason, Director of Legal Information for the Foundation. "But across America, teachers are fed up with union officials pouring their compulsory dues into the campaign coffers of [the union's] favorite radical politicians."[61]

At the December 3, 1998, fairness hearing, United States District Judge Thomas S. Zilly ruled the settlement fair and binding on all parties. The settlement's two-part resolution was strongly in favor of the teachers who filed suit against NEA, WEA, and numerous UniServe Councils.

Under part one of the settlement, *Hudson* Notice, the unions are required to take the following steps:

1. All UniServe Councils of any size and all local associations with 850 members or more would provide audited chargeable/non-chargeable financial statements in the *Hudson* notices, and base their nonchargeable rebates on the audited reduced fee amount;
2. local associations with less than 850 members would provide explanatory declarations, signed under oath by a local officer, and unaudited financial statements detailing the chargeable and nonchargeable expenditures, but base their rebate on the

lower of their unaudited nonchargeable calculation or the WEA's audited nonchargeable percentage;*

3. objectors and challenger would get the same (larger) rebate amount at the same time during the school year, within a month of objecting or challenging;
4. challengers would receive additional rebates for the last four school years so that their rebates would be equal to the rebates objectors already received; and
5. the figures and year basis for both the *Hudson* notice and the *Hudson* 'arbitration' would be the same.[62]

Under part two of the settlement, *Lehnert* Chargeability, the unions are required to take the following steps:

1. The 250 challengers will receive additional rebates for the last four school years during which they had paid fees (and had not previously settled their challenges) so the actual agency fees paid for those years will equal an average of 47 percent of the amount members paid the NEA and 62 percent [of the amount] paid the WEA and the respective UniServe Council for an average of 59 percent of the amount members paid the NEA, WEA, and UniServe Councils (by contrast, the average chargeable percentage of the WEA alone during that period was 81 percent); and
2. In the future the union will move all of the items listed above which they previously had treated as 100 percent chargeable to either 100 percent nonchargeable or, for the administrative actions like staff meetings, training sessions, general meetings, or general office work, they will allocate those activities and costs between chargeable and nonchargeable totals.[63]

---

* "Plaintiffs agreed to the small local association audit exemption, not because it is legal, but because many plaintiffs: a) did not want to name their local as a defendant in this litigation; b) did not have a major concern about their local's activities and expenditures; or c) did not want to 'burden' their local with additional requirements, even if they are legally required." (Taken from the settlement statement that Stefan Gleason of the National Right to Work Legal Defense Foundation faxed to the author on 8 March 1999, 3.)

In another part of Washington State, the Federal Way School District offers teachers two options for union compulsory dues deductions. The first is the usual method, wherein teachers authorize the district to deduct compulsory membership dues from their salaries and transfer the dues to the NEA affiliate. The second is a declaration of exemption from deduction of dues or fees. This option directs the school district "to refrain from making any deductions from my salary for membership dues, representation fees, or charitable contributions for bona fide religious objections."[64]

Elsewhere in Washington State, Seattle School District No. 1's agreement with its NEA affiliate specifies that "employees that fail to authorize payroll deduction will have the agency shop fee deducted from their salary and paid to the Association."[65] Employees who obtain an exemption from paying compulsory union dues under the bona fide religious objection "pay an amount of money equivalent to the agency shop fee to a non-religious charity designated by the Association."[66]

These declarations of exemption are only for those who object to union dues and fees on religious grounds, and the union still gets to choose where the teachers' money goes. Nonetheless, this exception in the master contract is evidence that some teachers are winning their battle not to pay money to a union that lobbies for causes that violate their beliefs. It is also evidence of WEA and NEA's recognition that this battle can no longer be easily won in either the public or legal arenas. More teachers need to know about this movement and the options it offers. As teachers learn their choices, one of the "sticks" NEA uses to control them may begin to lose its force.

THE TAX-MONEY FUNNEL TO NEA

Through an unbroken chain of money-transfer tactics, NEA funnels tax money directly into its coffers. This money-transfer scheme begins when taxpayers pay taxes to support schools. Approximately 83 percent of school-support tax money goes to salaries and benefits.[67] Of the salaries school districts pay teachers, NEA and its state and local affiliates collect unified dues that nationally average about $400 per teacher per year. Teachers pay compulsory dues through the automatic dues deduction process, and because NEA has been successful in forcing teachers to pay union dues, the tax money collected to pay for education is, in effect, directly transferred from citizens' pockets to NEA union bosses by local school districts. Through this mechanism, a significant portion of citizens' taxes go not to education but to support NEA and NEA-PAC,* NEA's political action committee, which aggressively and effectively fights legislation to place caps on federal taxation, derails balanced budget amendments, and supports NEA's ultraliberal political and social agendas.

NEA might argue that teachers have a right to do as they choose with their salaries. While this argument carries in most situations, in the case of compulsory union dues payments, it does not. Paying NEA dues is not a matter of free choice; it is a condition of employment. Because teachers' salaries come from tax money and because teachers are forced to pay union dues before they even receive their paychecks, it follows that from the moment citizens pay taxes, a

---

*"Federal restrictions on PAC funds do not apply to elections for state and local office or ballot measures. The latter are governed by state statutes that vary widely.... In any event, each state must comply with the federal campaign finance laws applicable to candidates for federal office. Federal law specifies that (1) money contributed to federal candidates must be collected separately from dues; (2) voluntary contributions must be kept in a separate account; and (3) members must not be coerced into contributing to the PAC fund. Nevertheless, unions that collect funds for national PACs can contribute to candidates for state and local offices. In addition, the unions can use general funds, or dues revenues to pay political staff, to publish articles or to purchase materials used to collect PAC funds. Unions can also legally employ political directors who direct political campaigns and coordinate fundraising and are paid from dues revenues. Such revenues can also be used to print and distribute literature asking for PAC contributions, although agency fee payors must not be charged for this." Taken from: Myron Lieberman, Charlene K. Haar, and Leo Troy, *The NEA and AFT: Teacher Unions in Power and Politics* (Rockport, Mass, Pro>Active Publications, 1994), 67–68.

portion of their tax money is on the fast track to NEA's bank account. What makes this strong-arm technique all the more objectionable is that, because of the special classification NEA garnered from Congress in 1907, it pays no taxes on its $65 million[68] office building in Washington, D.C. NEA's classification as a volunteer educational services provider protects it from paying about $1.4 million a year in taxes—taxes other labor unions must pay.[69] So, while our property taxes go from taxpayers' pockets to NEA's coffers, NEA, a private concern, pays no property taxes in support of education on the $109 million in property it owns. [70]

FEAR, THE GREAT MOTIVATOR

NEA bosses use this traditional labor union stick to great advantage. For teachers who waver or refuse to toe the union line, sufficient social pressure can most often bring them back. In her study of unions in teachers' professional lives, Nina Bascia discovered, "Some teachers struggled with the notion of striking, and social pressure clearly played a role in their decisions, but many believed they ultimately had no choice... because [they] didn't want to deal with the hassles [from union colleagues]."[71] As Bascia observed, "For one of the few teachers unsympathetic with the union, it was 'constant turmoil.'"[72]

Union activity before and during strikes is legendary. Just as communities and school boards fear union action, teachers are fearful of resisting NEA militants' desired ends or the means used to achieve them. The National Institute for Labor Relations Research tracks incidents of union violence in both public and private sectors. According to the institute's data files, from 1975 through 1993, NEA was the tenth most violent of both public- and private-sector unions; and, with 170 incidents of recorded violence, it ranked as the most violent public-sector union.[73]

Newspaper after newspaper tells stories of striking union militants inflicting personal injury and property damage on fellow teachers who chose not to strike and on substitute teachers hired by local school boards to teach children whom striking teachers chose not to teach.

At Pedro High School, Los Angeles police formed a human wedge to escort nonstriking teachers across the picket line. Union activists shouted, threw eggs, and kicked cars. Police arrested one such teacher for allegedly hitting and spitting at a substitute teacher.[74] During the same strike action, police arrested a thirty-year-old teacher for throwing a rock that injured a twelve-year-old girl who was walking to class. The teacher, whom police charged with suspicion of felony assault with a deadly weapon and throwing a substance at a car, explained the incident by saying he was throwing a rock at a substitute teacher's car, but missed and hit the child.[75]

In Ohio in 1991 students of Kettering Fairmont and Van Buren schools said their teachers told them to call substitute teachers "scabs" and promised them that if students got discipline slips during the strike, the regular teachers would disregard them upon their return.[76]

Parents, too, have experienced union violence. In East Palestine, Ohio, a guidance counselor faced criminal charges after she allegedly kicked the passenger-side door of a car driven by a parent who was leaving an elementary school.[77] Following a similar strike-related incident in Ohio, a substitute who had been asked to teach students during the strike said, "Our cars were trashed, I had acid poured on the entire side of my car, and nails put in my tires. My windows were hit so hard they don't close properly."[78]

We are concerned that children are more violent today. The union-perpetrated violence that students witness certainly does not help; if violence is an acceptable means to an end for union-activist teachers, why not for students?

The list of such cases goes on; the point is that those teachers who prefer not to participate in strikes are well aware of NEA's tactics and its insistence that they actively support strikes. Teachers who contemplate behaviors different from those espoused by NEA bosses, UniServ operatives, and local union militants know that if they do not strike they might suffer violence against their person or property as well as social and psychological pressure from union activists and local union officials.

Sadly, union bosses who incite violence can be protected under the U.S. Supreme Court's 5-4 ruling in the *U.S. v. Enmons* case wherein the Court "held that union officials and their agents are exempt from prosecution under the Hobbs Act for acts of violence committed to achieve 'legitimate union objectives.'"[79]

SURCHARGES AS A TOOL OF UNIFICATION AND POWER

Carrot-and-stick strategies often combine to give NEA the control of teachers it uses to fight parents and taxpayers' wishes for school choice. In recent incidents, NEA played teachers' concern for their own financial welfare against their concern for student welfare. NEA has convinced teachers to fear competition and has used teachers' fear of how vouchers might affect their job security as the springboard from which to raise money for its fight against school-choice initiatives.

In California in 1993 NEA's state affiliate assessed each of its 225,000 members a $57[80] surcharge to raise over $14 million in its campaign to defeat Proposition 174, the school-voucher initiative.[81] In New Jersey, NEA's state affiliate promised its membership that it would fight vouchers and then assessed them a $50 surcharge to raise money for the antivoucher campaign.[82] NEA's state affiliates can assess this sort of money because it has created a culture of fear among teachers. Teachers know what happens to those who do not abide by NEA's rules.

NEA is eager to keep real school-choice options away from the public. Yet, "40 percent of all urban public-school teachers," admitted Keith Geiger, past president of NEA, "send their children to private schools."[83] And 22 percent of all NEA teachers, twice the national average, send their children to private schools.[84] Something is out of kilter here. What allows NEA to charge its members $63 and $50 surcharges in defense of a near-monopoly school system to which 40 percent of urban teachers and 22 percent of all NEA teachers do not send their own children? Is it short-sightedness—or fear?

Do NEA officials tell members that good teachers, the majority of public schoolteachers, will be in demand when private schools open their doors to the public's children? You can bet they don't. NEA, on the other hand, may be in considerable trouble if its members leave public schools to teach in private schools where teachers are not—yet—forced to belong to labor unions. Perhaps NEA bosses are using teachers to protect the union's interests. Perhaps NEA's ability to do so derives from its long-standing control of teachers.

An Expanding NEA

The largest teachers' union in the nation is no longer just a union for K-12 teachers. It is moving onto college and university campuses. If NEA has the same success in this arena, our colleges and universities will move toward the union-centered focus we see in our K-12 public schools. NEA is also expanding union membership to educational support personnel, such as bus drivers, cafeteria workers, and custodial and maintenance workers.[85] NEA will use the same tactics with these groups that have been so successful with teachers. When every employee in the school system must dance to NEA's tune, our public schools will even more strongly resist the wishes of parents, school board, students, and taxpayers.

What Next?

Will NEA's takeover of public education continue? Will our children attend classes in NEA-dominated classrooms from pre-K through university Ph.D. programs?

As is becoming more evident every day, many teachers have been forced to lend their support to and follow the wrong leaders. They have been forced to accept NEA's view of a world of lifetime, protected guarantees and increasing union control of schools. Moreover, an activist faction of teachers within many local schools has become one with the status-quo, big-government labor union and has, in so doing, publicly declared self-interest its primary focus—over the interests of students, parents, and the local community.

At the root of the power of militant unionists are laws that give union officials the ability to force teachers to join a union, accept union bosses' exclusive representation, and pay compulsory dues. While the actions of a few local union activists are visible and irksome, it is the web of power that NEA bosses have spun over decades that steals teachers' freedoms and threatens our schools.

If parents and taxpayers do not confront NEA and its assault on public schoolteachers' rights to work and to choose to join or not join a labor union, NEA will use its coercive powers eventually to reach into private schools to organize and control their teachers. Parents who hoped they could run away from NEA-spawned troubles in public education may find that, unless it is challenged now, NEA will follow them and their children into private-sector schools.

NEA is caught in an outdated metaphor that sees tomorrow's world through the lens of labor-versus-management battles culminating in win-lose solutions; and NEA has carefully constructed the system so the union wins.

As public schools lose students to private schools and the demand for teachers increases in private schools, public schoolteachers will seek and find employment in these schools. Some of these teachers, newly employed in what could be a world of fresh teaching opportunities, will carry with them the mindset of labor-versus-management that has shaped NEA's successful takeover of public schools. NEA will follow these teachers and their union attitudes into private schools, and it could eventually take over.

Jo Seker, veteran Ohio teacher and crusader against forced unionism, observed, "The majority of teachers across the country do not know what is standing in their way. I really believe that the union convinces them that it's the school board and the administrators standing in their way... I've seen teachers wake up by hearing about some of the horror stories out there.... It's the union that's getting in the way."[86] In the words of Peter Brimelow and Leslie Spencer, who investigated and wrote about NEA for *Forbes*, "NEA is a political science textbook case: It exemplifies the so-called iron law of oligarchy, the tendency of membership organizations to degenerate from democracies into elite-driven groups serving the interests of their leaders."[87] Somehow parents and taxpayers need to get past the union to talk with the teachers—before NEA's powerful national, state, and local elite stop even that possibility.

NEA has used false hope and real fear to gain control of many teachers, and through teachers NEA controls local schools. But NEA could not control local schools if it did not similarly influence and control superintendents and school boards.

5

....

Controlling Local Control

"A school board acts in the public interest; therefore, its larger constituent body is the public, and specifically the students of the district. On the other hand, a union is a private interest group, existing to serve the specific needs of its constituency—the employees covered by the negotiated agreement.... [T]he union's primary intent must always be to improve the employee's, not the student's well-being."[1]

—*Marc Gaswirth and Garry Whalen*, Collective Negotiations

From its beginning, NEA worked first to create a government-controlled system of public education and then to defeat a fundamental principle of public education: Public schools belong to the public, and the people who work in them are public servants who take direction from the public about what it wants its schools to be.

Certainly a school board should seek input from and listen to the educators it hires when considering how best to accomplish the goals it sets for its schools and school district. And educators have a responsibility to advise school boards. But educators are not the same thing as NEA. NEA is a union run by union bosses. And NEA wants to do more than advise; NEA wants to control local school boards, set goals for local school districts, and direct the operation of local schools. NEA would have parents and taxpayers believe it knows better than they what is best for each community's children. In reality, NEA only wants what is best for NEA, its agenda, and its high command.

NEA's CONTROL OF SCHOOL BOARDS AND SUPERINTENDENTS

NEA's philosophy and goals are national, yet it acts on the knowledge that all politics are local. NEA uses its regional UniServ agents to keep teachers toeing the union line while hiding its real agenda behind teachers' good names.* NEA bosses use local teachers, whose faces parents know, to persuade and pressure parents to support union goals over those of the local board of education. From the successes of its local affiliates, NEA activists draw the support they need to achieve state and national agendas.

NEA-national, its state affiliates, and its local unions then bombard local boards of education and superintendents with federal legislation, Department of Education mandates, state laws, case law, agency regulations, local union grievances, and negotiations demands. As a result, school board members and superintendents spend time and public resources attending to militant union-member wants rather than student needs. They also spend a good bit of their time and energy anticipating what NEA activists want, avoiding confrontation with them, and meeting NEA's demands. While defense is important, it is the good offense that sets the game plan and wins the game. In public education, NEA militants are most often on the offense and school boards and superintendents are most often on the defense.

NEA, a no-holds-barred labor union, would have the public believe its officials act first and always in the best interests of chil-

---

*Both the Kamber Group and Sol Alinsky recommended that NEA use local teachers to push its agenda within home communities. In 1997, the Kamber report recommended, "[I]f the NEA is to define itself to the outside world... then it must put teachers first—explicitly out front—as its primary messengers to the outside world." Some thirty years earlier, Saul Alinsky directed, "Get those teacher leaders to organize the community.... [S]end teachers into the homes. Once teachers show interest in kids by visiting homes, they develop a relationship with parents.... Once one or two teacher leaders begin to push and get near community-wide success, the rest of the teachers will go along."

dren. How then to reconcile this claim with its blatant efforts to wrest policy-setting authority from local school boards and educational leadership from local superintendents and principals—not to improve teaching and learning, mind you, but to gain control of public education for its own purposes?

DEMOCRACY BE DAMMED—"PAY UP OR WE'LL SHUT YOU DOWN"[2]

Something other than concern for children and commitment to democratic process motivated Keith Geiger, then-NEA-national's president, to travel to Kalkaska, Michigan, to shut down its schools. In March of 1993, Geiger acted in response to a citizen vote against the tax hikes required to give teachers a 6 percent salary increase each year for three years.

Kalkaska was a 1,600-person town in a poor, rural area of northern Michigan, where the average annual income for nonteachers was about $22,000 and teachers' average income was $32,000—plus benefits and a retirement plan. Absent the assent of local people to tax themselves and their neighbors, the school board could have cut support staff and laid off bus drivers to free up money local NEA militants demanded for increased teachers' salaries. Or it could have gone into debt to meet the union negotiators' salary demand. It chose to do neither. Perhaps the board's leaders believed in the democratic process, or perhaps they agreed with Gaswirth and Whalen that "the money the school board gives to its employees in the form of salary increases or fringe benefit improvements equals an exact decrease in the money [a] board has available to purchase textbooks, audio-visual equipment, sports equipment, and even to hire new employees for new or expanded programs."[3] In Kalkaska, the school board chose to hold the line on the union negotiators' salary and benefits demands.

Whatever the board's reasons, Keith Geiger and Al Short, the Michigan Education Association's chief lobbyist, descended upon this small town to teach it a lesson and send a message to other Michigan school boards. In what Brimelow and Spencer described as "nothing more than a union-orchestrated stunt,"[4] NEA shut down the Kalkaska school system. The school shutdown cost the district $1.1 million; the district had to pay teachers' retirement benefits, even though teachers did not work. They could also receive unemployment benefits. As Brimelow and Spencer described it in *Forbes*, NEA-national and its state affiliate as much as said to the small community and its school board: "Pay up or we'll shut you down."

NEA did not care that the school board had presented its case for tax increases and that the local people, through the democratic process, had voted "no" on the ballot issue. NEA militants wanted raises, and they wanted the raises now. A vote to determine the will of the people was only a minor inconvenience that NEA bosses dealt with quickly and forcefully. In the words of a journalist who investigated NEA's invasion of this small town, "So complete was the union capture of Kalkaska's school board that an editorial writer from the *Detroit News*.... found his phone call asking for the board's viewpoint referred to the local NEA office."[5]

IT's THE NEA WAY OR IT's NO WAY—FAIRFAX, A STUDY IN UNION DUPLICITY

It seems NEA bosses can stop any program or reform effort. In Fairfax, Virginia, the story of NEA's ability to stop a promising program began in 1987, when Robert Spillane, superintendent of Fairfax schools, instituted a creative and aggressive merit pay program for teachers.

Many hailed the program as the most innovative and productive in the land. Mary Hartwood Futrell, NEA's president at the time, deviated from NEA's long-standing condemnation of merit pay and actively supported the plan. Praising the plan, Hartwood Futrell said, "Other districts around the nation might learn something from Fairfax County."[6] Former assistant education secretary, Chester E. Finn, Jr., said of the Fairfax plan, "It's good news. It's a break in the dam."[7] The merit pay program was popular with almost everyone who knew anything about it; Fairfax teachers gave their support to the plan and its consequences for their careers. And a short time after the program was implemented, standardized test scores for all students, and especially for minority students, increased significantly.

Also in a short time, NEA bosses withdrew their support of the merit pay program. Eventually, in early 1992, the Fairfax County School Board voted seven to four to end merit pay.

What happened? How could a program that initially received unequivocal support from almost everyone, produced measurable gains in student learning, and enjoyed healthy lifesigns in the district's schools be declared terminally ill and, like so many other efforts to bring productive focus to public education, die a painful public death?

Although the high visibility of the program and the involvement of national notables added a unique flavor to Fairfax's situation, the facts of the Fairfax case followed a predictable pattern: NEA militants gladly accepted financial inducements to gain their support for change, and then, because merit pay threatened NEA's monopoly control of education, they turned around and rejected the change.

The *New York Times* reported that, in Fairfax, the inducement "called for each of the 9,000 teachers in the district, the 10th largest school district in the country, to receive a 30 percent pay raise over three years. In return, every teacher's classroom performance would be evaluated. The worst teachers would be dismissed, but the best could qualify for a 10 percent bonus."[8] NEA and its members accepted the 30 percent pay raise, at a $9.5 million cost to the district, and initial bonuses of $2,100 to $3,500 for its strongest teachers.[9] The district later increased these bonuses in attempts to gain flagging union support.

The merit pay program worked well for students. In 1993 Superintendent Spillane reported, "The rate of increase in minority achievement has been nothing less than solid—some would say spectacular. African Americans' scores on the Scholastic Aptitude Test are up 16 points, up 20 points for Hispanics. Fairfax may be the only school district in America with an increasing Hispanic population and decreasing drop-out rate."[10] Good things were happening for teachers, too. Fairfax school board member Carla Yock observed, "Virtually every teacher, even those who have not measured up, say it has improved instruction in their school."[11]

A chronological listing of newspaper headlines and a brief synopsis of each article serve as an autopsy of Fairfax's efforts to bring reform to its schools. The chronology also serves as a testimony to NEA militants' ability to block any reform a school board or a superintendent tries to implement.

- January 28, 1989, **"NEA Lauds Fairfax Merit Pay"**
  Then-NEA President Mary Hartwood Futrell endorsed Fairfax's merit pay program, saying, "Other districts around the nation might learn something from Fairfax County." Giving reasons why she supported the merit pay program, Futrell cited "heavy involvement of teachers and major across-the-board pay raises that are being awarded before merit pay is finally in place this fall."[12] (*Washington Post*)

- February 15, 1989, **"Fairfax Board to Give Top Teachers 9% Bonus"** The Fairfax School Board, after debating how to balance the district's $809 million operating budget and how not to overburden the county's financial contribution to the teachers' retirement plan, voted to implement a revised merit pay program. The Board decided it could not afford the 10 percent pay increases previously discussed and instead approved a 9 percent bonus for qualifying teachers. The revised merit pay program would save the district $2.7 million and give "skillful" and "exemplary" teachers bonuses of $2,600 to $3,900 annually. These bonuses replaced pay increases that would also have increased teacher retirement benefits, thus adding significantly to the county's costs for contributing to the teachers' retirement plan. Mary Hartwood Futrell withdrew her support of the merit pay program. Even with a $2.7 million savings, the Fairfax budget increased 8.2 percent overall, and the district still gave an average 8 percent raise to teachers.[13] (*Washington Post*)

- March 16, 1989, **"Fairfax Teachers Drop Support of Merit Pay"** After accepting across-the-board pay raises for all teachers, NEA local union leaders said, "Merit pay must go because we cannot accept any more false promises." School officials said union leadership was taking advantage of the change from 10 percent pay increases to 9 percent bonuses to pull away from a program that made some of their members uneasy. Observers of NEA's actions charged the union "is exploiting any opportunity to sink merit pay, now that teachers have received the three across-the-board raises."[14] (*Washington Post*)

■ April 12, 1989, "**Lessons: In a Virginia School District, a Bold Experiment in Merit Pay Falters**" "Teachers, having pocketed their across-the-board pay raises, are balking at the merit evaluation," wrote this reporter. The journalist observed that merit pay originated in the business world and "is based on the idea that employees who perform at a higher level should be rewarded by their superiors." The writer found that "to the board's delight, the plan succeeded in weeding out weak teachers. In the first year of operation, a school district that rarely dismissed more than a handful of teachers discharged 150 judged ineffective. Another 165 were rated 'marginal' and given a year to shape up or be dismissed." Meanwhile, the president of the local NEA chapter "urged teachers to stop cooperating with the voluntary assessments required for the additional salaries."[15] (*New York Times*)

■ December 26, 1991, "**Merit Pay Revisited**" Both of Fairfax County's teachers' unions opposed the $9.5 million merit pay program, as did the PTA. According to the article, "The merit program has resulted in the removal or retirement of some 450 instructors." Before the merit pay program, the district fired fewer than six teachers a year. A teacher said of the merit pay program, "It has also helped the school system weed out

the weak instructors. Previously, that is exactly what
it had been unable to do."[16] (*Washington Post*)

■ February 18, 1992, **"Fairfax Teacher Merit Pay Plan
May Fall to Budget Ax"** The superintendent vowed to
stay in the district and fight forces trying to scuttle the
merit pay program. Some teachers whose teaching was
judged "skillful" and "exemplary" asked school board
members to "please do something about the hostility
we are getting from our colleagues because we are
receiving a bonus and they are not."[17] (*Washington
Post*)

■ February 19, 1992, **"Fairfax Votes to Suspend Merit
Pay for Teachers"** On a 7 to 4 vote, Fairfax School
Board members suspended the district's merit pay program. The local union president said NEA was in favor
of phasing out the program rather than suspending it
immediately. "We're disappointed that a portion of our
employees would be losing money out of their checks,"
he said.[18] (*Washington Post*)

■ February 20, 1992, **"There's No Merit in Their
Decision"** In his Washington Post article about the
Fairfax County school board's decision to suspend the
merit pay program, Steve Twomey claimed, "In the real
world—any place that's not government, that is—merit
pay and evaluations often come with the job. The idea
is as obvious as the weather: He who performs better
earns more.... We're all evaluated subjectively every
day. That's life. Class-free society went out with the
Soviet Union."[19] (*Washington Post*)

■ March 15, 1993, **"An F for Merit in Fairfax Schools?"**
"The merits of merit pay," pointed out the article's
author, "far outweigh the arguments of stay-pay systems that simply reward teachers for growing older on

the job regardless of whether the job is monitored and done."[20] (*Washington Post*)

■ March 25, 1994, **"Va. District to Give Bonuses to Top-Rated Teachers"** "The Fairfax County, Va., school board has voted to restore parts of a controversial performance-pay program over the objections of the local teachers' union and some school-board members.... But union leaders criticized the cost of the plan and claimed it will undermine collegiality in the schools. 'We tried this several years ago and it didn't work,' said Kelly Peaks Horner, the president of the [local NEA affiliate]."[21] (*Education Week*)

NEA militants bargained for and got substantial multiyear raises for all teachers; then they withdrew their support for the merit pay program and eventually attacked the program, the superintendent, and the school board until the board voted to discontinue the program. But of course, the multiyear, across-the-board salary increases remained and raised the base salary; NEA negotiators will forever start at a higher dollar level when bargaining salaries for the district's nine thousand teachers.

Lost are the benefits the merit pay program brought to students and exemplary teachers. Although the district reinstalled parts of the program in a much-diminished form, the original merit pay system will never be fully reinstated. Aside from the fact that merit pay proved to be good for students and teachers, the point here is that NEA will continue its stratagem of agreeing to programs that bring money into its hands. Then it will find reason, any reason, not to live up to its part of the bargain.

BE WARNED, NEA WILL TAKE ACTION

Michigan has recently made several productive educational innovations. The state enacted school charter laws that allow teachers to cooperate—often under suspension of state laws, school board policy, and union contract rules—to direct and deliver unique educational services to some students.

NEA bosses, fearful that change would give teachers independence, are less than enthusiastic about charter schools. As noted by the Hudson Institute, "A regional director of the Michigan Education Association warned the president of Saginaw Valley State University that the union would take action if the university authorized 'unplanned, uncontrolled charter schools.'"[22] The union representative also threatened to cause the university's graduates to stop donating to the university's various programs. Finally, the union spokesperson threatened to encourage local school boards and superintendents to end their participation in the university's educational programs.

Upon learning of these threats, a spokesperson for Michigan Governor John Engler, who strongly supports educational reform, described the union's approach as "goon squad tactics."[23]

NEA's attempt to stop one university from supporting educational reform in Michigan is distressing. Herbert J. Walberg, research professor of education at the University of Illinois at Chicago, thinks that move is part of a trend. Walberg believes, "Teachers' and administrators' unions that dominate education legislation have already ensured that charter schools won't be seriously tried."[24] To the extent Walberg is right, the opportunities charter schools offer students, teachers, parents, and taxpayers are lost to a union power grab.

NEA's "In-the-Best-Interests-of-Children" Gambit

NEA often conceals its efforts to add more teachers to school district payrolls—thereby forcing more union membership and more dues money—by claiming that what it demands, it demands in the best interests of children. As we have seen in Chapter four, current efforts to reduce class size are designed to generate more members and, therefore, money for NEA. Since this effort was so successful, NEA bosses are now using the same in-the-best-interests-of-children tactic to force school districts to hire elementary school "specialists."

In the fall of 1994 NEA negotiators demanded that the Federal Way School District in Washington State add thirty physical education (PE) specialists to the district's teaching roster. School district administrators estimated this demand would cost taxpayers $1.3 million in the first year alone.

But cost was not the most significant issue. By considering this demand, the school board would set a precedent, and the board would thereafter have to negotiate staffing levels and staffing decisions with NEA. This would widen the union's power to include determining what teaching specialists each school must hire and how many teaching staff each school must employ.

Staffing decisions are management responsibilities that school boards must protect from union encroachment if elected boards are to retain the ability to direct educational programs, control costs, and respond to the will of the people. A school board that gives over this power is a school board in name only. In such a district, it is NEA bosses who will run the schools and determine the level of taxing required to support the union's staffing plan.

Hiring elementary PE specialists clearly meets the union's need to increase its membership. Whether PE specialists meet a legitimate educational need is not clear. However, like the arguments union militants used to support demands for smaller classes, the arguments for PE specialists were inventive, if not persuasive. First, according to the *Seattle Times*, the union stated that "specialists-taught PE 'is a major benefit to children.'"[25] Later the union said the thirty PE specialists would give teachers more time for academics. Still later the union added that children who have scheduled and routine PE activities are more likely to settle down in the classroom and have fewer playground conflicts than those who do not. Finally, the union maintained that studies show today's children are less fit and more fat than previous generations of children and that much of this is attributable to poor educational programs.[26]

Why can't students engage in scheduled PE activities under the direction of their own teacher, just as they routinely sing, paint, and do other nonacademic activities? The union's argument skips over this obvious question and ignores the way elementary schools have successfully worked for generations. High schools tend to be subject-matter–driven; elementary schools are child-centered. Elementary teachers are generalists who are well versed in children's developmental needs and in the elementary school's whole curriculum. They are trained to teach elementary-age children in all subject areas—PE included. But, as usual, the union bosses' intent is to redesign elementary schools around their money-making preferences rather than around what is best for children. And, most certainly, NEA is not particularly attentive to the rising cost to taxpayers that additional staff would bring.

In Burnsville, Minnesota, the high cost of NEA-style staffing—featherbedding designed to cut the flexibility of teachers, parents, and administrators—came back to haunt taxpayers and school district officials. In its March 26, 1995, article about forced budget cuts, the local paper observed, "Bowing to pressure, board members softened administrators' controversial proposal to eliminate science and physical education specialists in the district's nine elementary schools. Instead they reduced positions to half time."[27] The Burnsville school board "soften[ed]" the impact on teachers "through a one-student increase in the elementary staff ratio instead of the half-student proposed by administrators."[28] The ratios at the senior high increased by 2.5 students and at the junior high by 1.7 students.[29] One elementary teacher said he was not certain that using science and physical education specialists at the elementary level was educationally sound.[30]

Indeed, many Burnsville teachers and parents probably questioned the educational soundness of raising class sizes to over thirty while maintaining the subject-matter specialists at the elementary level. But within the harsh realities of high taxes and limited budgets, when one costly and questionable educational practice bumps up against another, the concerns of students, teachers, parents, and taxpayers often become secondary to the power of union bosses to protect all union job slots.

If parents, teachers, and taxpayers are not vigilant, elementary schools will evolve away from the time-honored, generalist classroom teacher in favor of math specialists, science specialists, reading specialists, and writing specialists. These specialists, like their secondary counterparts, will meet with one hundred-plus students. And elementary students, like their high school big brothers and sisters, will be shuffled from the reading specialist to the science specialist to whatever specialist on different days of different weeks. All of this in the name of child-centered education? I doubt it.

It is not surprising that union chieftains ignore the cost of all these specialists. Far worse, elementary schools modeled after the one-room schoolhouse—in which students and teachers knew each other as whole people—may disappear. The world is already much too controlled by experts who wish to deal only with portions of people, as if their parts were more important than the whole person. President James Abram Garfield spoke of this problem in 1865 when he described his image of true teaching: "Give me a log hut, with only a simple bench, Mark Hopkins*on one end and I on the other, and you may have all the buildings, apparatus, and libraries without him."[31]

Like the elementary music specialist argument, and the elementary art specialist argument, and the elementary bilingual specialist argument, the elementary PE specialist argument is, in major part, an NEA strategy to add more teachers to its membership roles, at the expense of children and taxpayers. When many secondary schools and universities are trying to address the best interests of students by creating more intimate student-teacher groupings, increased human interactions, and more integrated learning, why would NEA bosses wish to specialize, departmentalize, and compartmentalize elementary schools?

One force driving this issue is a product of NEA's labor-management conflict model. Union-activist elementary teachers claim to want the same no-student-contact preparation periods secondary teachers have. The addition of specialists to the elementary school would allow elementary classroom teachers to be without students while subject-matter specialists teach PE, art, music, and a number of other subjects. Elementary union militants charge the union has not negotiated lesson preparation time as effectively for them as it

---

*Hopkins, Mark. "b. Feb. 4 1802, d. June 17, 1887, was an American minister and educator who taught moral philosophy and rhetoric at Williams College (1830-87).... Hopkins served as president of Williams College from 1836 to 1872." Grolier Electronic Publishing, Inc.

has for their high school counterparts. This issue has been bubbling for a long time in elementary teacher ranks.

The elementary-preparation-period issue is difficult for NEA bosses to resolve because of the huge amounts of money required to fill elementary specialist positions. For NEA, it is a matter of timing, of choosing which districts to target first. Once NEA labor chieftains negotiate elementary specialists into a few contracts, the existence of these contracts becomes the new benchmark other NEA locals will point to as they negotiate with their own local school boards. NEA militants will turn to their misinformed ally, the PTA, to speak at public meetings in favor of elementary specialists. Over time, this new idea will become an established standard, and NEA bosses will be off in pursuit of another conquest.

In the August 1996 edition of the *Quarterly Journal of Economics*, Harvard Assistant Professor of Economics, Caroline Minter Hoxey, summarized her extensive research concerning teacher unions' effect on schools. She wrote, "I find that teachers' unions are primarily rent seeking, raising school budgets and school inputs but lowering student achievement by decreasing the productivity of inputs."[32] Hoxey's second conclusion was also condemning. She found that "[t]eachers' unions may be the primary means whereby a lack of competition among public schools translates into more generous school inputs and worse student performance."[33]

Is the union bosses' push for elementary specialists working? In early July of 1997, Seattle School District administrators proposed that elementary teachers teach four days each week, using the fifth day for planning while specialists teach art, drama, and music.

THE SITE-BASED MANAGEMENT GAMBIT

Site-based management looms large in current school reform efforts. But site-based management, like its older sibling school decentralization, is plagued by disagreement over what it will become and how districts will achieve it. In general, site-based management keeps the responsibility for general policies with the district's school board and central office but moves to the schools the locus of control for operational decisions about how to effect these general policies. Agreement about what site-based management is and how it is to work stops here. For some, site-based management means making the principal the central force in the school. Others believe teachers should take the central role in making decisions about how to conduct the school's business. Still others believe site-based management calls for more parent and community participation in school governance, or even its operations.

Site-based management holds promise, or so some educational management theorists and public policy makers believe. The basic idea seems sound: Those who do the work should have a major voice in determining how to accomplish the work. Who can argue with this?

But site-based management, in its present ill-defined state, can be a real hornets' nest. If there are problems, and there are always problems when implementing new ways to do business, NEA spokespeople will publicly charge that the problems exist because school boards and administrators have not taken a strong enough leadership position or have taken too strong a leadership position. NEA bosses will claim boards and administrators have not defined it well enough, have defined it too narrowly, or have not otherwise sufficiently identified the scope of what site-based management will manage.

Yet, in closed faculty and curriculum meetings, NEA activists will take every opportunity to chip at issues and decisions and increase their control of the site team until their agents and their agendas dominate.* The strategy is all the more effective because "NEA" is seldom visibly present. Instead, individual teachers—whom parents

---

*I witnessed this behavior in site-council meetings when parent, teacher, and administrative representatives would discuss an issue and approach agreement. Often, one or more union representatives would table action on the issue until the next meeting. This behavior seemed out of step with the spirit of the new site-council movement, so I began to ponder what might be happening. At one such revisiting of a previously tabled issue, the union activist's "rephrased" position on the issue was word-for-word from NEA's handbook. I learned that the site council was not truly a forum for give-and-take discussion and group decisions about what best to do for our school; it was instead a launching platform for NEA's agenda.

know and like—are pushed out front in these below-the-surface operations. Site-based management, as NEA would have it, gives decision-making authority to militant union teachers. To use a syllogistic analysis: If union members hold authority over the decision, and NEA bosses control the union members, then NEA bosses control the decision.

It is clearly not just any teacher to whom NEA's bosses want to give power. In Indiana, attorneys for the National Right to Work Legal Defense Foundation filed charges on behalf of Spanish teacher Mary Terkoski when NEA local union officials put pressure on school officials to throw Terkoski off a key school committee because she was not a member of the union.[34] Speaking for the National Right to Work Legal Defense Foundation, Rex Reed observed, "Increasingly, the National Education Association (NEA) union bosses' *modus operandi* is to illegally control who gets admitted to teacher groups and professional committees. Once they've got their militants in, they use these committees to pass their radical agenda and secure more power for themselves."[35]

Incidentally, NEA rejects the term "site-based management." It prefers "site-based decision making" and states in its handbook that it "supports site-based decision making processes that are based on contractual/formal agreements between districts and local associations."[36]

NEA wants to make site councils yet another component of public education that it will control through collective bargaining negotiations. Further, NEA states in *Handbook 1996–1997*, "The scope of local site decision making should be limited only by the contractual/formal agreement."[37] In other words, the decision-making team could usurp local control, board of education direction, and parent involvement. NEA bosses do not want just to "manage"; that's not where the action is. NEA bosses want to make "decisions." Over time, NEA will gain increased control of schools if allowed to expand its definition of and control of site-based decision making. It is the collective bargaining and binding arbitration nose-in-the-tent strategy all over again.

In *NEA Handbook 1996–1997*, NEA proclaims that site-based decision making agreements between districts and local associations must include certain provisions, of which NEA lists six. Two of these provisions deal with additional compensation for teachers who serve on site-based decision-making teams, and one requires "a district-association structure for processing conflict resolution." Evidently if union activists who serve on the democratically based decision-making team are not successful in gaining a particular objective through reasoned argument and persuasion, NEA can resort to the old standbys: object, arbitrate, and then apply power-politics until it gets what it wants. This is not site-based management; this is NEA-based management. This is NEA control of local education.

How far might this control go? In 1993, a reporter for the *Courier-Journal* in Louisville, Kentucky, wrote, "The Court of Appeals ruled that school councils, rather than school boards, have the 'real authority' to run Kentucky's public schools."[38] Reflecting concern that the three-teacher, two-parent, one-principal site council could operate outside the purview of democratically elected local school boards, a representative of the Kentucky School Boards association observed, "Under this decision... the councils really have no one at the local level they are accountable to."[39]

One can easily become lost in arguments about whether one plan for site-based management is better than another plan. The point is not so much whether site-based management is good or bad, or even if it will work or not work. The point is that NEA bosses are using "site-based decision making" to take control of schools away from school boards and parents. Chubb and Moe, in their landmark book *Politics, Markets, and America's Schools*, commented on NEA's and others' attempts to "empower" teachers. They wrote, "All these reforms to empower and professionalize teaching are institutionally crippled from the outset; they are destined to disappoint. The kind of power that teachers have in effective schools cannot be imposed by formal rule."[40]

Chief among the norms that make up a union culture is that union members do not step on other union members' toes. This norm takes many forms. When union activists sit on site-based management teams with decision-making authority over how limited budgets should be allocated, their solution often is to base the next year's allocation on the current year's allocation, uniformly adjusting up or down, depending upon the amount of money allotted to the school. The norms of union culture preclude critical examination of individual jobs and almost never is the effectiveness of a program examined with an eye toward its possible elimination. Yet, cutting some programs (or positions) might be the best way to do the least harm to students and teachers within the confines of limited resources. But NEA's focus is resource input, not student-learning output. The not-so-hidden hand of NEA has a predictable effect: "Go-along-to-get-along" and "protect the status quo" are the guiding rules.

NEA is using site-based management to advance its argument that unless teachers have total control of schools and school programs, teachers cannot be held accountable for a school or program's success.[41] This notion is preposterous. Who among us has total independence and total control of what he or she does in the workplace? Yet we do have responsibility for some level of achievement, market-share growth, same-store sales, return on investment, or other measures of production. NEA's form of site-based management disconnects its members from the need to follow direction set by parents, school boards, superintendents, and principals; it is another NEA attack on local control.

For all its problems, site-based management has promise. Its success depends on at least four factors: (1) tying performance to compensation and job retention as a form of direct accountability, (2) training staff so they have the necessary communications and problem-solving skills, (3) defining the role and responsibilities of the principal, and (4) protecting teachers and school communities from imposition of NEA's agenda and its control of all actions taken at the school level.

Its success also depends on understanding that site-based management is a derivative of the decentralization movement and that decentralization is about moving the locus of control from the district's central office to the school. Most importantly, decentralization does not mean that local leadership in the form of a strong school principal is to be avoided—quite to the contrary.[42] For now, however, site-based management is a potentially promising practice NEA bosses are hijacking to their own ends.

Why is this happening? Because militant NEA activists have beaten and badgered school boards until they are often eager to give over vital elements of their responsibility just to have some semblance of civility and peace in their districts. Boards know that if they do not cater to the requests and outright demands of local NEA union officials, they will be attacked. Under this pressure, boards abdicate one of their core responsibilities—oversight of curriculum and instruction. Boards pass on these responsibilities to school sites without fulfilling their duty to establish curricular direction, set learning standards, or clearly define areas of responsibility and limits of authority.

Some observers believe that school board meetings have become meetings in public, not public meetings. Too often, the real players at these meetings are the board and NEA power brokers; parents, teachers, and principals just sit by, waiting for the latest decision.

Yet implementation of the management philosophies and development of the working relationships inherent in site-based management can be desirable. Today's organizations must develop ways to involve people who do the work in the decisions about how the work is to get done. Because organizations exist in competitive environments, their members must cooperate and have a common purpose in order for the organization to survive.

In public education, there is too often neither the feeling nor the reality that "we are in this together." The feeling has become: "I am forced to belong to and pay dues to the union. I am prevented from being compensated for individual performance. I have tenure for the remainder of my working life, the board of education must pay my salary and fund my retirement plan, and NEA protects me—why should I do anything differently than I am now doing?" Given public education's environment of conflicting purposes, management strategies that are possible and necessary elsewhere may be misused and misdirected to NEA's unproductive ends.

Jack Welch, while CEO of General Electric, shared his thoughts about being part of an organization dependent for its survival on everyone working together through common purposes to meet market demands. Welch said he continually tests his own performance by asking, "Are we regenerating? Are you dealing with new things? When you find yourself in a new environment, do you come up with a fundamentally different approach?"[43] How different from this approach to challenges are the norms and the culture that NEA bosses would have define and limit public education.

NEA: SELECTING AND ELECTING SCHOOL BOARD MEMBERS

NEA's tactics for controlling who sits on local school boards take two forms: electing NEA puppets to local boards and recalling board members who do not further NEA's agenda.

In some states, teachers can serve on the governing board of the school district in which they teach. States that disallow this practice do allow teachers who live in one community and teach in another to sit on the school boards of communities in which they live. We can safely assume that most of these teacher-school board members do a fine job. On the other hand, having teachers elected to school boards is a good way for NEA to ensure that it will have union activists on school boards and an inside track on the board's business.

The more common practice for gaining the sympathy of board members is for an NEA local to spend compulsory union dues money to support the election of selected people. NEA also knows that timing is important. The typical school board election draws few voters. In the words of a 1994 *Wall Street Journal* article, NEA knows that "low-turnout elections are a better way to achieve their goals than striking."[44] When few private citizens get involved, NEA can support its candidates and, with its teacher block and political action committee at the ready, it can control enough votes to win.

But NEA is ever at the watch for who might be similarly well organized. In the September issue of *NEA Today*, NEA advised its membership to look for "'stealth candidates'—experienced right-wing activists who conceal their extremist views to win elections to local school boards."[45] In the same article, NEA provided a six-point list describing how to "unearth a stealth candidate *before* election day."[46] Adding more than a little stealth itself, NEA bosses recom-

mended that its activists members "recruit third party advocates—
parents and community leaders—to speak out."[47]

Besides controlling who gets elected, NEA locals use recall campaigns to punish and remove board members who do not behave as
NEA would like. Unlike getting candidates elected to office, which
occurs only at certain times and only once each year, NEA officials
can mount a recall campaign anytime an NEA local is dissatisfied
with a school board member's performance. Such was the case in the
Union Elementary School District of San Jose, California, in 1993.
According to the *Wall Street Journal*, "The district board angered
the union in two basic ways: by not agreeing to use $11.4 million
in proceeds from sale of a surplus school site to give raises, and by
retaining a superintendent who sought to shake up established rou-
tines among personnel."[48] Local union militants ran the recall
campaign, and the California Teachers Association provided a con
sultant—and, of course, lots of money. The union bosses' efforts successfully removed three board members but failed to oust a fourth,
who hung on by a scant two hundred votes garnered through "extra-
ordinary effort." Opponents of the recall did file a complaint with
elections authorities alleging that the teachers' union sought to keep
secret its involvement in the recall effort. But later union activists
conducted both "sickout" and "work-to-rule" labor actions. The
Wall Street Journal reported that "the [board members] subsequently agreed to the ongoing raise from one-time revenues and a
buyout of the superintendent's contract."[49]

NEA's Misuse of Academic Freedom

NEA uses the cloak of academic freedom to shield its members from
those who try to hold union militants accountable for using their
positions to inappropriately influence students.

Academic freedom dates back to Socrates' time and also has roots
in European medieval universities. It grew out of a need to protect
the academic work of university professors and researchers from
undue influence and control that could restrain their legitimate
efforts to develop new knowledge. In their book *The Development
of Academic Freedom in the United States*, Richard Hofstadter and

Walter P. Metzger cited the American Association of Colleges' agreement on academic freedom reached in 1940. That agreement stated, "Institutions of higher education are conducted for the common good and not to further the interests of either the individual teacher or the institution as a whole."[50] Furthering the interests of a labor union at the expense of the common good would conflict with the principles of academic freedom and, therefore, fall outside the intent of this agreement.

Academic freedom has history, purpose, and limitations. Issues of academic freedom are very much alive and deserve careful consideration, especially regarding how and to what degree these long-standing protections apply to those who teach kindergarten through twelfth grade in public schools. Teachers need latitude to discuss with students issues that, while they may be sensitive, are appropriate to students' maturity level and connected to that portion of the school-board–approved curriculum for which the teacher is responsible.

According to NEA, however, academic freedom is now to be combined with "professional freedom." Resolution E-10 Academic and Professional Freedom declares that teachers are free to discuss "divergent points of view" and "controversial issues." And because "professional freedom" leads to declared "teachers' rights," each teacher, according to NEA, has the "right to evaluate, criticize, and/or advocate his or her personal point of view concerning the policies and programs of the schools."[51] Presumably, since NEA's constitution does not limit these "rights" to particular venues, union activists can use their classrooms and school time to convince students, for example, that a particular bond issue should pass or that a certain school board member does not care about children because he or she voted against a school budget.

NEA's tactic is bold and obvious: begin with a time-honored and respected article of academe and, through purposeful extension, intermingle it with a political objective. The result is a pulpit for the expression of political ideas that a school board would never willingly grant. Through this political gambit, NEA would make union militants unaccountable for any spoken act. Teachers, according to NEA, are free agents, with the "right" actively to "criticize, and/or advocate their personal point of view" regarding the policies or directives set by legitimately constituted school boards and authorized administrative staff.[52] NEA's incremental logic looks like this:

> Academic Freedom *becomes* Professional Freedom
> *becomes* Union Activist Rights

At the University of Oregon, the story is told of a dean who was under pressure to make a decision, the outcome of which would eventually change the direction of that division. The dean had sought to assure colleagues, with whom he was exploring options prior to making the needed decision, that there could be no insubordination of ideas during the discussion and debate stage of decision making. But then the dean reminded the professors that once discussion ended and a decision was made, these same professors had the obligation to support and carry out the decision.

NEA apparently does not follow this principle of corporate life. NEA does not say that union activists can speak their personal point of view in the classroom and community only if a policy with which they disagree is illegal, unethical, or immoral. NEA demands that union activists who do not personally agree with a policy or an administrative decision "can evaluate, criticize, and express their own point of view" anytime and anywhere they choose.

It was a dark and stormy night in mid-November 1994. In a small, pastoral community, the school board president and the district's superintendent held a town meeting following the third defeat of a bond levy. Seated at the front table with the board president and superintendent was a teacher representative of the local NEA affiliate. During the course of the meeting, this NEA local president and middle school English teacher matter-of-factly explained to the audience that, after the third failed bond levy election, she took it upon herself to lead her twelve- and thirteen-year-old English students in a tax-examination exercise. Her students, she assured the audience, had come to the conclusion that parents and taxpayers would not suffer undue financial burden if they were to support the next bond-levy effort.

In some states, laws strictly prohibit school board members and school district personnel from using school resources, including tax-supported time, to lobby for additional revenues gained though taxation. These prohibitions apply to school personnel who improperly attempt to influence adults. This local NEA union official, however, thought nothing of subjecting her middle school students to her beliefs about their parents' obligations to pay more taxes to support an end she and the union desired. Before concluding her remarks that stormy November evening, this NEA chapter president also shared her belief that the nation's tax structure needed complete overhauling because the rich were not paying enough taxes, and she felt that the evening's discussion showed that the salary for beginning teachers was too low.

Unfortunately, this is not an isolated case. Pattie Christensen of Longmont, California, wrote *Forbes* to say, "My daughter is in kindergarten, where they do not have enough 'time or money' to teach children to read, but they have the time to tell the children how their parents should vote! It is disgusting."[53]

And in the summer of 1999, Pennsylvania State Education Secretary Eugene Hickok chastised PSAE—NEA's state affiliate—for directing teachers to use their classrooms to speak against vouchers. In his statement, Secretary Hickok said, "I am stunned at the June 7 statement I have just read from David J. Gondak, the head of the state's largest teachers union. Mr. Gondak is telling PSEA members to use their classrooms—to use the positions of authority we have given them over our children—to denigrate school choice.... What Mr. Gondak is advocating is an outrageous violation of the trust we rightly enjoy with our teachers. Their job is to teach the information our children need to succeed—not to teach the PSEA position on school choice."[54]

NEA's efforts are persistent and consistent. We must challenge union militants' "right" to use the classroom as a bully pulpit from which to advance personally held beliefs and NEA's agenda.

Educational leadership under these circumstances becomes a cascading inconsistency of illogic. In NEA's world, principals must lead teachers; but union members are, for any reason, free to accept or reject any effort by a principal to lead. Further, union activists have the professional freedom and right to use their classrooms to criticize anyone and anything they do not personally agree with.

THE PTA—NEA'S PARENT PUPPET

"We will pull the PTA Charter of any unit that goes beyond the PTA agenda—as we would have with any PTA that supported vouchers!"[55] According to Charlene Haar in "PTA: It's Not 'Parents Taking Action,'" this was the threat a California PTA executive made to delegates at the May 5, 1994, state convention of the California Congress of Parents, Teachers, and Students.[56]

Can this be right? Is it true the PTA takes an active role in opposing educational reforms that would give parents choices about where and how their children will be educated?

Indeed, not only does the PTA forbid member organizations from supporting parental-choice school reform, in California in 1994 the state PTA took an active role in defeating Proposition 174, the school-choice ballot initiative. Haar said that a speaker at the 1994 PTA state convention congratulated the state's PTA delegates by declaring, "PTA volunteers defeated Proposition 174; all the California Teachers Association [NEA state affiliate] did was put up the money."[57] And put up the money the teachers' union did— some $13 million to defeat Proposition 174 on November 2, 1993, with a strong 69.7 percent vote to reject and only a 30.3 percent vote to accept school choice.[58]

The PTA is no longer an independent organization of parents. When the PTA began, its members described themselves as "united in the holiest purpose"—to gain the best education for children. However, since 1887, when it began as the National Congress of Mothers, the venerable PTA has increasingly come under NEA control. At first, the PTA was an association of women "who feared because the nation's children were at risk, the nation was at risk."[59] In 1908 the organization became the National Council of Mothers and Parent-Teacher Association, and its membership began including teachers.

As education became more professionalized, teachers and administrators gained specialized credentials. The purposes and workings of education became less open to parental influence, and teachers worked more independently of parental wishes. Fellow teachers and the professional groups to which the teachers belonged began to influence teachers' professional beliefs and actions. In the early 1920s the PTA's national office was housed in NEA's Washington, D.C., headquarters building.

In 1961, as NEA began using collective bargaining as its primary tool for gaining control of public education, teacher strikes became a fact of life for parents and taxpayers. By 1968 NEA had persuaded the PTA to take a neutral position whenever union bosses ordered strikes. By 1987 the PTA position statement on "teacher negotiations, sanctions, and strikes" reaffirmed its 1968 resolution and "prohibit[ed] its members from staffing classrooms even when members [were] teachers and the staffing [was] not illegal."[60] Today the PTA defers to NEA in times of teacher strikes, thus effectively losing its potential to add an independent voice to the development of educational policy.

PTA's membership today is six million, down from twelve million in 1966. Because—for some reason—it stopped keeping membership records, the PTA does not officially know how many of its six million are teachers and NEA members. If some of its members ever did want the PTA to take positions against NEA dogma, its $6 million annual revenues would be no match for NEA-national's $173 million. But as it stands now, the PTA has no plans to do anything other than continue to support NEA's policies. Instead of investigating why public schools have become so self-serving, PTA conferences focus on programs that echo and support NEA's agenda.

Charlene K. Haar, an author and authority on the PTA's sad state, maintains that it is natural for teachers and parents to have conflicting views about some educational issues.[61] By taking a subservient role to NEA, however, PTA parents have ceased to advocate for changes that benefit students or even pursue alternate ideas for their own children. Worse still, many PTA parents have learned to fear union activists' reprisals against their children if, as parents and PTA members, they criticize a program, fail to support union politics, or speak out against union actions.

When, in 1992, the union demanded that teachers in Montgomery County, Maryland, refuse to complete scholarship forms or write student recommendations because their contract did not specifically demand these services, parents were all but helpless. And when the union asked teachers to refuse to meet with parents in the evening or on weekends unless additionally compensated, parents had no forum for discussing the contracts NEA bargained with school boards.[62] Unless the PTA develops an identity and a purpose of its own, apart from NEA's, it will never be able to serve independent teachers, parents, and students. It will only help advance NEA's takeover of local schools.

There are success stories, however. A few people have broken away from PTA's business-as-usual mentality to make improvements in their local schools. Kay Wall transformed the Greenwich, Connecticut, PTA into a group focused on maintaining and improving academic standards. Wall admits that some parents were uncomfortable with the idea of challenging the PTA's orientation to support NEA on every issue.[63]

Public education has taken one more step toward becoming a closed cartel that operates primarily for the benefit of those inside and at the expense of students, parents, and taxpayers. In specific reference to Ohio's vote on educational vouchers, Marilyn Cross, president of the Ohio Education Association, clearly set out NEA's views on parental input. She declared, "Public schools weren't invented for the benefit of parents. They were invented because society decided it was to society's benefit to have an educated populace."[63] Evidently only NEA—not democratically elected local school boards, not school superintendents hired by school boards, and not even parents—will decide how schools will educate children or what schools will require children to learn.

School board members and school boards, however, are not powerless to act on the will of the people. State laws and state-level department of education regulations give school boards both responsibility and power.

In light of this fact, how can NEA have the effect on local public education governance that it so obviously has? While school boards do have laws and regulations that define and establish their responsibilities, case law and union actions have eroded and continue to erode school board powers. NEA bosses use case law derived from carefully chosen lawsuits and carefully crafted regulations to take school boards' powers away while transferring tremendous power to the union.

6

·····················

The Unholy Alliance: Faust Comes to Public Education

"One of the major themes in public administration is the tendency for producers to gain control over the agencies that are supposed to regulate them on behalf of consumers...., A large body of literature is devoted to 'regulatory capture' and its undesirable consequences."[1]

—*Myron Lieberman,* Public Education: An Autopsy

ORGANIZATIONAL THEORISTS WHO ASCRIBE to the power-and-politics model warn that organizational goals are rarely established by those in positions of authority. Goals, say these theorists, come from ongoing maneuvering and bargaining among individuals and coalitions.[2]

While other models help explain the internal workings of organizations whose primary purpose is to accomplish certain goals, the power-and-politics model applies particularly well to public education, where individuals and coalitions constantly jockey for position and bargain for agreements that, quite apart from educational goals, satisfy their own desires.[3] In private-sector businesses, market forces work to keep individual and coalition interests aligned with organizational goals, but no similar forces exist in tax-supported, public-sector monopolies. Within the house of public education, organizational goals, thought by parents and taxpayers to be well established and focused on students, are often lost to the self-interests of those who have power and play politics.

Many think of the school board as the one entity in public education that is faithful to the public trust and works to make those "best possible decisions" that provide quality education to students at reasonable cost to communities. But the leadership and control that many assume schools boards provide often do not exist, at least not in the ways and to the degree parents and taxpayers like to think.

Decision making in public education is not about weighing what is best for students against what taxpayers can afford and then making the best choice from an array of uplifting options. In public education, school boards, superintendents, and teacher union officials, each with their own desires, comprise an uneasy alliance that determines policies, sets priorities, and dictates prices. It is an alliance of reluctant, mutual dependence fashioned through time to sustain a stumbling balance among the three partners who grudgingly work together to acquire and apportion limited public resources. It is a political alliance that assures the protection and continued survival of alliance members while achieving some gains for each constituency. It is not an alliance born of principles and possibilities. It is, all too often, an unholy alliance derived from self-interests and misused public trust. With its trade-offs, accommodations, and appeasements, this alliance fuels and makes possible NEA's control of teachers and public education.

THE UNHOLY ALLIANCE

How can this happen? How can committed, conscientious school board members and superintendents take part in a conspiracy that works against the public good? To illustrate, it will help to examine something most know and hold in high regard—the public school classroom.

In the bag of tricks of classroom teaching, some teachers have developed a strategy for getting along with, rather than teaching, a classroom of students. The strategy can be called the "agreement." This "agreement" is the most basic of contracts: The teacher communicates to students that if they do not cause the teacher problems, the teacher will not cause the students problems. Students, after all, have the power to disrupt class, complain to the principal, or tell parents the class is a zero. And the teacher has the power to demand a lot from students—assign homework, refer errant students to the principal, or write notes to parents. So, the teacher cuts a deal with students and the students cut a deal with the teacher. It is a system in perfect balance.

This classroom gives the appearance of being a smooth-running, albeit not-too-exciting, laboratory of learning. The teacher is in front of the room, the students are seated neatly in orderly fashion, the room is quiet, and there are no discipline problems.

In reality, it is a classroom founded on a breach of public trust and a violation of professional ethics. In "agreement" classrooms, the teacher does not really teach, and students learn only superficially and minimally, if they learn it at all. It is a classroom where the teacher has traded educational goals for a risk-free, easy ride to retirement. It is a classroom where students trade away their exuberance, natural curiosity, and the opportunity to learn for an easy class and a passing grade.

I hasten to add that in my experience the vast majority of classrooms are not "agreement" classrooms. Most teachers work hard to challenge students. Good teaching involves stretching, pushing, and pulling students to levels they have not previously achieved. Students react, resist, and sometimes even rebel at this. The classrooms of good teachers may not be neat or orderly or quiet. People in these classrooms are busy teaching and learning, and the ambiance is often spontaneous and energetic. Learning can be messy.

The purpose of explaining "agreement" classrooms is to show that agreements counterproductive to official purposes do exist within public education. They also exist by virtue of long-established practices and unspoken agreements between and among members of the Unholy Alliance. The ground rules are much the same. If you do not cause me too much trouble, say members of the Unholy Alliance to one another, I will not cause you too much trouble, and public education in our community will run smoothly (if fraudulently). The differences between the classroom agreement and this unspoken agreement are two: first, in school board/superintendent/union agreements, the scope is much larger; and second, each member of the Unholy Alliance knows that the NEA-local holds the trump card—it can call in the area UniServ operative or even NEA-national personnel to make life ugly until NEA bosses get what they want.

These agreements create a closed system. The system operates, in large measure, for the benefit of the three major players; and it gives NEA the leverage it enjoys in school district after school district across the states. These out-of-view agreements create the Unholy Alliance, and they allow NEA bosses the power to exact their booty from school districts at the expense of students, teachers, taxpayers, and the democratic process.

This, more than I wish, is a condemnation of school boards; at least it is a condemnation of some school board members. Over the years, I have watched as good people newly elected to school boards experienced the crushing realities of the Unholy Alliance. The same socialization process used to ensure that teachers and principals hold the "correct" worldview brings new school board members into line, too.

Criticizing newly elected school board members, one county commissioner in Minnesota said, "It's kind of like someone does a lobotomy on them once they're elected." What board members understand and how they change once elected largely depends on the character of their superintendent. They will either clearly see the raw power NEA bosses and activists hold and use, or they will be kept at arm's length from the real issues of schools and teaching and, thereby, prevented from ever knowing how NEA uses its power to shape and direct their district.

In *Managers of Virtue*, David Tyack and Elisabeth Hansot contrasted two views of how superintendents operate in socially and politically turbulent times. One view stressed how the superintendent "is compelled by the pressures around him to organize his thoughts and activities in accordance with the demands made upon him by the people who wield the power in the community."[4] Tyack and Hansot also pointed out that "a number of scholars" hold the view that

> school administrators have their own distinct
> professional cultures, values, and interests and have
> demonstrated considerable ingenuity in co-opting the lay
> boards that supposedly decided public policy. By
> controlling the flow of information to school board
> members, by claiming impartial expertise, and by
> obfuscation when necessary, they have turned school
> boards into rubber stamps for their policies. This has
> been particularly true, political scientists assert, in large
> and heterogeneous urban districts where bureaucracies
> seem opaque to public scrutiny and so multilayered that
> even the officials at the top could not penetrate the
> maze. With its apolitical ideology, public education has
> become a textbook case of a closed system.[5]

From my observation, these explanations of how and why school boards get their information are accurate, if not timid. Moreover, and to make matters even more complicated, too many superintendents who are trying to bring about productive changes despite pressure by NEA militants find it difficult to share sensitive information with school board members who may have been elected because of union support. Whatever the scenario, it seems certain that board members find it difficult to understand clearly how their school districts really work.

NEA spokespeople make it clear to school boards and to superintendents that if they venture too far from the accepted NEA line, the union will bear down on them until they no longer hold the title of school board member or superintendent. Through this process, school boards and superintendents, whether willingly or reluctantly, become members of the Unholy Alliance that gives up legitimate authority to NEA.

Like the three legs of a tripod that push against each other to hold up the cauldron and its boiling brew, the three members of the Unholy Alliance push against each other in measured force designed more to prop up the Alliance than to support the needs of children and the public. The public never sees how the Unholy Alliance works. Laws, regulations, and formal agreements often institutionalize the process and keep it from the public's view. Chief among the mechanisms NEA bosses use to enforce the rules of the Unholy Alliance and expand their empire is collective bargaining.

COLLECTIVE BARGAINING

Collective bargaining is the tool NEA bosses have used to gain control at the local level and power at the national level. Many believe that school boards, because they have statutory authority, set school district policy. In reality, through its use of collective bargaining, NEA negotiators often set and enforce public policy about issues critical to the long-term direction and the near-term operation of districts.

Although private-sector collective bargaining had been in use since enactment of the National Labor Relations Act in 1935, public-sector collective bargaining did not come until 1959 in Wisconsin and 1960 in New York.[6] Once collective bargaining got the green light for public-sector application, it developed more quickly and more aggressively than had its private-sector counterpart.

As discussed in Chapter One, until 1960 NEA did not favor collective bargaining. After losing the New York City union ratification election to the American Federation of Teachers (AFT), in large measure because the AFT supported teachers' use of collective bargaining, NEA quickly got on the collective bargaining bandwagon. At first NEA bargained only for wages and benefits. But by the 1970s, shrinking student enrollments threatened the educational status quo, and NEA bosses seized the opportunity to use their resources and collective bargaining power to influence educational policy decisions. Over the past thirty years, contract negotiations have led to union involvement in virtually every facet of a school district's being.

To understand public policy issues associated with collective bargaining and the effect it has on public education's long-term direction and everyday operation, it is necessary to know more about how collective bargaining affects the democratic process that the public believes governs school districts.

COLLECTIVE BARGAINING AND DEMOCRATIC PROCESS

Because collective bargaining distorts school governance and impedes democracy in public education, it is counterproductive to both the purpose and the operation of public education. Ideally, teachers, administrators, and school boards work in collaboration within a school district to make decisions that are best for students. The NEA high command has thwarted this process through monopoly bargaining—also known as compulsory public-sector collective bargaining—that forces teachers to accept and work within the agreement that union officials reach during contract negotiations. Because of forced unionism and monopoly bargaining, teachers are not free to work cooperatively with administrators and boards. The premise that compulsory public-sector collective bargaining is a positive and efficient means to manage personnel issues in the work place is false in theory and in practice. Compulsory public-sector collective bargaining neither meets a compelling government interest nor serves as the least-restrictive option by which to achieve individual freedom.

One of the principal goals of collective bargaining is to limit management's freedom and latitude for making decisions.[7] Since the public elects boards of education to represent them in determining educational policy, NEA's goal of limiting the decision-making freedom of school boards works against democratic control of public education.

Much research has focused on the effect public-sector labor unions have on the ability of public-sector boards to set policy and make decisions. As the editor stated in an introduction to a paper by Professor Steven M. Goldschmidt and Leland E. Stuart from the University of Oregon, "Extensive policy bargaining [by teacher unions] has reduced the capacity of many districts to respond to changing expectations for public education."[8]

In her research for the Rand Corporation, Lorraine McDonnell made a critical assessment of the effects of collective bargaining on school governance when she cautioned, "This process has imposed serious constraints on other actors in the education governance system. Collective bargaining reduces public access to decision-making; makes boards less directly accountable; reduces management latitude; and gives one group significant advantage over competing interests."[9] McDonnell also observed that collective bargaining usurps traditional democratic controls and blocks citizen participation.

At its best, collective bargaining is a bilateral system of decision making that closes out public access. However, because public education is virtually a closed system in which NEA holds the power, collective bargaining is hardly a bilateral system. Clearly, the collective bargaining model most prevalent in school districts does not serve well the interests of participatory democracy. But it does serve the interests of the Unholy Alliance.

If collective bargaining works against participatory democracy and greatly restricts decision-making latitude for elected boards, why have boards of education not worked to alter or even replace collective bargaining? A look at collective bargaining's history helps explain.

Collective bargaining came to public education from the private sector, where it had origins in the European industrial revolution. In their research on public policy, Charles D. King and Mark van de Vall found that collective bargaining, or closely related forms of "industrial democracy," began over a hundred years ago as a way to incorporate political democracy into the workplace.[10] Unions in the United States have been working since that time to achieve their concepts of workplace democracy. In many states, the "right" for public employees to organize, have labor organization representation, and engage in collective bargaining became possible when state legislatures and courts modified the doctrine of sovereign immunity*

---

*"As it applies to labor relations, sovereign immunity refers to the government's power to fix, through law, the terms of its employees'

and allowed citizens to sue the state for personal injuries. This action opened the door to public employee collective bargaining.[11]

Prior to modification of state-level immunity, a number of acts passed on the national level in the arena of labor relations. This legislation also gave support to the labor movement. In 1935 the Wagner Act established the National Labor Relations Board to certify private-sector employee representatives for collective bargaining and to prevent unfair labor practices. In 1947 Congress passed the Taft-Hartley Act, which outlawed "closed shops" but allowed "union shops." The difference is timing. "Closed shops" demanded that perspective employees join a union before they were hired; "union shops" required that they join after being hired. Today, statutes in some states grant union officials a monopoly over workplace bargaining and, therefore, monopoly power to organize employees.

This labor history and enabling legislation[12] have given public-employee union bosses political power and legal might to continue using compulsory collective bargaining in the public-sector workplace. How well does this form of collective bargaining transfer from the private to the public sector?

In the private sector, market forces provide a controlling balance to collective bargaining. As Harry H. Wellington and Ralph K. Winter, Jr., pointed out in the *Yale Law Journal*:

---

employment. In the case of public schools, the people are sovereign but have delegated their governing powers to their elected representatives—the school board. The school board is responsible to the public. The school board acts in trust and historically could not redelegate its power to set conditions of employment to labor organizations. Therefore, contracts between school boards and teacher unions represented an illegal delegation of sovereign constitutional powers. The sovereign immunity doctrine attempted to maximize the public's right to make all public policy decisions. This constitutional concept had the effect, and still does in a number of states, of prohibiting public employee collective bargaining." (page 5 of: Goldschmidt, S (1982). *An Overview of the Evolution of Collective Bargaining and Its Impact on Education*. In K. Duckworth & W. DeBevoise, (Eds.), *The Effects of Collective Bargain on School Administrative Leadership* (pp. 3–9). Eugene, OR: Center for Education Policy and Management.

> Union power is frequently constrained by the fact that consumers react to a relative increase in the price of a product by purchasing less of it. As a result any significant real financial benefit... which accrues to workers through collective bargaining, may well cause significant unemployment among union members. Because of this employment-benefit relationship, the economic costs imposed by collective bargaining as it presently exists in the private sector seem inherently limited.[13]

The market disciplines that limit union power in the private sector, however, do not exist in the same way in the public sector. In the private sector, collective bargaining is an economic model, and market-imposed economics control it. In public education, union officials are likely to bargain for as much of the budget as they can get and may even force a tax increase (liquidate taxing power[14]) to pay for the gains they command beyond what the current budget can support.[15] Collective bargaining in public education involves allocation of public resources.[16] School boards, however, can spend the public's money only once. Money spent to meet union bosses' demands cannot also be used to buy textbooks, teaching materials, new or replacement equipment, or hire more staff.[17] In the public sector, collective bargaining is more a political model in which, as Wellington and Winter noted, "economic considerations are but one criterion among many."[18]

The "political" component of the collective bargaining model bears on public education in two ways. First, the elected or hired public officials who generally administer public-sector organizations need to remain "politically viable"[19] in their communities. Political viability often depends directly on the public official's ability to balance interests and keep people content. This is particularly true of superintendents, who must work with union officials to achieve the goals of a district. To the extent unions affect the reelection and rehiring of public officials, it is incumbent upon public officials to meet the union's expectations.

Second, the standard of acceptance in the public sector is often set by how smoothly services are delivered to a community. When union officials threaten to withdraw or limit services, political constituencies regularly apply pressure to public officials for immediate restoration of services, without regard for the near-term or long-term costs of meeting union demands.[20] In these ways, the ability of public-sector management to bargain on the merits of issues and hold a position in the bargaining process is greatly hampered by the politics of collective bargaining.

Examining the limits of collective bargaining in the public sector, Wellington and Winter found that "collective bargaining cannot be fully transplanted from the private sector to the public."[21] And, as she studied teacher unions, McDonnell observed that a fundamental difference between making decisions in an open political process and in closed collective bargaining is people's access to the decision-making process.[22] In his public policy research, E. E. Schattschneider found that collective bargaining drastically limits the public's access to decisions about public education. He wrote:

> Above everything, the people are powerless if the political enterprise is not competitive. It is the competition of political organizations that provides the people with the opportunity to make a choice. Without this opportunity popular sovereignty amounts to nothing.
>
> Democracy is a competitive political system in which competing leaders and organizations define the alternatives of public policy in such a way that the public can participate in the decision-making process.[23]

The version of collective bargaining transplanted into public education is not the same as the model practiced in the private sector. It is not different because the mechanics of bargaining are different, or because the employees are different, or even because the work is different. It is different because the employer is the government; and those who act at the behest of the employer are elected public board members who work for and are answerable to citizens and voters. Public employees are supposed to take direction from the public through elected officials, and, thereby, be accountable to the public.[24] Of this significant difference between the public and private sectors, Wellington and Winter wrote, "If we consider the ultimate result of this tendency to stretch collective bargaining to comprehend any subject that a union leader may desire to bargain on, we come out with the union leaders really running the economy of the country; but with no legal or public responsibility."[25]

An interesting—but not much discussed—outcome of NEA's use of collective bargaining is the negative impact public-sector bargaining has on private-sector unions. Examining unions, Leo Troy, professor of economics at Rutgers University, observed:

> Public sector unions want a larger share of the economy
> and society. However, I believe that this goal puts them
> at odds with the goals of private sector unions,
> especially in the long run. While public sector unions
> focus on the distribution of economic resources between
> the public and private sectors of the economy, private
> sector unions focus on the growth of the economy and
> can expect their members to prosper only if the gains to
> the private economy are retained by their members....
> Although public sector unions may claim they, too, favor
> economic growth (so as to enlarge their share of
> resources) their redistributional objectives can be
> expected to have a contrary effect.[26]

From NEA's point of view, the principal means of wealth redistribution is taxation. As we earlier learned, NEA has lobbied to stop any legislation that would cap government spending or require a balanced budget. Through increased taxation, gains made in the private sector are taxed and the tax money is then available for public-sector unions to slip into their coffers.

Teacher strikes, sometimes an outcome of compulsory public-sector collective bargaining, are another way NEA negates democratic control of public services. Strikes by public employees disrupt essential services and cause considerable inconvenience. Often constituents apply pressure to public-policy decision makers to settle with employee groups no matter what must be done to reach agreement. In this way, even the few market restraints that find their way to the public sector are abridged as management is put at a significant disadvantage.[27]

Few would argue that teachers should not be allowed to negotiate their salaries and benefits individually. But the growing power of union officials to bargain for teachers as a group and thereby gain control over matters of educational policy decreases the latitude boards have to exercise responsible leadership in our republican form of government. So, too, does blocking the public from access to decision-making have a negative affect on public control of public education.

Although the desire to bring more democracy to the workplace was, ostensibly, an initial reason for bringing collective bargaining into public education, the outcome has been privilege for union bosses and loss of democratic process for parents and taxpayers. Robert Summers, when he was a law professor at Cornell University, observed that public-sector collective bargaining

> redistributes government authority to one major
> participant—the union—which is not publicly
> accountable at all for its actions. Under a bargaining
> statute, the voters of a school district, for example, do
> not elect a union, nor can they vote a union out of office
> after it has successfully negotiated a collective
> bargaining agreement objectionable to voters. This
> particular law-making and budget-creating entity is
> neither elected by nor accountable to the public.[28]

In 1982 Kendrick Scott, then director of membership services for the Kentucky School Board's Association, found in his research on collective bargaining that: "(A) the public is opposed [to collective bargaining]; (B) it is expensive; (C) it diminishes local control of education; and (D) it is detrimental to the educational process."[29] Other researchers have since found that education is more expensive in districts where unions have collective bargaining powers. Still others have found that this increased cost of education does not necessarily correspond to improved student learning. Often the contrary is true.

The impact of compulsory public-sector collective bargaining on teachers, students, schools, parents, taxpayers, and democratic processes is significant. Is it not apparent that this brand of "industrial democracy" conflicts with the need for clear leadership and responsible, responsive school board decision making? In the last paragraph of his book on representative government and compulsory private-sector collective bargaining, Edwin Vieira, Jr., Harvard Ph.D. and J.D., wrote:

> The unconstitutionality of compulsory public-sector collective bargaining, then, is absolute, because compulsory bargaining through the exclusive-representation device neither satisfies a compelling government interest nor constitutes the means least-restrictive of individual or public liberty to achieve such an interest. Instead, it promotes the uniquely private advantage of special-interest political parties, by the means most restrictive both of dissenting public employees' first-amendment freedoms and of the people's claim to a republican government characterized by an equality of legal opportunity for all citizens to attempt to influence the political process. It is, in short, unconstitutional per se.[30]

How NEA Works Its Magic

Compulsory public-sector collective bargaining works in concert with grievances and binding arbitration to reinforce and expand the control NEA activists take from school boards. In addition to affecting public policy issues, NEA's representatives also use collective bargaining and its helpmates—grievances and binding arbitration—to control the everyday workings of many school districts.

Friends in High Places—NEA and AAA

It is obvious that collective bargaining has powerful effects on students, teachers, school boards, superintendents, and local school districts.

Not so obvious are the effects of decisions the American Arbitration Association (AAA) routinely renders in binding arbitration hearings.

The AAA enjoys a public perception that it is an independent organization whose purpose is to arbitrate fairly labor disputes between employees and employers. But independent the AAA is not. According to the National Right to Work Legal Defense Foundation, the AAA is notoriously pro-union. As the Foundation observed, "One of [union's] favorite tricks is to call in Big Labor's number one mouthpiece—the union-boss dominated AAA—to legitimize their illegal compulsory unionism schemes."[31] In an article entitled, "Phony 'Arbitrators' Rubber Stamp Union-Boss Coercion," the foundation pointed out that the AAA's "board of directors reads like a 'Who's Who in Big Labor:[32] A Foundation briefing paper listed AAA board members:

- **Bernard Ashe** is the top New York lawyer for the American Federation of Teachers (AFT) union.
- **Don Cameron** is the executive director of the National Education Association (NEA) teachers union.
- **Robert Coulson**, former president of the American Arbitration Association, has criticized several U.S. Supreme Court rulings, saying: "The labor-management community's ability to manage its own affairs is being threatened by this constant barrage of individual rights decisions."
- **Thomas Donahue** is the former secretary-treasurer of the AFL-CIO.
- **Sandra Feldman** is president of the American Federation of Teachers (AFT) union.
- **Bernard T. King** is a career union lawyer who has often defended compulsory unionism abuses in federal court.
- **Jay Mazur** is the president of the Union of Needletrades, Industrial, and Textile Employees (UNITE).
- **Gerald W. McEntee** is the international president of the American Federation of State, County, and Municipal Employees (AFSCME) union.
- **Betty Southard Murphy** is a lifelong management and union lawyer and staunch advocate of compulsory unionism. During

Ronald Reagan's 1980 search for a suitable labor secretary nominee, she was quickly drubbed out of the running for precisely this reason.

- **Carl M. Sapers** is a union lawyer whose law firm represents the NEA in many cases.
- **Jacob Sheinkman** is the former secretary-treasurer of the Amalgamated Clothing Workers (ACW) union.
- **John Sweeney** is the president of the AFL-CIO and former president of the Service Employees International Union (SEIU)—an aggressive pro-compulsion union known for its militancy.
- **Robert Tobias** is the national president of the National Treasury Employees Union (NTEU).
- **Judith P. Vladeck** is a union lawyer whose law firm represents the International Union of Electronic Workers (IUE).[33]

Clearly, the deck is stacked against any who find themselves on the other side of the table from NEA in an AAA-arbitrated case. As shown in Chapter 4, a continuous stream of grievance and binding arbitration decisions results in incremental union gains as arbitrators give away a little each time issues comes to arbitration. If the National Right to Work Legal Defense Foundation is correct and AAA arbitrators are typically pro-union, one can expect these arbitrators to give NEA bosses all the help they can through rendering NEA-friendly decisions.

NEGOTIATIONS AND THE FALLACY OF BOND LEVIES

Bond levy after bond levy failed in the November 1994 off-year election. Schools in many communities were in poor condition, and superintendents called on local taxpayers to pony up one more time to repair existing school buildings or build new ones. The poor physical condition of many schools was obvious. But bond levies failed anyway. Why?

Maybe it is because voters are sensing that NEA bosses and the Unholy Alliance are redirecting tax money away from needed maintenance projects and into budget areas more favored by the union.

Maybe it is because voters are aware of two ploys NEA representatives successfully use to influence where tax money goes. First is the take-the-maintenance-and-operations-money-for-union-goals gambit, and second is the ever-expanding-demands gambit. Alone, each is powerful; together, they are another cash cow for NEA.

The take-the-maintenance-and-operations-money-for-union-goals gambit works like this. When NEA's local union negotiators go to the bargaining table, they have active assistance from state-level UniServ representatives and, if needed, NEA-national. One job of these operatives is to research the amount of money in the district's budget. School districts are public agencies, and public agencies must share financial information. NEA knows how to inspect school district budgets. So, when NEA officials negotiate, they know how much money is in the budget for the instructional program, maintenance program, and other budget categories.

Building a budget each school year is an important and involved task. If designed well, a district's budget specifies the amount of money the school board has authorized to deliver the educational program, maintain buildings, and provide the other services communities want for their children. If, however, budgets are designed poorly, they have little relationship to the actual costs of a community's educational programs. Poorly developed and written budgets are more a political ploy than a financial/educational document. Such budgets only show where the superintendent and the school board temporarily park money until they spend it to meet this crisis or satisfy that pressure. While good school boards and superintendents build and administer budgets as a contract with their communities, NEA bosses may see school district budgets as a wonderfully accessible and delicious smorgasbord from which to take whatever they can through compulsory collective bargaining, grievances, binding arbitration, power politics, and intimidation.

Union officials often negotiate agreements that require funding beyond what the district can afford to pay from, for example, that portion of the district's budget designated for instructional costs. Perhaps NEA demands a pet program that requires more teachers and generates more dues money for NEA's coffers. Money to cover a union-negotiated increase must come from somewhere, and often it comes from the maintenance and operations budget. School boards can spend money only once. So, when the maintenance and operations money goes to pay for union demands, less money remains to maintain buildings or make improvements. (This results in what is euphemistically called deferred maintenance.) With the maintenance and operations money reduced and the school board still needing to repair buildings, an appeal must go to the public to authorize the sale of bonds or increase taxes to raise the "extra" money.

In this way, NEA gets money from currently existing funds and forces boards to go to the public to ask for additional money—a request that has at least two windfall benefits for NEA. First, a board's successful request for additional tax money means that new money is on the way and frees up even more current money—money that is immediately accessible for NEA's wants. Second, the request strains the board's relationship with the public which, in turn, helps NEA militants during times when they need public support to go up against the board.

The General Accounting Office recently reported to Congress that the nation's eighty thousand public schools need $112 billion for building repairs and upgrades.[34]

Just how does NEA take the money in negotiations? Isn't this a David-and-Goliath situation in which local unions negotiate against a powerful school board with the superintendent, administrators, and attorneys at their beck and call? How can a little ol' local teacher union ever hope to prevail against such management might?

One reason local teacher unions wield so much power is that NEA negotiators are masters at using a second strategy, the ever-expanding-demands gambit, to get what union officials want. This second strategy is more complicated than the take-the-maintenance-and-operations-money-for-union-goals strategy. We earlier examined the policy implications of collective bargaining to understand its inherently antidemocratic nature. Now we examine the nitty-gritty workings of collective bargaining, or contract negotiations as it is often called, to understand how the ever-expanding-demands gambit works for NEA.

Since 1960, boards and NEA-local representatives have negotiated thousands of contract agreements. Over the years, NEA contracts with school boards have become more complex, more demanding, and more controlling. In her study of teachers' unions, Nina Bascia found "that teachers' employment contracts tend to increase in scope, both becoming more detailed and covering a broader range of issues, as union and school boards interact over time."[35] In part to demonstrate their might to dues-paying members, union negotiators will always demand more of everything, especially more rights and more control.

In the private sector, market forces work to limit the demands a union can make. If union demands increase the cost of a company's product beyond a point where consumers can afford to buy, workers may be laid off or the company may even go bankrupt.

In government-protected, tax-supported public education, however, NEA militants continually bargain for more and require the school board to go again and again to the taxpayer for increased taxes and special levies. In the state of Washington, the Evergreen Freedom Foundation discovered "that over a 12-year period, state and local employees' average [hourly] compensation rose $4.78 compared to $1.00 received by a person employed in the private sector (adjusted for inflation)."[36] This public policy research center recommends "that all compensation of public employees be frozen until private sector wages catch up with the public sector."[37]

Myron Lieberman, in his book *Public Education: An Autopsy*, highlighted differences between public- and private-sector unions. In the context of a discussion about bringing market forces to education, Lieberman wrote:

> In order for a market initiative to succeed, it must also attract support from noneducational constituencies for noneducational reasons. Workers in competitive industries might be one such constituency. As previously noted, public school teachers are amply protected against risk. Although some private-sector employees enjoy various job protections, public school teachers enjoy much stronger protections than most workers in our society. From an equity standpoint, why should

private-sector workers but not teachers face the threat of competition? Inasmuch as a system based on competition is the general rule, the burden of proof should be on the exceptions to it. Furthermore, if protection from competition is justified, employment that incurs the risk of competition should pay more than employment that does not. The underlying issue here has important strategic as well as policy dimensions.[38]

Books, training manuals, and all manner of course work teach the simple and complex strategies of collective bargaining. While NEA uses many of the collective bargaining strategies described in these sources, we will look here at two: nose-in-the-tent and incremental-gains.

The nose-in-the-tent strategy is simple and effective. Consider, for example, a teacher-union proposal to include this statement as a part of the preamble to its labor contract with a school district:

In order to effectuate the provisions of the state negotiations law and to encourage and increase effective and harmonious working relationships between the School District and its professional employees represented by the Teachers Association (hereinafter referred to as the "Association") and to enable the professional employees more fully to participate in and contribute to the development of local policies for the school district as they pertain to the terms and conditions of employment of teachers, this agreement is made.[39]

Seems innocent enough. This, after all, is just the preamble to the contract; the real stuff comes later—right? And who can disagree with the enlightened philosophy expressed in these seventy-nine words? Any school board would want to "encourage and increase effective and harmonious working relationships" with its employee groups, especially teachers. As for "enabl[ing] the professional employees more fully to participate in and contribute to the development of local policies for the school district," any modern, sensitive, egalitarian school board would gladly embrace this concept.

But those experienced in the art of teacher contract negotiations see this preamble as a series of contract demands, and they react to it much differently than would our enlightened, trusting, fictitious school board. I will quote in its entirety the demand analysis of this preamble paragraph that Thealan Associates, Inc., offered in *Teacher Contract Demands: Analysis and Response for the School Board Negotiator*.

> Since the contract is a document to spell out terms and conditions of employment within the framework of the law, it is a labor document, not a statement of either educational nor metaphysical philosophy.
>
> This preamble calls for the employees to "participate in and contribute to the development of local policies." Even though there is an apparent conditioning of this participatory right to policies concerning "terms and conditions of employment" it is merely the tip of the iceberg. There is great dispute as to what constitutes a term and condition, and the union will take the position that all policies affect them. The school board is endowed by the state law and by the voters to be the legislative body for the school district. It has the sole right to make policy and approve rules and regulations. A demand such as this one can have an impact not envisioned by the district. (While it is possible to utilize the suggestions of the teaching staff in policy formulations, it should not be a contract right.) It is entirely conceivable that, in an arbitration proceeding, an arbitrator can hold that the board is not empowered to act on a policy until it has the input of the union. Indeed, by extension it might be taken that policy cannot be enacted without the permission of the Association. Lest the reader think this advice is too harsh please note that every word[,] phrase and clause in a negotiated contract has meaning—and the teacher

organization will eventually attempt to give meaning to the words, no matter how innocuous they may appear at first glance. Consequently, school boards should not agree to language that appears harmless just for the sake of agreeing. The words may come back to haunt your district years later. If the words are so meaningless the teachers' organization should be willing to withdraw them. Such terms as "morale," "harmonious working relationships," "quality education" are very subjective terms. The district may find that an arbitrator, the Commissioner, or other agencies will interpret these terms in a fashion the district did not envision. After all, it could be taken that the failure of the district to agree to the union (association) demands has impacted the morale and well-being of the staff and, thus, affected the quality of education in the district. Such emotive terms really have no proper place in a labor contract.[40]

The nose-in-the-tent gambit is a fundamental strategy in NEA's ongoing efforts first to negotiate contract language that gives it some small right, and then use this newly established right as a fulcrum from which it incrementally leverages more power and money. The earlier cited example of negotiated class-size limits is but one way NEA does this.

One small nose is hard to see in a big tent, especially when you do not spend much time in the tent. Because of demands on school board members' time and energy and because of the political nature of public office, board members often serve only a short time. New board members spend the first year of their term absorbing educational jargon, identifying issues, and learning what the board of education does. By the time new members understand what is happening around them, they are thinking about whether to run for reelection. Many do not—and the process starts all over again.

As sitting board members face the decision to accept or reject the proposed contract, they are confronted with contract language that is the result of long months of negotiations and is often written in the arcane vernacular of educational legalize. At the same time, the magnitude of the expenditures, the complexities of policy, and the pressure of a possible teacher strike weigh heavily on them. Under these conditions, board members sometimes approve a contract mostly to bring a nasty process to conclusion and restore a level of peace to the district. Union activists often claim that during negotiations their morale is low because the board is not treating them well. Boards become reluctant to stand firm on issues that would result in another charge of harming the morale of the teaching corps. In this union-engineered atmosphere, boards approve contracts with language that sooner or later causes the district and its taxpayers considerable difficulty.

Contract negotiations are never completed; one agreement sets the stage for the next negotiation, and the next for the next. Teacher contract negotiations, à la NEA, are a machine in constant motion. Like any machine fashioned through years of fine tuning, the parts of NEA's contract-negotiations machine fit together to amplify force and effect. So it is with the incremental-gains strategy.

Again, Thealan Associates, Inc., offered a sample clause to examine. The "Building Representation" clause initially asks only that a union representative have the "right" to meet every two weeks with the building principal. If the school board's negotiating team agrees to this seemingly innocuous request, a chain of events is set in motion. Over the next several years, this newly acquired "right" gains force and effect and soon requires the principal to give over more and more control of the school to the union. It is worth reemphasizing that this is not an argument against involving teachers in what to do and how best to do it. Teachers need to be involved. The operative word here is union; it is NEA bosses who must not control the school.

Thealan Associates, Inc., examined the incremental-gains strategy by first looking at the union "demand" and then offering a "demand analysis" school boards and their contract negotiators should consider.

Union Demand Number One

The [union] shall select a building representative for each school building who shall meet with the principal at least once every two weeks to review and discuss local school problems and practices.

Demand Analysis

The selection of a building representative by the [union] is not a suitable provision for a collective agreement because the board of education should not have a contractual involvement in the internal operations of an employee [union].

The requirement "a representative and the principal" is too restrictive and too structured. The purpose of conferences with the building representative should not be to handle or discuss "local school problems or practices" but should be related directly to the agreement or the settlement of grievances or potential grievances. In other words, there should be a specified reference to terms and conditions of employment. This demand, as written, has the effect of establishing a dual administrative structure. In practice, the implementation of the provision would place the building representative and the principal in a bargaining situation.

Union Demand Number Two

The building representative shall have the right to schedule [union] meetings before or after school or during lunch periods.

Demand Analysis

Teacher [union] meetings should be held after the regular school day. Meetings held during lunch hours often impair the effectiveness of teachers who have supervisory responsibilities during the lunch hour. This provision also enables the building representative to schedule meetings in conflict with meetings scheduled by the district.

Union Demand Number Three

The building representative shall be provided ten (10) minutes' time at all building faculty meetings to report on matters involving representation of the teachers by the [union].

Demand Analysis

"Faculty meetings" are meetings of educators. The building representative is a representative of the teachers as "employees" not as educators. The distinction is significant in this case. Faculty meetings should not be [union] meetings. This type of provision provides the [union] with a captive audience. There will be teachers present at faculty meetings who are not [union] members. If this type of provision is granted, competing [unions] may demand equal time.

Union Demand Number Four

The building representative shall be allowed one (1) free period each week to perform his [or her], duties under this Agreement.

Demand Analysis

A commonly accepted principle in labor relations is that one party does not provide financial support for the other. Therefore, it is improper to require the taxpayers of a district to pay a teacher for time in which he [or she] functions on behalf of the teachers' [union] and not as a teacher. If building representatives are established by the [union], they should be compensated by the [union].

Union Demand Number Five

The building representative shall be permitted to meet with teachers at times and places convenient to him [or her], provided that such meetings can be scheduled without disturbing the regular academic program.

Demand Analysis

Generally, a building representative should have access to the people he [or she] represents. However, it is not wise to grant a provision with such wide latitude. Teachers in the same building will make arrangements for "informal" meetings regardless of the contract provisions or school district policies. Therefore, a contract provision should include language that will attempt to inhibit "general" or "formalized" meetings during the school day that can disrupt a school.

The term "time and places convenient to him [or her]" is totally unacceptable. The needs of the school and the students it serves should supersede the convenience of the building representative.[41]

In these scenarios, several significant strategies happen sequentially. The nose-in-the-tent is the first step—getting the district to agree initially to contract language, for example, that requires the building principal to meet biweekly with a union-selected building representative. Then there is incremental expansion of the first, seemingly innocent, request into successively more aggressive and controlling union demands. Ultimately, the principal is unable to make decisions, involve people, and lead the school without the prior knowledge and consent of the union's building representative.

The most invisible part of this scenario is that contract negotiations are typically conducted in meetings closed to the public and closed even to the building principals who will have to live with and administer the terms and conditions of the contract. Issues that would not be brought up and agreements that would never be struck in the full view of a scrutinizing public are accomplished in the closed negotiations that establish district policy. As a result, taxpayer money supports an educational program that increasingly becomes defined by the demands and constraints of contracts on which taxpayer have had no input.

As Myron Lieberman, former AFT union negotiator and author of several books about the deleterious affects of teacher unions on public education, recently commented, "The basic problem is that democracy suffers when school boards end up 'swapping public policies in the middle of the night with one interest group.'"[42]

In 1994, a reporter for the *Minneapolis Star and Tribune* observed that "statewide, student programs are being cut to pay for teacher contracts that districts can't afford."[43] For what do NEA negotiators negotiate? Often, NEA negotiators gain concessions for the union. In fact, establishing, protecting, and expanding union power is the primary aim of NEA bosses. One union benefit NEA widely enjoys is taxpayer-supported union communication with union members.

UNION COMMUNICATION AT PUBLIC EXPENSE

NEA officials negotiate for, and districts give away, access to public-owned communication "tools" that NEA uses to conduct union business.

How much money does the taxpaying public spend each year to support NEA's use of:

- district trucks and delivery drivers to transport union mail to its members in the district schools,
- secretaries to sort and distribute union mail,
- telephone systems to conduct union business,
- networked computer systems to communicate with union members,
- school equipment, such as computers and copy machines, to support union business, and
- school facilities to host union meetings?

It is mind-boggling to consider on a nationwide basis the direct costs to taxpayers for teacher-union business. Nationwide numbers become meaningless. Because of their huge size and their remoteness from our lives, national figures inform us little and overwhelm us greatly. It would be more informative to calculate what these and other union privileges cost your local school district, and, therefore, what they cost you and other local taxpayers. And if an administrator tells you there is no cost to the district because, for example, delivery trucks were going to the schools anyway, ask the administrator to try that same logic on FedEx or UPS.

With the help of the school district's business manager, you can calculate these costs. Or perhaps the school board could direct the superintendent to calculate the costs. Remember, however, that school boards and district administrators pay a heavy price for offending NEA; they must choose their battles carefully. Remember also that some of the data must come from secretaries and truck drivers, who also are union members and have every reason not to alienate NEA militants. They may not be able to be as forthcoming as you, or they, would like. Curious taxpayers may encounter reluctance, or even refusal, to calculate such costs. If administrators do agree to do the calculations, they may calculate on the low side to avoid the appearance of being spendthrifts who give away taxpayer money. It is best to ask the district to show its work and for you to check the numbers. But do not get lost in numbers, because the real point is that *no* tax money should be used to support the union and pay NEA's costs.

While local boards of education must decide whether to stop or continue this practice, taxpayers and parents have a right to know the costs involved.

It is common practice in many districts to rent publicly owned school facilities to local clubs and groups. One wonders why districts do not apply the same policies and fee schedules to NEA for its private use of publicly owned property—especially when NEA's meetings are often about ways to take more tax money and control from citizens. The least the union should do in return for using a school facility is help pay to maintain the building.

Alex Gimarc, a parent in the Anchorage school district, wrote an article for the March 16, 1995, *Anchorage Daily News* in which he pointed out, "Association benefits pay Anchorage Education Association members $297,000 to make up for classroom time spent negotiating contracts. The tax-payers are essentially subsidizing the union negotiations against them."[44] What else has the union negotiated that costs the taxpayer and siphons off money that could go to the education of children?

Unfortunately, school boards seem to spend a good deal of time learning how to get more money from the taxpayer rather than how to spend less taxpayer money or even how to spend money more effectively. In a recent issue of *The American School Board Journal*, an article entitled "Getting Voters to Say Yes" outlined the art of "[w]inning voter support for higher property taxes."[45] Certainly there are times for this kind of information sharing, but the presumption of the article was that school boards must only master techniques to convince citizens to pay more taxes. Do school boards consider that they might listen and respond to the cost-containing wishes of the tax-paying public? Or that they might learn how to manage better the money taxpayers have already entrusted to them?

School boards get caught in an awful fix when they assume that their job is to take money from the public to support the ever-growing needs of the insatiable education bureaucracy. A *Seattle Post-Intelligencer* front-page headline told of the Seattle school board's fifth effort to "promote" a school bond measure. The article's title was "Backing May Be Illegal: Seattle District Spent $100,000 to Promote School Bond Issue."[46]

Evidently the board interpreted the four previous failed bond measures to mean that it had to become better at politics and more effective at voter campaigns. The board did not interpret the four failed bond measures as a message that it should work to understand the public's concerns, better manage costs, and provide a school district more in keeping with the wishes of the taxpayers.

Of course, the teacher union, from a safe distance, supported the board's effort. Once again, a school board in need of more money was caught between the proverbial rock and a hard place: either go to the public for more money or go toe-to-toe with the union to control costs. As NEA-controlled public education exists today, there is little choice but for school boards to go after what union negotiators call "new money."

NEA's primary tool for putting boards and districts at such a disadvantage is collective bargaining. Speaking for NEA, Keith Geiger made it clear that NEA wants a national collective bargaining law—and the sooner, the better. For now, however, NEA will be content with gaining a few statewide collective bargaining laws as a foundation upon which it can build its campaign for one national collective bargaining law.[47]

NEA's Field Agents: UniServ Operatives

NEA uses another force to rein in out-of-step teachers, control school boards, intimidate school administrators, and enforce the Unholy Alliance's unwritten rules. In its state-level hierarchy of power, midway between its national officers and its school-level foot soldiers, NEA has created its powerful UniServ program.

NEA began the UniServ (unified service) program in 1970. According to Allan West, past NEA deputy executive secretary, UniServ "provided full-time salaried professional personnel to strengthen the programs and services of local affiliates. In 1972 there were 600 UniServ personnel at work with local associations."[48] Today over 1,500 UniServ operatives "strengthen and serve" NEA's local affiliates.[49] The typical UniServ representative makes between $60,000 and $100,000 in annual salary with a benefits package of about 35 percent.[50] According to a 1995 publication from the National Institute for Labor Relations Research, the "average salary of a UniServ Staffer is $72,000 per year."[51] The Institute also discovered that "22% of the $92 NEA National Dues [that each member annually pays] went to UniServ in 1991. [The] UniServ program in Indiana as of August of 1991 cost $5.8 million."[52]

By region, UniServ staffing and funding for school year 1993–1994 was:

Region	Unit Employees	NEA Funds
Pacific	278	$6,264,925
Midwestern	361	7,869,144
Southeastern	201	4,521,464
Mid-Atlantic	239	5,450,200
Northeast	119	6,280,567
Western	165	3,828,880
TOTALS	**1,363**	**$34,215,180**[53]

In her research on teacher unions, Charlene K. Haar found that "NEA operates six regional offices that employ field representatives who are NEA employees. These field representatives are represented by Association of Field Staff Employees (AFSE), which negotiates on their behalf with the NEA. These are also well-paid positions... so generous that the NEA does not publicize the salaries and dollar value of all fringe benefits to NEA members."[54]

This adds up to a lot of money. It is an investment willingly made. Haar found that "UniServe staff accords the highest priority to contract language that maximizes the union's income stream."[55] Of course, the money comes from dues, mostly compulsory dues, and the origin of dues money is tax money.

Among other duties, UniServ operatives develop and execute the local affiliates' political action plan, advise on or handle the local affiliates' contract negotiations and grievances, and coordinate and advocate national and state association programs and priorities with the local union and its members. According to the National Institute for Labor Relations Research, UniServ operatives learn the Saul Alinsky theory and methods of organizing local NEA affiliates. This training teaches conflict as an important means to achieve NEA bosses' goals.

Alinsky, until his death in June 1972, conducted training programs for NEA's UniServ personnel. In January and February of 1972, he conducted such training programs for Kentucky and Illinois UniServ operatives. NEA is a private organization and keeps certain information tightly controlled. It is difficult to obtain copies of NEA training programs; therefore, it is also difficult to determine to what extent NEA operatives still use Alinsky training manuals. Nonetheless, excerpts from "Alinsky for Teacher Organizers" give insight into what NEA expects Alinsky-trained UniServ operatives to think and do. (The wording and underlining are from the document. These are not my words.)

- Alinsky believes that the teacher association's real <u>power</u> base is not in teachers, but in the community. He [Alinsky] does not see our task of organizing them as any different from those of his own community organizers.
- Because he sees teacher's <u>power</u> base outside the membership and in the community, Alinsky offers a straight line route to organization of that <u>power</u> base:
  - Get those teacher leaders to organize the community to <u>put pressure on the superintendent</u> or the <u>school board</u> to get things done for education. Develop a multi-issue base in getting to the community.
  - <u>Organize the community by using the natural interests in the children to get into the homes. That is, send teachers into the homes. Once teachers show interest in kids by visiting homes, they develop a relationship with parents.</u>
  - Once one or two teacher leaders begin to push and get near community-wide success, the rest of the teachers will go along.

- Alinsky believes that the organizer can tap into the boredom and routine of the teaching profession by providing an active, exciting alternative in the association structure to this routine.
- According to Alinsky, the organizer never has issues to begin with. People are resigned. The organizer has to touch the person's self-interest to find the issues around which the person is willing to organize. This means the organizer must take some chances in the beginning.
- The real training does not take place with words, but only with actions, which means that in order to train leaders, the <u>organization must set enough brush fires to keep them active and to keep the action going</u>.
- <u>After sending leaders in to the power people to express grievances, you must get hold of them as soon as they come out to keep them from getting off alone and scared about their future</u>.
- The worst thing the organizer can do in terms of tactics is to get together with his people and lay out a structured campaign because the structured campaign allows you to rationalize failure and to stop the action any time you run into a barrier.
- Certainly, Alinsky would not recommend exchanges of letters or private discussions with the superintendent as a way of building the organization. Such meetings or such correspondence might solve the problem, but they would not provide the kind of action that is exciting and what makes your people want to get involved with the organization, to participate. Going to court is likewise a local anesthetic; it freezes the action and prevents exploitation of the issue.
- <u>Generally, the Alinsky advice on tactics is guerrilla war advice. To win: know the enemy, divide the enemy, know who all the players are, conduct the action on several levels, and personalize the conflict</u>.
- <u>It is hard to deal with an enemy with whom you have a personal relationship. You should not let your people fraternize with the enemy. Distance helps you to polarize the issue—to make it an us/them affair</u>.

- Your record on small issues will convince your allies you are for real. If you're going to get the superintendent fired, win small child-oriented battles against his administrators. Once your people see you winning and are together, you can go to parents' groups, church groups, community groups for their support in taking on the superintendent.
- Alinsky's strategic and tactical essence is built around conflict.
- He uses confrontation much as teacher groups used confrontation at the negotiations table in order to buy a piece of power. Alinsky does not believe you can reason away from the power groups slices of their power. He believes they will attempt to buy you off by giving you, in exchange for real power, apparent power. Confrontation is then a way to apply pressure until you get real power.[56]

NEA's affinity for conflict and its eagerness to manipulate teachers and parents makes it difficult for school administrators to practice professional cooperation and collegial leadership to assist teachers and lead school communities.

Given Alinsky's incredible contempt for the role of teachers, school administrators, and parents, and for the democratic process, it is not surprising to see how his conflict theory has translated into practice. Examples of UniServ operative activities include:

- **October 19, 1978,** *Cleveland Press* Teachers crossing picket lines had windows shot out and homes and cars splattered with paint. The rally supporting the strike was put together by the UniServ Coordinating Council.
- **May 28, 1981,** *Boardman News*, **Youngstown, Ohio** Strike manuals [were found] entitled "Strategy UniServ Directors" outlining procedures to follow before and during a teachers' strike in Ravenna-Kent, Ohio. Strategies listed include: Mislead Own Membership; Nail the Negotiator; Neighborhood Nuisance; Blast the Boss; and Telephone Campaign. This strike result[ed] in the president of the union being found guilty of disorderly conduct, and there were many incidents of vandalism.

- **April 3, 1985,** *Indianapolis Star* Richard Cornstuble, Indiana State Teachers Association and UniServ staffer, was caught holding a bag with white spray paint and varnish remover over a school board member's car. In Cornstuble's car, officials found a sledgehammer, spray paint, a piece of concrete, and a city map with X's indicating the location of school board members' homes.

- **May 20, 1992,** *Education Week* Walter Galvin, UniServ director of Des Moines Education Association, was accused of violating "House ethic rules that bar lobbyists from tying campaign contributions to a vote." Galvin said, "I have noting to lose. As I understand it, the only penalty they can put on me is to revoke my lobbying privileges, and I am not a registered lobbyist in the first place."

- **June 3, 1992,** *Washington Post* Rick Willis, Fairfax Education Association member and UniServ staffer, helped manipulate the selection of Prudential Life Insurance as health insurance carrier for Fairfax Education Association, at an additional cost to the county taxpayers of $2.1 million. Prudential is a major contributor to NEA's National Foundation for the Improvement of Education.[57]

In practice and by design, UniServ operatives are specifically chosen, specially trained, highly paid shock troops.

They are one reason why school board members and superintendents are often afraid of the union and its bosses. But fear of NEA bosses is not limited to those who hold top-level posts. Principals and parents, too, fear union militants. In fact, public education operates under an NEA-created shroud of fear that controls the behavior of any who might come in conflict with the giant union's interests.

I have many times witnessed the effect UniServ operatives have on teachers and administrators. In many respects, they are like the Communist Party's *zampolits* who were attached to every Soviet military unit to keep troops and officers in compliance with party objectives.

NEA presents itself as a professional, caring organization dedicated to the well-being of children, the strength of communities, and the survival of the nation. In a 1994 speech to NEA's nine thousand Representative Assembly delegates, Keith Geiger told his audience, "The National Education Association is in the forefront of educational change.... Our Association is 2.2 million strong. At a time when public education and our Association are under relentless attack, NEA continues to grow. The NEA family stands as the largest, most influential, most effective child and youth advocacy organization on this planet."[58]

God help us all.

NEA's plan for creating and controlling public education goes well beyond coercion of teachers, intimidation of school superintendents, and control of local school boards. To achieve the level and degree of control NEA desires, NEA must have ready access to and control of public policymakers at the national level.

7

....

The Partnership:
NEA and the
Federal Government

"If I become President, you'll become my partners. I won't forget who brought me to the White House."[1]

—*Bill Clinton, Promise to NEA, December 1991*

THE *QUID PRO QUO* AGREEMENTS that prop up and support NEA reach beyond the Unholy Alliance. Many of the strategies and payoffs that join NEA, school boards, and superintendents also bind NEA and various government entities. NEA's continued achievement of its educational and social agendas is possible in large part because of the federal government's active aid and assistance.

It was not always so. In 1939 President Franklin D. Roosevelt, contending that unionization of public sector employees was "unthinkable and intolerable,"[2] signed the Hatch Act to limit the political activity of federal workers. Roosevelt believed public sector employees enjoyed special privileges—guaranteed salaries, good benefits, and protected jobs—and felt they should not strike and therein "obstruct the operations of government until their demands are satisfied."[3]

Presidential politics and standards of leadership have since changed. In 1962 President John F. Kennedy gave public-sector unions the powerful privilege of monopoly representation, thus beginning a momentous and far-reaching policy change. While this move brought immediate union support to his presidency, it also began what was to become a calamitous shift of power. The privilege of monopoly representation coupled with forced unionism and compulsory public-sector collective bargaining led to a loss of independence for tens of thousands of teachers and a loss of control for thousands of public school districts across the fifty states.

In 1965 President Lyndon B. Johnson championed the NEA-sponsored $1.5 billion federal aid package that became the Elementary and Secondary Education Act. To that date, the act was "the single largest federal aid to education program ever enacted by Congress."[4]

In 1979 President Jimmy Carter repaid NEA for its campaign support by creating a cabinet-level Department of Education, complete with a secretary of education who had a direct path to the president.

And in 1992 President Bill Clinton, after vowing not to forget who brought him to the White House, promised labor union officials that he would support a watering down of the Hatch Act.[5] As this book was going to print, President Clinton was aggressively pursuing a billion-plus dollar legislative package to (1) buy an additional one hundred thousand classroom teachers and (2) pay for deferred maintenance on elementary and secondary schools.

Some consider the Democrat Party "the education party." In view of its history since 1939, it would be more accurate to describe it as "the NEA party."

Many of NEA's "educational agenda" issues are more connected to labor union interests than educational interests. Frequently, however, NEA bosses use their muscle to promote social goals that have nothing to do with even labor union interests. This practice continues despite the fact that many NEA members object to the union bosses' passionate pursuit of its ultraliberal social agenda.

NEA resolutions show a commitment to ultraliberal causes and numerous social issues that are completely unrelated to teachers and teaching. Why is a teacher union so strident on these issues? In fact, why is it involved in these issues at all? In her book, *NEA: Propaganda Front of the Radical Left*, Sally D. Reed included a copy of an NEA telegram to members of the U.S. Senate:

To: All Members of the U.S. Senate
From: Linda Tarr-Whelan
           Director, Government Relations
           National Education Association

On behalf of NEA's 1.7 million members, I urge you to oppose S.J. Res. 3, a constitutional amendment to ban abortions.

NEA believes that reproductive freedom is one of the most fundamental human and civil rights. The decision about abortions is an economic one for millions of American working women and their families. Whether or not a woman chooses to have a child is a matter for her to decide, based on imput [sic] from her family, her doctor & her pastor—not the government.

NEA considers reproductive freedom of choice the constitutional right of every woman and strongly opposes any amendment to the constitution or statute which would limit or eradicate this right.

End message[6]

How can an NEA officer pretend that all NEA's then-1.7 million members—now 2.264 million—support this position on abortion? Even if it were true, what does abortion have to do with public education?

NEA takes a position on affirmative action, too. In one of six resolutions dealing with this issue, and after lengthy discussion of "societal needs," NEA advises, "It may be necessary, therefore, to give preference in recruitment, hiring, retention, and promotion policies to certain ethnic-minority groups or women or men to overcome past discrimination."[7]

Delegates at the 1995 NEA Representative Assembly adopted literally hundreds of resolutions and legislative targets they want Congress to make into national law. In his research for an article on teacher unions, Sol Stern found that "if Congress passed all NEA's legislative proposals, the annual additional charge to the federal treasury would be $800 billion, requiring an average tax increase of $10,000 for a family of four."[8]

Some NEA resolutions are tangentially related to educational issues; some are not even remotely related. Almost all reflect an ultraliberal bias. The nine items listed here are taken from *The 1995–96 Resolutions of the National Education Association* report that chronicled resolutions the Representative Assembly adopted at its 1995 annual meeting.

- **English as the Official Language:** The Association believes that... efforts to legislate English as the official language disregard cultural pluralism; deprive those in need of education, social services, and employment; and must be challenged.[9]
- **Family Planning:** The Association... urges the implementation of community-operated, school-based family planning clinics that will provide intensive counseling by trained personnel.[10]
- **Education of Refugee Children and Children of Undocumented Immigrants:** The association urges that... impacted school districts receive federal and state assistance to provide educational facilities, personnel, special programs, and instructional materials [for]... refugee children and children of undocumented immigrants.[11]
- **Federal Financial Support for Education:** The Association will continually seek general federal support for the whole of public elementary, secondary, and post secondary education. The federal monies must be expended solely and equitably for public education.[12]
- **Voucher Plans:** The National Education Association believes that voucher plans or funding formulas that have the same effect as vouchers—under which education is financed by fed-

eral, state, or local grants to parents, schools, or school systems—could lead to racial, economic, and social isolation of
students and weaken or destroy public education.[13] [Note: The
1994–95 "Voucher Plans" resolution was worded the same
except the last three words changed from "public school system" to "public education."]

- **Labor Movement Education:** The National Education Association believes that the influence of the labor movement and
unionism on the growth of the United States should be an inte-
gral part of the curriculum in our schools.[14]

- **Immigration:** The National Education Association supports
efforts to improve the immigration process, including the provision of due process, political asylum, and timely legalization
without regard to national origin.[15]

- **Control of Guns and Other Deadly Weapons:** The National
Education Association believes that stricter legislation is needed
to control guns and other deadly weapons. The Association
supports legislation that provides for prescriptive controls on
the manufacture, distribution, and sale of handguns.[16]

- **Telephone/Telemarketing Programs:** The National Education
Association recognizes the potential for telephone and telemar-
keting programs to exploit children. The Association believes
that electronic blocking devices should be available to parents,
at no cost, to limit children's access to these programs.[17]

These nine resolutions give a glimpse of NEA's ambitious plan to
shape American society according to its ideology and social agenda.
The means to accomplish its controlling agenda are well established
in the federal government's departments and agencies. NEA is a
good student of the workings of government and the people who
make government work. To encourage those in power to proactive
support of its agenda, NEA has developed its powerful and effective Government Relations Division.

GOVERNMENT RELATIONS

According the *National Education Association Handbook 1994–
1995*, NEA's division of "Government Relations" carries lead respon-

sibilities for organizing and training NEA members to elect pro-education candidates to federal office; influencing the executive branch in its development of legislative proposals and its regulation of programs of interest to NEA; working with organizations of education policymakers at the state, local, and regional levels to adopt positions compatible with NEA's; and advancing NEA's Legislative Program in Congress. To implement its broad agenda, Government Relations is comprised of the following sections: Federal Relations, Political Advocacy, Information Resources, and Administrative Services."[18]

Each of these four sections holds specific responsibilities to further NEA's Legislative Program. Among a host of duties, the Information Resources section has responsibility for "the development of congressional testimony,"[19] and the Federal Relations section is to achieve "a true partnership of the federal, state, and local levels of government."[20] (The question: What, in NEA's view, constitutes "a true partnership"?) The Field Services section offers "[t]wo field service teams [to] provide on-site consultation and assistance, as well as training in political action, lobbying, PAC fundraising, and assistance on state and local issues."[21] And NEA's Political Advocacy section "compliment[s] and facilitate[s] NEA's lobbying efforts by helping to secure the election to federal office of candidates who support public education."[22]

Since NEA admits to "550 staff members, who work in Washington, D.C., and in six regional offices,"[23] an organization of 2.2 million members, and a 1994–1995 operating budget of $179,157,000,[24] few can doubt that NEA is strong on the "influence" part of its mission statement.

The NEA-government partnership works, and it works well. A good example is NEA's support of Bill Clinton's first campaign for the presidency. Aside from $3.1 million in direct NEA contributions,[25] the union also kicked in $528,000 in "soft money."[26]* Ignoring the fact that NEA bosses spent millions of compulsory-dues dollars in support of a candidate many NEA members opposed, then-NEA President Keith Geiger arrogantly told the faithful in a September 1992 newsletter article, "This is the President we've awaited, the President we need."[27] Geiger also told the members that Bill Clinton spoke before an "audience that was nothing less than a multi-ethnic, multi-racial mosaic of strong-willed, independent-minded individuals [who] rose to their feet. Their applause was thunderous. They cheered, they stomped, they whistled and screamed. Some even cried.... Bill Clinton captured more that 88 percent of the votes.... He intends to be our partner."[28]

NEA's high command supports a candidate, the candidate becomes president, and the new president chooses a secretary of education who supports NEA's Legislative Program and social agenda. Secretary of Education Richard Riley is a longtime friend of NEA-style education. As the *Wall Street Journal* pointed out, during his term as governor of South Carolina, Riley "vastly increased spending on schools."[29] Speaking before the California Teachers Association, Secretary Riley assured NEA loyalists that he would resist voucher-based parental school choice and foreswore any such option being provided to private schools.[30] The secretary assured them of his support of "longer-range Clinton plans to 'focus on the whole child for the whole day and beyond.'"[31] A reporter for the *Wall Street Journal* surmised this was "the opening for using the school building as a base for an expansive social-service program."[32] Faithful to NEA's pet solution to all educational problems, Riley proudly proclaimed that billions of dollars in added spending would be committed to already existing federal programs.[33] It is no coincidence that the Department of Education's goals for reengineering America are also NEA's goals. NEA's Political Action Committee sees to it.

NEA-PAC

NEA-PAC is also under the Government Relations Division. According to NEA, "NEA-PAC is the political action arm of NEA members nationwide.... Its objective is to help elect to federal office those candidates who support federal legislation consistent with the

---

*According to "Democrats Surpass GOP in 'Soft Money,'" in the 25 August 1993 edition of *The Washington Post*, "'Soft money' refers to funds that go to the national parties for party-building activities such as voter registration and get-out-the-vote drives." Whereas there is a $20,000 limit on individual donation to candidates, there is no limit on "soft money" donations to the parties.

policies established by the NEA Representative Assembly. NEA-PAC supports friends of education by making financial contributions to the candidates' campaigns and by encouraging members to volunteer their services to those campaigns."[34]

Federal law prohibits use of union membership dues for PAC activities. Hardly deterred by the laws of the land, NEA officials find ways to use union dues to political ends. NEA bosses also continue to coerce members to make annual "contributions" of at least $10 to NEA-PAC.[35] State* and local NEA affiliates ask for similar contributions, and in some cases NEA or its affiliates request individual contributions of $50 or more. That these contributions add up to big money is plainly evident in the numerous campaign contributions NEA annually makes to "friends of education."

Nationally, NEA-PAC ranked fourth in money contributed to federal candidates in 1986–1987 and fifth in 1990.[36] In 1972 NEA-PAC raised $36,000. In 1990 NEA-PAC raised $4.2 million; wealthier big-money players included "the Teamster's Democratic Republican Independent Voter Education Committee, followed by the American Medical Association PAC, the Realtors PAC, and Voter Guide, a one-time California group that collected money for ballot initiatives."[37]

The *American School Board Journal* reported that in 1980 Walter Mondale told a crowd at the New York Democrat Convention, "If you want to go somewhere in national politics these days, you'd better get NEA behind you."[38] That same year, NEA sent 464 members to the Democrat convention as delegates or alternates and

---

*From Jeanne Allen in The Center for Education Reform's February/March 1995 newsletter we learned: "The Michigan Education Association has committed to spend $8 million for a three year PR blitz. Members are angry that their dues have been hiked $30 to finance this campaign, which is targeted at reviving MEA's marginal political influence in the Capital and poor public image statewide.... The New Jersey Education Association is also assessing each of its members $50 over the next year for its new $10 million Pride in Public Education campaign. This effort is devoted to hyping a more rosy picture of the schools' progress and creating a climate for more favorable collective bargaining in the future."

twenty-two members to the Republican Convention.[39] Does all this time, money, and effort pay off for NEA? In 1990 NEA won 247 of the 285 seats it backed in House of Representatives races (87 percent) and 19 of the 27 seats it endorsed for the Senate (70 percent).[40] At the 1992 Democrat Convention, 512 of the 4,928 delegates (over 10 percent) were either NEA or AFT members—the single largest interest-group contingent among the delegates.[41]

But NEA is still not satisfied. Mickey Ibarra, political advocacy manager in NEA's Government Relations division, explained that to buttress and enforce their plan for growth, NEA installed a new computer system to track and record members' political contributions.[42] In the years to come, NEA will continue to coerce its members to pay money for numerous special political causes, the goals of which will be strikingly similar: to support NEA's bosses, advance their agenda, and promote ultraliberal social issues.

As successful as their campaigns have been in electing chosen people to national office and as effective as they have been in raising huge sums of money to support PAC activities, NEA chieftains know that the personal involvement of members is their most effective weapon. Past NEA Acting Executive Secretary Allan West wrote in *The National Education Association: The Power Base for Education*, "The greatest resource possessed by teachers is the sum total of personal resources of almost two million members [now 2.264 million] residing in every congressional district in the United States. Their collective influence as active local citizens in their own communities, *coordinated by a national strategy*, can add up to a tremendous political force beyond the limits of what money can buy"[43] (emphasis added).

The "collective influence" to achieve NEA's "national strategy" has been very effective. But do the concepts of local control, neighborhood schools, and parents' wishes fit into NEA's vision of a one-size-fits-all national system of education?

THE U.S. DEPARTMENT OF EDUCATION

President Carter's elevation of the Department of Education in 1979 to a cabinet-level post has given NEA power brokers increased political leverage and a path to the president. The Department of Education, however, was not intended to be as it is today. Since NEA's earliest days, it has come to its present stature through 140 years of incremental expansion of its responsibilities and authority.

The idea for the Department of Education began when NEA began, and it has taken several paths on its way from wish to reality. As long ago as February 10, 1866, the National Association of State and City School Superintendents issued a communiqué to the Senate and House of Representatives requesting they establish a national bureau of education.[44] According to a report from the U.S. Department of Education, that next year

> the Congress of the United States passed legislation providing "That there shall be established at the City of Washington, a department of education, for the purpose of collecting such statistics and facts as shall show the condition and progress of education in the several States and Territories, and of diffusing such information respecting the organization and management of schools and school systems, and methods of teaching, as shall aid the people of the United States in the establishment and maintenance of efficient school systems, and otherwise promote the causes of education throughout the country."[45]

In 1867 the United States Office of Education, as it was then called, had a staff of six and a budget of $13,000.[46] It was headed by a commissioner of education who received a salary of $4,000 annually. The commissioner had three clerks with annual salaries of $2,000, $1,800, and $1,600.[47]

Over the next eight decades, the mission of the United States Office of Education changed little, but its staff and budget grew. According to authors David Tyack and Elisabeth Hansot, "In 1950 the United States Office of Education (USOE) was a minor bureaucracy with a staff of 300 and a budget of $40 million; its duties, as in the nineteenth century, were largely those of collecting and providing educational information."[48]

The department is considerably different today. As shown in its *FY 1998 Budget Summary* report, the Department of Education employed 4,655 people in 1996.[49] Down from 4,816 in 1995, the department explained that it "has maintained operations in spite of low staffing levels in part by relying on automation and private contractors."[50] The department also reported a 1997 appropriated budget of $29,366,057,000 and a 1998 estimated budget of $39,470,231,000—a 34 percent increase in one year.[51]

The original Department of Education had a limited charge; but as early as the February 10, 1866, communiqué to Congress, the seeds were planted for its present omnibus role in public education. In that document, the superintendents argued, "The assistance and encouragement of the General Government are needed to secure the adoption of school systems throughout the country. Just where education is most needed, there it is always least appreciated and valued." The superintendents claimed "that the demand for education must be awakened by *external influences and agencies*"[52] (emphasis added).

Wanting what has never been and can never be—federal assistance without federal control—these apparently well-meaning but politically naive petitioners cautioned Congress to create a bureau "without its being invested with any official control of the school authorities therein." "Indeed," they contended, "the highest value of such a bureau would be its quickening and informing, rather than its authoritative and direct control."[53]

That was then and this is now. Now NEA policymakers want a national system of education they can control, and the Department of Education plays prominently in their plans.

In their 1994 book on teacher unions, Lieberman, Haar, and Troy emphasized that, in 1979, President Jimmy Carter "vigorously supported legislation creating a U.S. Department of Education, a longtime NEA goal."[54] On October 17, 1979, legislation authorizing the new cabinet became law, and the Department of Education was official on May 4, 1980.[55] Although the 262-page *Education Department 1990: A Resource Manual for the Federal Education Department* did not, unbelievable as it is, include a statement of the department's mission or congressional charge, it did state the responsibilities of the secretary of the Department of Education:

The Secretary of Education advises the President on education plans, policies, and programs of the federal government. The Secretary directs Department staff in carrying out the approved programs and activities of the Department and promotes general public understanding of the Department's goals, programs, and objectives. The Secretary also carries out certain federal responsibilities for four federally aided programs: The American Printing House of the Blind, Gallaudet University, Howard University, and the National Technical Institute for the Deaf.[56]

As earlier noted, today's Department of Education is an amazing conglomeration. In 1990 its *Resource Manual* listed fifty-five acts of "Authorizing Legislation" and 146 "Major Programs." The major programs were listed alphabetically beginning with the "Anti-Drug Abuse Act" and ending with the "Women's Educational Equity Act."[57] According to its "all purpose table," the department's estimated 1991 budget was $24,954,800,000, and its estimated administrative cost to manage those programs was $406,700,000.[58]

Also according to the *Resource Manual*, the Pell Grants program received the largest funding—$5,277,000,000.[59] The Pell Grant "[p]rovides need-based grants to low-income undergraduate students to promote access to postsecondary education and to lower the burden of its financing.... Applicants must be U.S. citizens or eligible non-citizens."[60]

One of the smaller programs, English Literacy, with requested funding of $1,000,000, provides "[g]rants to states to conduct English literacy projects for individuals of limited English proficiency."[61]

Under the College Work-Study Program, the department budgeted $601,765,000 to make "[d]irect payments to provide part-time employment to eligible postsecondary students, to help them meet educational expenses."[62]

The department set aside $487,619,000 to "[f]ormula grants to provide financial assistance to establish programs of alcohol and drug abuse education and prevention"[63] and another $15,959,000 to "maintain five regional centers, which train school teams to assess alcohol- and drug-related problems confronting their schools and mobilize communities in response to those problems."[64]

In another program, the department allocated $285,375,000 to fund "formula grants providing financial assistance to SEA's [state education agencies, i.e., state departments of education] for compensatory education services of migrant agricultural workers and fishermen."[65,*]

This review leads you to wonder why the federal government takes money from citizens living in the fifty states to fund programs in neighborhood schools. The government collects money from the states and transfers it to the federal level where, after subtracting for various handling charges, the remaining money is sent back to the states with certain federal mandates attached. This is a costly way to fund education.

On Jim Lehrer's February 10, 1999, *NewsHour* program, Representative William Goodling and Secretary Riley were interviewed in a point-counterpoint format. In response to questions, Secretary Riley said, "What the federal government is trying to do is to expand on what's working in the states using information that we have gleaned from the states."[66] Then commenting on the federal government's ever-expanding role in education, he said, "We've got to see to it that those dollars are spent in an accountable way."[67]

Confronting this display of federal government intrusion in states' affairs, Representative Goodling pointed out that the Department

---

*As a parent, I have knowledge of this program. When my wife, children, and I lived in Alaska, we left our Mainland home each summer and traveled to a small island north of Kodiak Island where we owned and operated a commercial salmon fishing business. Since our sons, as fishermen, "migrated" to the fishing grounds and worked with us to run the operation, they qualified as migrant students. Yet, the Moo brothers migrated only during the summer and never missed a day of school due to commercial fishing—some migration. I was told the money from migrant students went to buy computers for the district's elementary schools.

of Education was planning to "require" more and more of states and local school districts. Representative Goodling noted that Secretary Riley, referring to the federal government said, "*[W]e'll require* states and school districts to end social promotion. *We'll require* students to get more help. *We'll require* you to adopt performance examinations"[68] (emphasis added).

Unbelievably, Secretary Riley responded that if states and school districts "refuse accountability, then we have no choice but to pull back on administrative funds or something."[69] Or something! What is the or something to which the secretary refers?

This attack on states and local control is not limited to the Department of Education. Central control of education is a growing movement within the Democrat Party. On the February 22, 1999, NewsHour program, Senator Richard Durbin, Democrat from Illinois, said as a prelude to his defense of President Clinton's plans for an increased federal-government role in education, "I hope we do not get all caught up in these old clichés, the Washington political clichés about education and local control and federal regulation."[70] Six days later, in a February 28, 1999, article, California's newly elected Democrat Governor Gary Davis was quoted as saying, "We've had local control of schools for 50 years, and it's been an abject failure."[71]

Translation from Riley, Durbin, and Davis—centrally contrived, one-size-fits-all programs will be imposed on school districts and neighborhood schools. Good-bye local control.

Of course, true local control would be unacceptable to NEA's power brokers and their federal government allies; so, from this point of view, centralization of power and legislated control makes sense. How better to force teachers and local schools, state colleges, and universities to provide the educational programs the Department of Education wants? Considering that the Constitution does not give the federal government authority over public education, the $39 billion budget the Department of Education estimated for 1998 seems a sizable sum. Imagine what the Department of Education's annual budget could be if it had constitutional authority.

THE CONNECTIONS THAT BIND

In what ways are there connections between NEA and the Department of Education? When former NEA president, Keith Geiger, addressed this question in his July 1993 report to NEA's Representative Assembly, he told those assembled, "The U.S. Department of Education set out to test the proposition that a strong [labor] contract is the route to greater professionalism. They hired the prestigious Rand Corporation. The Rand researchers did a very thorough job. They reviewed 150 collective bargaining contracts, they interviewed 600 educators and policymakers, and they visited 52 school buildings. And what did they find? The Rand report concluded, and I quote, 'Obtaining key bread-and-butter items that regulate basic working conditions is a precondition for securing contract provisions that enhance teacher professionalism.'"[72]

Why should this particular question be of such interest to the Department of Education? The Rand Corporation's conclusions are consistent with NEA's contention that collective bargaining is the key to teacher professionalism. How exactly "teacher professionalism" derives from "bread-and-butter items" garnered through collective bargaining is unanswered in Geiger's speech. Nevertheless, in a February 1993 newsletter article addressing this same study, Geiger proclaimed, "It is time for every district office in America to concede that instructional issues are appropriate bargaining issues."[73] Imagine the effect negotiating "instructional issues" with NEA militants would have on local schools and communities.

Laws in some states preclude collective bargaining, and other states specify what issues the districts must open to collective bargaining while leaving to the discretion of local school boards the appropriateness of all other issues. But on the strength of this one study commissioned by the Department of Education, Geiger and other NEA officials eagerly proclaimed the need to impose mandatory collective bargaining on all fifty states and their fifteen thousand school districts.

Geiger went even further. Stating that collective bargaining in every school district is the path to "universal excellence," Geiger challenged the membership. He proclaimed, "We need universal excellence," and added, "If we're to achieve that goal, we must bargain better, bargain smarter, and refute all those who would limit collective bargaining to bread-and-butter issues."[74] In this study, NEA finds justification to bargain all issues related to public education collectively, especially "instructional issues." Who needs boards of education or local control? NEA would gladly run every school district.

It is good to have friends in high places, such as the Department of Education.

GOALS 2000, EDUCATE AMERICA ACT

In a May 1994 article entitled, "Goals 2000, Is This the Most Important Federal Education Legislation in a Generation?" an NEA spokesperson proclaimed, "On March 31, at a public elementary school in San Diego, President Clinton signed the Goals 2000: Educate America Act, *establishing for the first time in history a national mission statement** for America's schools"[75] (emphasis added). The creation of a "national mission statement" takes each state and our nation one step closer to NEA's long-held goal for a single, national system of education. How strange that a federal agency established for the limited purposes of "collecting such statistics and facts as will show the condition and progress of education in the several States and Territories" should now decide that it, rather than the states, will be the focus for all things educational.

---

*The *Goals 2000: Educate America Act* sets eight goals to be achieved by the year 2000

1. All children in America will start school ready to learn.
2. The high school graduation rate will increase to at least 90 percent.
3. All students will leave grades 4, 8, and 12 having demonstrated competency over challenging subject matter..., and prepared for responsible citizenship, further learning, and productive employment....

The Department of Education is solidly behind the Goals 2000 program. Goals 2000 gives the department a badly needed purpose around which to justify its existence, and it offers the department a bully pulpit from which to argue for one national system of education controlled and directed by the department and its ideological allies.

In its monthly Goals 2000 newsletter, the department heralded Vice President Gore's book, *Earth in Balance*, and reminded states and communities of their eligibility for funding through the Department of Education if they "commit to the program."[76] The article told readers, "The Secretary outlined four major areas of national concern where the Department of Education plays an active role: helping to ensure *national security, economic security*, a responsible citizenry, and equal access to education"[77] (emphasis added). In the pursuit of all this, the secretary assured, "We seek to support and encourage: we do not dictate or determine local or state policy."[78]

Perhaps the secretary is not considering the federal government's history of incremental intrusion into matters of public education, or perhaps he is naive about the goals of the Department of Education. But obviously, to mention "national security" and "economic security" with reference to public education is to lay the foundation for federal takeover of public education under the guise of threats to national security and national interests.

Twenty years ago, in an effort to understand better the arguments for federal control of education, I wrote a research paper investigat-

---

4. The nation's teaching force will have access to programs for the continued improvement of their professional skills....
5. United States students will be first in the world in mathematics and science achievement.
6. Every adult in America will be literate.
7. Every school in America will be free of drugs and violence and will offer a disciplined environment conducive to learning.
8. Every school and home will engage in partnerships that will increase parental involvement and participation in promoting social, emotional, and academic growth of children. (Taken from *NEA Today*, May 1994.)

ing the issue. To my consternation, and notwithstanding the apparent violation of the Tenth Amendment, I discovered that arguments for federal control of education are not new.* The precedents that support federal intrusion in public education have come primarily through two channels: (1) declaring a state of emergency and having the federal government come to the rescue (Sputnik begot the National Defense Education Act, wherein millions of federal dollars—and federal control—flowed to states and local school districts), and (2) giving "free money" to citizens to cure social woes when the federal government wanted to control the solution (the

---

*The arguments I cited in 1975 to show the case for federal control of education were:

1. The main efforts of those who advocate federal control of education are to show that a national emergency exists and that this emergency resulted directly from the failure of local and state authorities to provide the quality of education needed for the Nation to survive in a fiercely competitive world market and threatening geo-political environment. It could then be shown that the federal government has not only the obligation but the means by which to effect a takeover of public education. Perhaps the "provide-for-the-common-defense-and-general-welfare-of-the-United-States" clause of the Constitution could be used to justify the federal government's assumption of educational powers.

2. Federal government action to provide for the general welfare is not unknown. Federal troops effected desegregation and the federal government has administered numerous educational programs. (Up to 1975, these programs included: Department of Defense schools, Bureau of Indian Affairs schools, Manpower Development Training Act schools, Comprehensive Employment Training Act schools, and military service academies.)

3. The federal government has provided money to local districts for quite some time. To qualify for federal funds, districts must agree to accomplish specified goals. In this way the federal government already has gained a level of control of local school districts.

4. Conversely, the federal government can withhold money it would normally award a district until the district agrees to stop a specific action.

Comprehensive Employment Training Act trained the unskilled in vocational education programs so they would be employable). Whatever the outcomes of these programs, the federal government clearly has increased its control over public education.

Others also think the U.S. Department and its Goals 2000 program are leading us in the wrong direction. The Department of Education and the secretary claim that the "goals" in the pages and pages of the Goals 2000 Act are voluntary. Of the onslaught of federal intrusion into education, Jeanne Allen in *The School Reform Handbook* wrote, "Even though laws emphasize the 'voluntary' nature of the goals, funds are linked to a federal seal of approval. The intent to further federalize education is clear—as the Secretary of Education stated in a speech to the National School Board Association, 'Education is back from the dead in Washington. Our budget is up $1.6 billion.'"[79] (More recently, of course, the Department's proposed budget is up some 50 billion dollars, and counting.)

Milton Chappell, staff attorney for the National Right to Work Legal Defense Foundation, analyzed S.1150, *Goals 2000: Educate America Act*. He concluded that the program President Clinton champions and Secretary of Education Richard Riley aggressively supports will assure that "representatives of labor unions will actively participate in setting the national educational goals and standards—both at the federal and state levels. Additionally, labor organizations, both directly and indirectly, will be entitled to receive massive federal and state grants under the spending sections of S.1150."[80]

In his report, Chappell observed, "S.1150 establishes four new boards: National Education Goals Panel, National Education Standards and Improvement Council, 52 State Improvement Plan Panels, and National Skill Standards Board."[81]

Chappell pointed out that the act "specifically mandates that membership on each of the 52 state panels must include 'school teachers'

Proponents for federal control of education can argue that the same reasoning that required and justified federal intervention to desegregate public schools in the 1960s now justifies the federal government's takeover of public education.

and 'representatives of teachers' organizations... and labor leaders, to be appointed by the governor and the chief state school officer." Further, "S.1150 gives these various boards and panels the authority to work with such broad-based entities," observed Chappell, "that it is certain that labor organizations, especially the NEA, will be supplying these panels with the criteria, goals and standards which the panels will eventually adopt and impose on the Nation."[82]

Chappell concluded his three-page report with this warning:

> The most dangerous part of [Goals 2000] is Title III—State and Local Education Systemic Improvement. It mandates teacher [*i.e.,* union] involvement at the state and local level in all programs, strategies and reforms to revitalize and improve, according to Title III's dictates,* the local public schools. Id. (301 [pp.48–51]). For instance, Title III requires each State improvement plan to "involve broad-based and ongoing classroom teacher input in... developing or recommending instructional materials and technology,... [and] the State's system of teacher... preparation and licensure, and of continuing professional development programs... Id. (306 (c) [pp.61–64]). It also mandates that federal funding be in addition to and above the current funding. Moreover, the funding provided under Title III cannot be used for current or existing projects. Id. (302-04 [pp.51–57]). Finally, both the State improvement and all funding under Title III must be reviewed by the Secretary of Education and a peer review panel consisting of "educators, classroom teachers, related services personnel, experts on educational innovations, and improvement,... advocates, and other appropriate

---

*Taken from the Act: "State and local education improvement efforts must incorporate strategies for providing students and families with coordinated access to appropriate social services, health care, nutrition, early childhood education, and child care." Id. (301(9) [p.50]

individuals [who] shall be representative of the diversity
of the United States with regard to geography, race,
ethnicity, gender and disability characteristics [and]
shall [make] at least 1 site visit to each state. (306 (j)
[pp.66–67]).[83]

Yes indeed, "If I become President, you'll become my partners. I
won't forget who brought me to the White House." So said candidate Clinton. And a promise made, in this case, is a promise kept.

From this promise, NEA has realized a tremendous return on
investment: The federal government continues and accelerates its
move to take over public education; the federal government spends
federal tax money in local communities to circumvent local control
by offering programs NEA wants; NEA power brokers figure prominently in decision making that will shape the workings and outcomes
of Goals 2000; teacher unions are mandated in legislation as partners who must be included in efforts to reform education; and NEA's
ultraliberal social agenda gains another tax-supported legislative
mandate.

The Department of Education's fervor for Goals 2000 seems to
know no bounds. According to Jeanne Allen of the Center for
Education Reform, which co-hosted a national Educational Summit
in January 1995, she and others at the summit experienced a "living,
breathing example of federal intrusion. Early in the day [of the summit meeting], a U.S. Department of Education representative showed
up, uninvited, to distribute some promotional material. Despite
objections, this official placed on all of the chairs glossy publications
touting Goals 2000 and other 'achievements' of the Administration.
He also demanded to see a list of press attending the event, claiming they 'needed' the info he had to offer."[84] With thousands of federal staff and seemingly limitless tax money, the Department of
Education can be everywhere at any time to promote its programs,
goals, and agenda.

The *Goals 2000 Act* and its companion *School-to-Work
Opportunity Act* fly in the face of common sense and long-
established practice. Before the nation's labor unions convinced legislators that adolescents should not work—because they take jobs

away from adults who need to work and who, not coincidentally, can join unions and pay dues—young boys and girls worked at all manner of jobs.

In those days, young people worked to earn money, acquire skills, gain pride and self-respect, and learn a work ethic. What adolescents learned at their first job was part of a rite of passage into the adult world. Now, the federal government has passed laws prohibiting young people from working at even the most routine jobs and has created a bureaucracy to enforce its anti-learn-to-work laws. As a result, the federal government has now discovered that young people need huge and expensive federal programs to learn "school-to-work" transition skills.

Where once it was a natural "home-to-work" process and parents, not federal bureaucrats, helped young men and women (then called "sons" and "daughters") to find jobs, get to work on time, and do a day's work for a day's pay, we now need the federal government and NEA.

This new *School-to-Work Act* is more a make-work program for federal employees and a chance for NEA to add new members than it is a way to help young people learn what they once learned in their neighborhoods and home towns under their family's watchful eye. In short, the federal government and the schools are taking over one more of the family's traditional responsibilities.

LEGAL BEAGLES—NEA'S DOGS OF WAR

If NEA-PAC money and NEA's powerful partner—the Department of Education—do not get for it what it wants, then NEA union officials unleash the dogs of war to block the democratic process.

In his 1997 research on NEA, Sol Stern discovered the depth of NEA's legal might. Stern found, "The NEA budgets $23 million a year for its legal arm, headed by a brilliant Washington lawyer named Robert Chanin. Chanin's primary mission, naturally, is to throw up legal challenges to every piece of legislation passed by democratically elected bodies that might free some children from the monopolistic public education system. But in addition, he intervenes in major court battles involving the pet issues of the Left."[85]

THE POLITICS OF EDUCATIONAL RESEARCH

It would be comforting to think that educational research is immune to the politics and power games that permeate so much of public education. Alas, the ideological war continues in the arena of educational research. Of the $60 million the Department of Education appropriated for research in 1990, $50 million supported studies mandated by Congress.[86] In 1990 the Democrats controlled Congress. NEA does not of course spend huge sums of money on congressional campaign support and lobbying without realizing substantial returns on its investments. Many Democrats look to NEA for direction on educational issues. In influencing congressional decisions, NEA has considerable control over the Department of Education's decisions about research funding.

In the private sector, market forces help to focus research and assure that organizations wisely use pertinent research findings. Privately owned companies cannot afford to do research and then not use its more promising findings in productive ways. In education, there are no particular incentives for anyone in the public schools to apply or otherwise use research findings.

Myron Lieberman charged, "Teacher unions not only oppose the introduction of [labor-saving] technology; they are adamantly opposed to R&D that might lead to it."[87] According to a 1990 report from the Hudson Institute, "Technology exists that can at least double the productivity of teaching."[88] In the hierarchy of teacher-union values, the financial and union interests of the providers of educational services take precedence over the best interests of the consumers of education; i.e., students, taxpayers, and the business community.

The money involved is staggering. The Department of Education's 1998 projected budget shows an estimated $510,693,000 to be budgeted just for the Office of Educational Research and Improvement (OERI).[89] And each of the department's divisions can commit additional money to educational research it wishes to pursue.

NEA has strong influence over the direction and outcome of educational research. But despite its power, it cannot always stop threatening research findings from finding the light of day. When this happens, teacher labor unions quickly work to refute the validity and block their use. To illustrate how this phenomenon works, return to a topic near and dear to NEA's heart: class size.

According to Myron Lieberman, "The research on class size indicates that within broad limits, reducing class size does not result in significant gains in pupil achievement. To achieve even modest gains, classes would have to be [substantially] smaller, and the costs would be prohibitive. Furthermore, as class size is reduced, more teachers are needed, exacerbating the problem of maintaining teacher quality. Generally speaking, therefore, smaller classes benefit teachers, not pupils."[90] Dr. Lieberman went on to explain, "When a U.S. Department of Education report drew this conclusion in 1988, the presidents of NEA and AFT charged that educational research was being politicized. In fact, both prior and subsequent researchers who could not reasonably be regarded as politically motivated reached the same conclusion."[91]

A similar chain of political events shut off research on contracting out the teaching of students. Lieberman observed, "In the 1970s teacher unions adamantly opposed federally funded experiments on contracting out instruction. The unions forced the research projects to adopt restrictions that crippled them educationally and destroyed their viability as experiments about anything. Subsequently, federal R&D projects in education have avoided labor-saving issues."[92]

Interestingly, the Department of Education[93] and NEA contract out for services. In fact, NEA's labor contracts with both its Washington, D.C., and regional staffs specifically provide for NEA and its affiliates to contract out work.[94] NEA does not broadcast this fact to its members or to the general public. It would be rather awkward for an NEA negotiator to explain to a school board why it is necessary and permissible for NEA to contract out work while it is absolutely not acceptable for school districts to do the same.

Considering that NEA now represents school cooks, bus drivers, and other nonteacher labor groups, the issue of contracting out becomes increasingly important to NEA's plan for membership growth and dues collection. In Resolution D-8 A Licensed Educator in Every Professional Position, NEA warned would-be contractors, "The Association will resist any attempts to diminish the quality of learning or services through the elimination of teaching positions, through the subcontracting of teaching and support services."[95] In Resolution F-26 Subcontracting/Contracting Out, NEA stated, "The Association believes that employees should not be displaced by private service providers or by temporary or part-time workers. The Association further believes that school districts should not enter into subcontracting agreements that transfer education employees or that abrogate previously contracted benefits, reduce compensation, deny fringe benefits, and/or reduce or eliminate accumulated retirement experiences and benefits."[96]

In summarizing the Department of Education's research role, Jeanne Allen of the Center for Education Reform wrote, "Large research centers have been funded to provide guidance and ideas to schools, but in reality, they become promoters for pet projects that have little effect on the classroom. Perhaps even more harmful, the use of federal money gives the impression that such programs are federally tested and approved."[97]

A Growing Backlash

Many are disenchanted with the Department of Education. Louis Grumet, executive director of the New York State School Boards Association, wrote about his and his association's view of the Department of Education:

> The New York State School Boards Association believes it is time to reinvent the federal role in public education. The U.S. Department of Education should be eliminated and its responsibilities transferred to the appropriate human service department.
>
> The Department of Education is far removed from the classroom and has become more of a burden to local school boards than a supportive partner. Using policy letters and program audits, the Department has abused its authority by threatening to withhold federal dollars from states and school boards unless they comply with edicts devoid of regulatory, legislative, or judicial

authority. The Department has become a tool for interest groups to place mandates on school boards outside the legislative process that are unrelated to the needs of children. We urge the dismantling of the U.S. Education Department and the return of educational governance to local school boards.

New York State School Boards Association
Executive Director
Louis Grumet
School Board News, January 17, 1995[98]

Because of these "interest groups," educational leaders waste much time, energy, and public money tending to adult wants rather than student needs. People are realizing that public education is not public in the sense that local public processes determine what happens in local schools.

NEA bosses have been successful in their work to control public education. They may have become too successful.

In the words of an old aphorism, be careful what you wish for, because you might get it. So it is with NEA. Through its 140-year history of clarity of purpose and achievement of task, NEA has steadily gained its ends. This is not to say NEA has no unrealized goals. Nothing could be further from reality. But NEA has fashioned a large, powerful, and well-organized national labor union and gained considerable leverage in federal law and regulation. The problem with NEA's near-perfect picture is that the public education system does not work. At least not with the consistency and degree of success that the public rightly demands. Many school principals watch with grim fascination while NEA spokespeople publicly mouth platitudes about meaningful systemic change. Later, these same principals will experience NEA's militants' unrelenting drive to protect the status quo with nonsolutions to real problems.

NEA has created a union-dominated educational system which it will protect through wave after wave of educational reform efforts. Public education, from NEA's perspective, exists primarily as a platform from which NEA can accomplish its union goals and advance its vision for social change. NEA bosses have a larger purpose than teaching America's children to read, write, calculate, and think. As NEA president Sam Lambert declared in 1967, NEA's goal is to "become a political power second to no other special interest group."[99] That goal is fast becoming a reality.

The stakes are high in the battle for control of public education, In financial terms, costs per student per year in some communities easily run to $9,000. According to the National Center for Educational Statistics, the estimated expenditure for all elementary and secondary schools in 1995 was $318,400,000,000—some 4.4 percent of the gross domestic product.[100]

Writing about the scope and intensity of the battle for control of public education, Chester Finn, Jr., cautioned, "It's an intellectual, conceptual, and ideological war. It's a war of ideas, and it's not a tea party. It's 50 million kids and $300 billion a year and 50 legislatures and governors, many of whom regard education as one of the most important things in their state."

NEA's partnership with government and the people whom government empowers has been phenomenally successful. As Chapter 8 will show, NEA is a master at the big game and the long-term plan.

8

....

Federal Follies: NEA's Dance of Politics and Power

"What I am talking about is the control of licensing, the control of admission to the profession, the control of standards of practice."[1]

—*Sam Lambert, NEA Executive Secretary, Address to Representative Assembly, 1971*

THE NATION IS EXPERIENCING a severe bout of education standards creep. Where once states and local school boards set education standards for local schools, now the debate begins with the assumption that education standards will be national in scope and elitist in origin. The only questions are what these standards should standardize and who will write and enforce them. Ignoring questions regarding the federal government's proper role in public education, discussions leap over constitutional issues to debate the mechanics of how this agency or that panel will develop, implement, and enforce national education standards.

National-level politicians are scrambling for media coverage to advocate their pet border-to-border education bromide. Listen closely and you will hear the underlying assumption—and demand—that the true solution to any education dilemma depends on citizens giving over control of local education to them and other omniscient career experts. Some professors in some departments of some universities are seeking and accepting federal research dollars to bring about federally controlled public education. And some national leaders generally thought to be conservative are supporting national education standards. These are strange bedfellows who have joined to bring about federal control of education.

THE NATIONAL EDUCATION STANDARDS GAME

Certainly we need education standards. Standards give us direction and focus. Standards give us goals toward which we strive. Standards help guide our discussions, inform our planning, and organize our resources. So what could be wrong with having national education standards?

The negative effects of national education standards are several. First and foremost is a loss of state control of education. Writers of the Constitution believed the states should be laboratories of democracy, individually testing solutions to both common and unique social, economic, and political problems. James Madison wrote in Federalist Paper Number 45, "The powers delegated by the proposed Constitution to the Federal Government, are few and defined. Those which are to remain in the State Governments are numerous and indefinite."[2] Since the Constitution does not specifically delegate the powers of education to the federal government, those powers "remain in the state governments." The framers of the Constitution knew the harmful effects of too strong a central government and of government controls that allow only one solution to issues of public policy.

The framers of the Constitution designed a government structure that encouraged multiple solutions to problems and inspired broad citizen involvement in the affairs of local, state, and federal governments. The current move to centralized education standards is without constitutional authority and directly obstructs states' rights to fashion educational systems by working independently, borrowing from each other, and collaborating through state-level consortiums to devise solutions to public education's problems.

How can a local school's education program reflect the unique wishes of local parents and taxpayers and allow for locally tailored solutions to questions of curriculum and school organization if the federal government writes curricula that, by federal decree, comprises the education program? Under such federal decree, local taxation pays for federally mandated programs that may require more funding than local parents and taxpayers wish to pay. Federally mandated standards will allocate resources differently than parents and taxpayers wish. If the federal government sets the education program, it also sets the education budget for local communities.

Federal funding to local school districts will moreover require that local districts make formal declarations of commitment to national standards. From then on, national student performance testing will determine if local communities have taught the "national standards." By attaching funding to the success or failure of student achievement of these standards, the federal government will control local schools, leaving local school board control in name only. Once the national standards, the national performance tests, the funding policies, and other mechanisms of enforcement are in place, the U.S. Department of Education will be the "super school board" of a federal system of education.

The University of California at Los Angeles recently wrote National Standards for U.S. History. The National Endowment of the Humanities funded the writing with $2 million of taxpayer money. Nationally syndicated columnist and education commentator Phyllis Schlafly took exception to this process. As she put it, "The idea of the federal government writing or financing public school curricula is an elitist, totalitarian notion that should be unacceptable in America."[3]

W. Edwards Deming, the quality control expert and father of total quality management (TQM), once warned, "If you control an industry's standards, you control that industry lock, stock, and ledger." He continued, "On the day that standards become a governmental function and responsibility, as is now being threatened, the government will take a very long step toward the control of American industry."[4] Deming was writing about the American manufacturing enterprise. His comments are no less appropriate for public education.

Another argument against national education standards is that they will aid and abet NEA's efforts to centralize and control public education. Few public policy changes could be more strategically advantageous for Washington, D.C.-based NEA than the consolidation of fifty separate state education governance systems (state governors, state legislatures, state departments of education, state school boards, and local school boards) into one conveniently located and centrally controlled national system of public school governance. From its vantage point in Washington, D.C., and through its symbiotic relationship with national power brokers, NEA lobbyists would then be able to focus their efforts on the few who would control a national system of public education across the fifty states and fifteen thousand school districts.

NEA does not want control of public education in the sense that it would replace federal departments and state and local boards of education. That would make NEA too visible and burden its bosses too much with accountability. NEA wants to control public education from a safe distance through manipulation of individuals and the boards and panels that set and control national education standards. This is NEA's strength, its strategy, and its protection.

The current feverish push for national standards goes beyond federalization of student learning goals. In 1986 the Carnegie Forum on Education and the Economy called for the formation of a National Board for Professional Teaching Standards to "establish standards of high levels of competence in the teaching profession, to assess the qualifications of those seeking board certification, and to grant certificates to those who meet standards."[5] Recently President Clinton's Goals 2000, Educate America Act formed a number of new boards:

- National Education Goals Panel,
- National Education Standards and Improvement Council,

- 50 State Improvement Plan Panels, and
- National Skill Standards Board.

Other national education-related groups include:

- the National Educational Research Policy and Priorities Board,
- the Office of Educational Technology, and
- the Office of Reform Assistance and Dissemination.

This multifront march to national standards and federal control is confusing because of the numerous offices, panels, boards, and councils involved. Perhaps the profusion of standards boards results from the perception of NEA's partner—the Department of Education—that the time is right for centralization. Whatever the motivation, the current advocacy for federal control is the most recent in a one-hundred-year history of similar efforts.

In general, efforts to create and impose national standards fall under two headings: (1) national student learning standards, and (2) national teaching skills standards.

NATIONAL STUDENT LEARNING STANDARDS BOARDS

Proposed as a way to bring public education into the twenty-first century, national education standards describe what students should know in the core subjects of math, science, English, and social studies.

The proposed national learning standards contain a second component: national performance testing. Delaware's Democrat governor, Thomas R. Carper, said national standards "are like a sandwich. The top piece of bread is the standard, the bottom piece of bread is the performance tests, but whatever is in the middle is up to the schools to decide."[6] Really? The federal government tells local schools what to teach through imposition of national learning standards and then measures the effectiveness of that teaching with national performance tests, but allows the local school to decide... WHAT? How to teach to the federally mandated standards as measured by federally mandated tests?

The governor's carefully worded simile judiciously avoids the phrase "national curriculum." But there can be no doubt that federally imposed national standards and national performance tests will create a national curriculum. Once "national education standards" are the law of the land for public schools, can their mandated imposition in private schools and home schooling programs be far behind?

Education standards and student performance testing make a great deal of sense—at local and state levels, but not at the federal level.

The call for a national curriculum is not new. The 1893 Committee of Ten proposed a classics curriculum in Latin, Greek, English, other modern languages, mathematics, physics, astronomy, chemistry, natural history, history, civil government, political economy, and geography,[7] that were intended to "train the mind" and "enhance the powers of observation [and] reasoning."[8] In 1918 the Cardinal Principles of Secondary Education largely replaced the earlier curriculum with one that emphasized "health, command of fundamental processes, worthy home membership, vocation, citizenship, worthy use of leisure, and ethical character."[9] In the 1930s the progressives proffered a national curriculum, as did the advocates of education reform in the 1960s. While each reform differed from its predecessor in what its prepackaged solutions sought to achieve, these earlier national curricula were the same in that public policymakers and educational experts assured parents and taxpayers that "one size fits all." Moreover, the experts proclaimed they knew the "one right way" to educational salvation. For the past 150 years, the American education elite have labored to eradicate local control of education and transfer it into the hands of professional educators. As AFT's Bella Rosenberg recently put it, "Yes, there will be parental involvement, but we shouldn't think that the patient can know more than the doctor."[10]

Currently, concern over the condition of public education causes many people to look for ways to help it become what it should and must be in a free society competing in an increasingly unforgiving world marketplace of ideas and economics. The May 1991 Gallop Poll showed that 68 percent of respondents favored "requiring the public schools in this country to use a standardized national curriculum."[11] Perhaps this support is an extension of the paradoxical phenomenon in which many parents voice deep concern about public schools as a whole but say they are content with the schools their own children attend. Perhaps 68 percent of respondents think a standardized national curriculum will not affect them, their children's education, or the local school with which they are satisfied. We would do well to remember Thomas Jefferson's warning: "The natural progress of things is for government to gain ground and for liberty to yield."

History is replete with accounts of citizens who voluntarily traded their freedoms for protection in times of threat only to lose those freedoms forever to governments whose natural tendency was "to gain ground." It is deceptively easy to turn to a distant federal government and ask that it solve our local problems. Proponents say national education standards will be voluntary. "But," as Phyllis Schlafly warned, "the receipt of federal money in the Elementary and Secondary Education Act is tied to the acceptance of 'voluntary' standards.' So much for voluntary!"[12] State departments around the nation are already writing the national standards into state law.[13] So much for state control of education.

Voluntary standards—like government recommendations—are not a strategy unknown to government as a way incrementally to impose its will over a citizenry. In *Managers of Virtue*, Tyack and Hansot described a mid-1800s' "issue of great significance for the future governance of public education" when they observed that the "power of recommendation" can "one day be turned into a power of regulation."[14] So it is today with the move to create the myriad education standards boards. Once these boards become accepted, they will forever be funded. Once they are funded, they will grow and continue to use taxpayer money to take local control away from parents and communities.

Democracy is not tidy; it is not even particularly efficient. But it can be effective, if informed citizens participate. Unless local citizens jealously keep control of their local schools, control will go to those who thirst for control.

Glen Cutlip, an NEA senior policy analyst, confided, "For the same reason we want national academic standards, we want *national resources standards*"[15] (emphasis added). First NEA wants national education standards to control curriculum, and then NEA wants national resources standards to control taxing and spending authority—both centrally controlled. The move for centralized standards will not end until NEA chieftains have complete control of what your children learn and what tax money you pay.

In a well-practiced, bargaining-table negotiations ploy, when the other side offers X, NEA negotiators demand X+10 percent or X+100 percent. In the application of this ploy, NEA's dual intent becomes more and more apparent: first, increase federal funding to public education to create growing dependency on federal funds; and second, tie federal funding to local delivery of programs over which NEA officials have significant influence.

Nations in the former USSR Eastern bloc learned that centralized government control does not work, and modern corporations are decentralizing to take better advantage of people's ability to make decisions and act according to local conditions. Why then are American public policymakers clamoring for a national curriculum brought through national education standards?

Except for one component in the move to a national curriculum, NEA wholeheartedly supports this current, multifront standards effort. NEA activists are a powerful force on various boards, panels, and commissions that set national public policy and the direction of public education. NEA, however, vigorously opposes national performance tests. In fact, NEA opposes even standardized testing mandated by local school boards. NEA's Resolution B-52 Standardized Testing of Students states, "The National Education Association opposes standardized testing that is mandated by local, state, or national authority. The Association also opposes the use of these tests to compare one student, staff member, school, or district with another, especially when the threat of loss of prestige, control, or resources is attached."[16]

Why is NEA for national academic standards but against national performance testing?

The answer is tied both to NEA's opposition to teacher evaluations based on student learning and to systems of merit pay where teacher compensation is based, in part, on student learning.

Evaluation of students using standardized performance testing moves public education one step closer to evaluating teachers based on what students learn. Since NEA has been phenomenally successful in perpetuating a lock-step pay system that mechanically pays teachers for years of teaching and credits earned, it is extremely unlikely NEA will embrace any reward system based on student learning. The current system, long in use, is simple to negotiate and easy to present to NEA members, many of whom have grown dependent on predictable salary increases regardless of the levels of student learning. The notion of individual recognition for meritorious teaching, or the idea of allowing teachers to step away from the pack, try something new, and earn rewards for their successes goes against NEA's strategies for controlling teachers.

Many teachers—perhaps most—support and use tests to measure learning. While good teachers hold students responsible for learning and frequently test students as a check on their own teaching effectiveness, NEA bosses do not want teachers to be held responsible for student learning or have their compensation based on it.

On the one hand, the union wants teachers to be responsible for choosing and evaluating principals and superintendents (Resolution D-19 Administrator Evaluations); but, on the other hand, NEA does not want students involved in choosing or evaluating teachers (Resolution D-18 Competency Testing and Evaluation).[17] A table comparing practices commonly available to teachers but not afforded students illustrates this:

What is Common Practice? Who Participates?

Practice	Teacher	Student
Choose Boss/Choose Teacher	Yes	No
Performance Tested	No	Yes
Input on Evaluation	Yes	No
Fired/Failed for Poor Performance	No	Yes
Input on School/Class Operations	Yes	No

Figure 8.1

Although it steadfastly resists use of mandated testing to measure student learning (measures of output), NEA policymakers energetically support mandating national standards (measures of input) for local schools. National student learning standards advance NEA's unrelenting move to standardize curriculum and centralize and control public education.

NATIONAL TEACHING SKILLS STANDARDS BOARDS

NEA harbors no similar split position in its advocacy for national teacher skills standards boards. At present two boards intend to set national standards for teacher training, teacher certification, and/or teacher hiring. NEA's representatives are actively involved in both.

The National Board for Professional Teaching Standards is the older of the boards and began in 1987 through a Carnegie Foundation task force. As described in the *Washington Times*, this "64-member Board, dominated by teachers" was charged with "establishing standards and assessments for the profession that would attest to a high level of teaching competence."[18] After eight years and $50 million, no one seemed certain that the board or its work "will make a difference in what cynics call a basically corrupt culture."[19] No one seemed certain except NEA. In a newsletter to the NEA membership, former president Geiger assured, "With your Association on the National Board, your voice *will* count."[20]

NEA bosses have demanded representation on reform boards under the cloak of advancing "the forefront of educational change"[21] and then stalled, blocked, and otherwise obfuscated issues until all but the most hearty yield. "The standards board is a case of putting the fox in charge of the henhouse," said Rita Kramer, author of *Ed School Follies: The Miseducation of America's Teachers*.[22] And Senator Jesse Helms said, "The control of... unions over the board will enable them to use taxpayers' money not so much to professionalize teachers as to finalize who does and does not teach in America."[23]

Carol Innerst, author of the *Washington Times* article "Little Merit Seen in Process of Setting Teaching Standards," observed, "From the beginning, the NEA was concerned that national certification would open the door to a pay scale based on teaching ability—the merit pay system that the NEA has always opposed."[24] With federal funding for the Teaching Standards Board giving NEA an additional $25 million in tax money to play with[25] and strong union representation on the board, NEA will continue to guard the public education henhouse.

Considering the issues at stake, it is not surprising that NEA representatives dominate the sixty-four–member board.[26] An issue the board will inevitably take up is merit pay. Merit pay is one of the "great evils" NEA policymakers have sworn to stop— witness the multiyear battle in Fairfax, Virginia, where NEA militants relentlessly worked to hobble the most promising of these programs.

NEA seldom shies from a challenge, or an opportunity. To combat what Chester Finn, Jr., observed is "the thing most taxpayers think is the most important indicator of teacher effectiveness: student achievement,"[27] NEA bosses make certain they and plenty of their followers sit on boards in order to block attempts to bring about merit pay.

Teachers, for example, who want national certification under the National Board for Professional Teaching Standards must pay $975 to participate in the certification process. Ever vigilant for opportunities to make the public pay to support NEA's agenda, former President Geiger wrote in his May 1994 newsletter article, "We might, for instance, want to consider bargaining subsidies for the certification fee, alternative scheduling to accommodate participation in certification, reimbursement for travel costs to assessment sites, role differentiation for Board certified teachers, and mentoring programs for certification candidates."[28]

This is what national teacher certification really means to NEA: it controls boards that control who becomes certified to teach and then uses certification as a bargaining chip to force the public to pay costs for national certification—all, of course, independent of student achievement.

Under President Clinton's Goals 2000, Educate America Act, signed into law in 1994, eight of the twenty-eight members sitting on the National Skill Standards Board must be "representative of organized labor selected from among individuals recommended by recognized labor federations."[29]

According to Milton Chappell, staff attorney for the National Right to Work Legal Defense Foundation:

> The purpose of the National Skills Standards Board
> includes the 'adoption of a voluntary system of skill
> standards and of assessment and certification... that can
> be used... by labor organizations, to enhance the
> employment security of workers by providing portable
> credentials and skills.' Id. at (502 [pp. 94–95].
> Accordingly, the Board must establish partnerships for
> each skill standards system it seeks to develop. These
> partnerships must include 'employee representatives
> who... shall be individuals [nonmanagerial employees]
> recommended by recognized national labor
> organizations representing employees in the occupation
> or industry for which a standard is being developed...
> and representatives of educational institutions...
> community-based organizations,... or nongovernmental
> [civil and minority rights advocacy] organizations.' Id.
> (504(c) [pp.107–09].[30]

With national teacher certification comes centralized control over who can teach. With centralized control of national teacher certification, student learning standards, and standardized student performance testing, comes loss of state control over who teaches and loss of state and local control over what is taught. Since teachers are one of the most important factors in the education enterprise, state-to-state differences in teacher certification support the states' acting as laboratories of democracy—free to find better ways to teach and to organize schools.

NEA top dogs do not want states and "We the People" to have this freedom, and they fight to maintain and expand their control over who teaches and who does not. Further, progress toward centralizing teacher certification moves important decisions into the national-level arena, and that is NEA's home court. States and local school districts have to play NEA's game—far, far away from hometowns and local control. As John Chubb and Terry Moe observed in *Politics, Markets, and America's Schools*, "This [teacher certification] board would be strongly influenced and perhaps dominated by the National Education Association and the American Federation of Teachers, adding to their already stifling hold on education personnel."[31]

While NEA actively supports national control of teacher certification, as a back-up, it also supports teacher-controlled state licensing boards. Chubb and Moe pointed out that "[t]he creation of teacher-controlled licensing boards within each of the states... would set legally binding standards and requirements for admission to the profession. In effect, government would delegate public authority to teachers, who would then use that authority to regulate themselves and control entry [into the teaching profession]."[32] Chubb and Moe further commented, "The proposal for state licensing boards is a bad idea,... [T]hese self-regulating boards—whether for doctors and lawyers or for cosmetologists, plumbers, and dog groomers—tend to use public authority in their own self-interest to restrict entry and enhance their incomes. And worse still, it would not really be 'teachers' who would control the boards, but most surely organized teachers—and far-and-away the largest, most geographically dispersed organization of teachers is the National Education Association."[33]

OF CENSURES, SANCTIONS, AND BOYCOTTS

Where NEA bosses cannot successfully play their power-politics game, they use economic censures, sanctions, and boycotts to gain their ends. Through these devices, the long arm of NEA extends into the business practices of private corporations, the politics of media personalities, and the actions of at least one local PTA.

The first step in activating a censure, sanction, or boycott happens at NEA's annual Representative Assembly meeting. Here the NEA faithful and their officials identify those persons and corporations most offensive to NEA. As a part of America's organized labor union community and with its own membership of 2.264 million, the teacher union can reach well beyond the schoolhouse to apply economic pressure to its "enemies."

In its *Handbook 1993–1994*, NEA stated, "NEA condemns the Marriott Corporation for its continued antilabor posture, in particular with regard to the Hotel and Restaurant Employees Union in

San Francisco and throughout the United States and in general with our local and state affiliates as Marriott *seeks to subcontract union-ized public school positions.* NEA will not patronize any Marriott locations in this country and will consider a boycott of the Marriott Corporation"[34] (emphasis added).

Why has Marriott incurred such wrath? NEA is aggressively expanding its union empire to represent all school employees, including school cooks. School cooks, who are often part-time and usually nine-month employees, are, in many locations, considerably more costly than their counterparts in the private sector. Serving good food at competitive prices, private-sector subcontractors can also save money for school districts by requiring fewer district-level food-service managers. Apparently not having read the golden goose fable, NEA representatives have charged into the negotiating arena to price food-service members out of their jobs. Where its negotiation common sense has failed, NEA uses its economic might—thus the boycott of Marriott Corporation, a chief player in school cafeteria contract services. Clearly, NEA union bosses are out of their element when they use old-world strategies to negotiate wages and benefits in an environment not protected by the monopoly status they enjoy when negotiating for teachers.

Marriott was only the first on NEA's 1993–1994 hit list. NEA put Fisher Scientific in its crosshairs to "investigate the employment practices" and "the company's treatment of its employees."[35] Philip Morris and Kraft General Foods made NEA's list too.[36]

NEA also decided "to immediately write a letter of protest to the president of the National Parent-Teachers Association (PTA) and board stating our displeasure with the violation by the North Little Rock PTA Council of the PTA national policy of neutrality during a job action; further, [NEA demanded] that the National PTA censure and/or reprimand the North Little Rock PTA Council to strictly observe the national PTA policy of neutrality should another job action occur in the future."[37]

"Job action" is NEA's code for a strike, work slow-down, work-to-rule, grievance campaign, or other strategy used to disrupt the teaching-learning process until it gains its goals. NEA feels strongly that PTAs must maintain neutrality when NEA calls a strike against a school district and withholds teaching from children. It is ironic that PTA groups cannot choose to "boycott" an NEA local, but NEA can strike schools and boycott businesses. By NEA's rules, it is the only player in the public education arena who can strike, boycott, or censure.

NEA's *Handbook 1994–1995* listed several new targets for its boycott and sanction campaign. NEA censured Heileman Brewing Company, maker of Crazy Horse Malt Liquor, for "marketing of an alcohol product that is highly offensive to minority groups and defames religious leaders."[38] Coca-Cola and the governor of Michigan committed transgressions against NEA and were sentenced to boycott and condemnation, respectively. The state of Florida, at least its orange juice industry, was threatened with boycott of Florida orange juice "[u]nless the Florida Department of Citrus cancel[ed] its contract with Rush Limbaugh."[39] It did.

In *Handbook 1996–1997*, NEA announced that it "shall publish a list of all identified corporations and their subsidiaries who subcontract or privatize public school employee positions and/or services in the first issue, the last issue, and the mid-year issue of *NEA Today*. NEA shall publish a column of abuses in each issue of *NEA Today* highlighting abuses to education which occur through privatization."[40]

In 1993 NEA could list all the "abusers"—a total of two—in its annual handbook. In 1997 NEA published an entire column in each of its monthly newsletters to list all those who dare to bring competition and economy to public education.

NEW THINGS, NEW THREATS

When someone tries something new, something that threatens NEA in any way, NEA militants can get downright nasty. Whittle Communications is trying something new. In doing so, it raised the ire of NEA officials by bringing privatization and competition to public education.

Channel One (Whittle's in-school, ten-minute, daily news program) and the accompanying electronic hardware Whittle's corporation gave to schools as an inducement were at first eagerly accepted in many schools. According to the *Washington Post*, educators "liked the idea of exposing students to current events and accepted on behalf of their ill-equipped schools the free classroom televisions, videocassette recorders and satellite dishes that came with the program."[41] *Channel One* reached eight million students.[42]

Then Whittle, the entrepreneur, announced his intention to begin the Edison Project, a plan to create a national system of privately run elementary and secondary schools. Still later, he contracted with school districts to administer schools. In 1994 Whittle announced plans for charter schools.[43]

Bringing ten-minute special news programs and free electronic equipment to classrooms was one thing. Bringing competition to NEA's world was something else.

NEA responded by attacking Whittle Communications. *Channel One* was no longer satisfactory. Of *Channel One*, Keith Geiger said, "We're proving that Americans want community-based, not corporate-imposed, education for their children."[44] NEA supported "Unplug," an anti-*Channel One* youth organization. NEA also announced it would use its financial strength in the form of stocks purchased with teacher pension funds to pressure *Channel One* advertisers and investors to dump Whittle.[45] According to Joe Mandese of *Advertising Age*, "NEA is organizing the nation's state and local teacher pension funds to withdraw more than $1.5 billion in investments from companies sponsoring the ad-supported, in-school TV programming venture."[46] To this end, NEA targeted Whittle sponsors: Procter & Gambel Co. ($800 million in P&G stock), McDonald's Corp. ($525 million), PepsiCo ($325 million), Time Warner ($176 million), and Reebok ($38 million).[47]

To push NEA's campaign, delegates at the 1994 Delegate Assembly "encouraged teachers and school employees to flag the firm for possible building and fire code hazards." The "firm," one can guess, was Whittle's *Channel One* enterprise. In a written resolution, NEA advised its members, "Some companies (i.e., Whittle) are installing wiring in the cheapest and fastest ways. Inadequate installations create safety and fire hazards."[48] This warning, of course, was a call for NEA members to harass Whittle and his *Channel One* program.

Also a target of the education cartel is John Shannon of *Hooked on Phonics* and *Hooked on Math* fame. Shannon seems to have been the target of the combined might of the government and the education establishment. As Shannon's two products became more successful in the marketplace, they also became more of a threat to the monopoly interests of educational status quoists.

For some reason the Federal Trade Commission (FTC) "charged *Hooked on Phonics* with deceptive and misleading advertising." According to Duncan Anderson and Michael Warsaw, who wrote for *Success* magazine, "past-FTC chairman James Miller warned the [FTC] against serving the interests of the education lobby. 'I detect rent-seeking behavior here—an effort not only to close off a competitor, but to eliminate a whole service.'"[49] So strongly did Miller believe this that he charged the FTC with using "the power of the State to suppress a competing technology."[50]

In an editorial comment in *Advertising Age*, Rance Crain observed, "Nero fiddles while Rome burns. Our public schools are the disgrace of America, and the NEA issues a call to arms against foes lurking around every corner. On the one side it resists all efforts to make its member teachers more productive. But maybe NEA's diversionary tactics make sense. If you were failing at your main job wouldn't you try to draw attention away from your failures?"[51]

THINKERS AND TINKERERS

What, if anything, can come from continuing to play by NEA's rules? Many of today's educational thinkers are really only systems tinkerers. They are stuck in the time metaphor of the agriculture calendar; in the space metaphor of the factory school; and in the old-world labor-union metaphor of NEA first, children and learning sometime later. They spend their creative energies rearranging an artifact of bygone eras.

Tinkerers do not challenge the basic assumptions, and, therefore, tinkerers will not challenge the basics of the current system of public education. They cling to familiar definitions of learning, education, school, and teacher. They think in terms of mass education, linear development, and standardized curriculum. They believe adolescence is a scientific fact rather than a social convention recently contrived to explain away that time in a young person's life that passed more productively when parents and community joined together to bring young adults into the community as full members. Educational systems tinkerers stand only on familiar ground and think only in small steps. Politics prevails over pedagogy.

NEA has established a reality others tiptoe around, as if NEA union bosses have a right to be the gatekeepers. School by school, town by town, and state by state, education could be a wellspring of strength, helping to keep us both competitive and compassionate. But now public education threatens to become a millstone that state by state, town by town, and school by school drags us down.

Writer Shirley McCune observed, "History suggests that it is difficult for any civilization that excelled in one age to maintain its achievements under a new set of conditions."[52] So long as NEA continues to force educational leaders and thinkers to spend their time and other people's money attending to teacher-union wants in preference to children's needs and community needs, our schools will not adjust to the new set of conditions that defines America today.

TIME FOR A SECOND REVOLUTION

If an organization has no soul, it can have no heart. America's teachers, the heart of public education, are lost. They are lost because they are forced to follow NEA, and NEA has no soul. NEA is a morally bankrupt, ultra-leftwing, political organization that does not represent the values of a good many of its members. When compulsory unionism forces teachers to support NEA's false lead, their mandatory dues payments go to further political and social agendas that ignore commitment to children—whether teachers like it or not. As a result of the union's political-predator mentality, we risk seeing parents and the public lose respect for teachers. And teachers must be the heart and soul of education.

From its inception in 1857 until 1910, an elite group of men led NEA. In 1920 a group of classroom teachers, the majority women, mounted a campaign within NEA to gain control of its agenda and internal workings. Out of this revolution came NEA's representative assembly, today a congress of nine thousand union activists who annually vote NEA's resolutions and legislative goals. Organizations being what they are, and given NEA's growth, it is not surprising that today's NEA high command resembles NEA's pre-1920 leadership— top-down rule coming from union bosses who are remote from the concerns and values of classroom teachers.

It is a common tenet of organizational theory that organizations resist change and often will not change of their own volition. It is time for classroom teachers once again to bring change to NEA. But this time, the revolution must focus less on the internal workings of the union and more on the organization's soul and purpose.

Section Five

Old Beginnings:
A Return to Local Control

....

Chapter Nine:
Foundations for Change

Chapter Ten:
Coloring Outside the Lines

Chapter Eleven:
Final Test: How to Regain Control

9

....

Foundations for Change

"We believe existing institutions cannot solve the problems, because they are the problem."[1]

—*John E. Chubb and Terry Moe*, Politics, Markets, and America's Schools

WE HAVE LOOKED AT NEA'S GOALS; its move to power; the national, state, and local systems it has created to control public education; and the tactics it uses to achieve its ends. As earlier stated, the intent of this book is to inform and, through informing, better enable parents, teachers, and taxpayers to confront NEA and regain control of schools. Previous chapters developed a knowledge of NEA's history and an understanding of how NEA came to be what it is today. The aim of this chapter is to build a deeper knowledge of larger issues that must be understood if NEA is to be successfully confronted and turned back. It also addresses the arguments that NEA bosses typically use to advance their causes. To those who would "poke a bear with a stick," Chapter 9 tells more about the bear and something about the stick.

THE SEARCH FOR NEW RULES AND NEW LEADERS

In his landmark book *The Structure of Scientific Revolution*, the eminent science historian Thomas Kuhn wrote, "Failure of existing rules is the prelude to a search for new ones."[2] The obvious failure of existing rules in schools today leads many parents and policymakers to search for new rules by which to reconstruct the house of public education.

While public education is not science in the same sense that Kuhn wrote of science, his analysis of change processes and his conclusions regarding the impetus for change are applicable to understanding the need to change public education and how that change might happen.

Kuhn writes of "normal science" as the usual state of affairs in which scientists "puzzle solve" within the well-established confines of a finite box. These scientists work to solve only those problems and, consequently, find only those solutions that exist within a limited and familiar universe. Puzzle solvers work hard at what they do, but they are locked into a bounded world and cannot, therefore, gain the insight needed to break out of the known box and find new ways to view the world or to ask new questions that will create new solutions. (These ways of viewing the world are what Kuhn calls paradigms.)

Within the context of public education, Kuhn's thinking suggests a comparison between NEA's bosses and people who are finding new solutions to education's problems. NEA militants—because of their old worldview, self-serving politics, and bunker mentality—will not ask new questions, devise new solutions, break out of the known box, and create new paradigms in education. Those who follow and support NEA are busy shoring up an old, outmoded system; they would have parents and taxpayers believe that puzzle-solving within the confines of the finite box is the only way to educate children. Meanwhile, many good educators, parents, and policymakers who are trying to free themselves from NEA's confining control, break out to find new ways to view the world, and create new solutions.

Chris Whittle, educational entrepreneur, commented:

> It is quite clear to me that the people of education, and
> particularly those who go to work every day in
> classrooms and in schools, are not the cause of our
> educational problems. The system, the whole construct
> of education, is our problem. The construct is based on

a set of assumptions, accumulated over literally
hundreds of years, that are in general no longer valid.
We need to disassemble the structure we currently have,
and then—combining old parts, many of which work
quite well, and new parts—we need to put it back
together in some fundamentally different way that
functions more effectively.[3]

In contrast to Whittle's quest for new ways, NEA's one-size-fits-all vision for public education quickly leads to the "one-best-way" approach espoused by Frederick W. Taylor at the turn of the century. Taylor's "scientific management" approach to resolving manufacturing problems grew from his belief that one best way existed to accomplish any task, and everyone should strictly follow this one best way everywhere they performed that task.[4]

Preposterous? Yes. People now regard many of Taylor's ideas as tyrannical. We have come a long way since Taylor's beliefs were popular.

Or have we? In 1989 then-NEA President Keith Geiger proclaimed, "I wish we could say that we could take a look at a national collective bargaining bill. I don't hold out much hope for that, but we can at least take a look at some states."[5] According to Geiger, federal law should mandate NEA's one-size-fits-all labor contract model and NEA's approach to working relationships in all the nation's fifteen thousand school districts.

A national, mandated collective bargaining bill would be the same as compelling all teachers in every state to pay dues to NEA as a condition of employment. NEA's heavy-handed control of people, however, may have unintended consequences. Kuhn observed that if, in the development of a new way of thinking, an individual or group is "able to attract most of the next generation's practitioners, the older schools [of thinking] gradually disappear."[6]

To some degree this may be happening to NEA and may negatively affect its ability to attract new teachers. NEA bosses and the Representative Assembly that votes NEA's agenda each year seem not to be in touch with many of NEA's rank-and-file classroom teachers. Although data in *NEA Handbook 1994–1995*[7] indicated an increase in membership, a *Wall Street Journal* article stated, "There are subtle signs the NEA's fortunes may change. A different clientele is coming into teaching—older, highly educated, experienced adults.... A 1986 National Center for Educational Information survey showed that while 75% of teachers with 25 or more years' experience and 70% with 15 or more years' experience belonged to the NEA, only 55% of those who had entered in the past five years were members of the union."[8] This article also suggested the growth claimed by NEA "is the result of administrators, college faculty, and other school personnel joining the union."[9]

Believing that shared values are essential to the functions that serve science, Kuhn observed, "The points at which values must be applied are invariably also those at which risk must be taken."[10] Kuhn believed that "[i]n matters like these the resort to shared values rather than to shared rules governing individual choice may be the community's way of distributing risk and assuring the long-term success of its enterprise."[11] Kuhn's observations about the science community apply equally well to the larger community.

In education, we are clearly at the point where we must take risks and "resort to shared values rather than to shared rules." The existing rules serve NEA union officials and allies well, but no one else. Nor do they serve education well. Parents, teachers, taxpayers, and policymakers must now act on shared values to distribute risk while creating long-term success in the form of parent/taxpayer-controlled, child-centered education. Without new solutions guided by shared values, we will continue to puzzle solve only within the familiar but limited box of public education as we know it today.

As John Chubb and Terry Moe insisted, "Existing institutions cannot solve the problems, because they are the problem." How did the existing institution of public education come to be the problem it is today?

CHANGE BY IMPOSITION—BACK TO THE FUTURE

In the middle and late 1800s, NEA officials began to believe that the local school boards governing public education were too resistant to the changes the officials wanted. Education was, according to them, too decentralized and too politically open. To combat this lay control, NEA policymakers (professional school reformers who, for the most part, were members of NEA's Department of Superintendents) moved to centralize control of education so, as "God's chosen agents,"[12] they could impose their brand of education on local schools.

While the nature of education programs changed from the 1890s through the Progressive Era, the belief of NEA's officials—that they were an "aristocracy of character"[13] whose responsibility it was to make fundamental changes in education—stayed the same. In *Managers of Virtue*, Tyack and Hansot explained that during this time these educators, believing that "reform by persuasion should perhaps give way to coercion by the state,"[14] began in earnest "to use the strong hand of the state to enforce their values"[15]—a powerful and effective strategy NEA bosses and their allies still use today.

The educational trust, as these NEA movers and shakers became known, decided to do away with or severely diminish the independent lay control that marked the governance of local schools at that time. To achieve this goal, NEA both centralized and professionalized education. No longer could members of the lay public become school superintendents. No longer did the lay public have a mechanism through which to determine the philosophies and policies under which public education would function. Determining the content and methods of education was now reserved for trained, certified, professional educators.

Encountering remarkably little resistance, the educational trust diligently watched over an increasingly centralized and standardized system of curricula, teaching methodologies, operational procedures, and governance. It took time, but the march was unrelenting. In 1937 America had over 119,000 school districts[16] serving a student population of approximately twenty-five million.[17] In 1997 approximately 15,000 school districts served a student population of about fifty-two million. NEA's membership grew from 181,000 in 1937 to over 2.2 million in 1994.[18] Today's system of public education is a product of a hundred-year effort to take local control away from parents, local educators, and the public through centralization and professionalization.

Public education has become a system of schools that are more alike across the fifty states than they are different. The question of whether this systemization of education serves students and their communities well goes to the heart of the debate. Centralization and professionalization have greatly reduced the lay public's ability to set policy for and operate local schools. Centralization and professionalization allow NEA to create and control one system of public education in all 86,000 public schools in America.

In an earlier time, centralization was thought to be the solution to a problem; today centralization is one of public education's major problems.

Many school districts and schools are too big, too remote, too impersonal, too unresponsive. Arguments for economy of scale have prevailed over concern for quality of learning and student safety. If public education continues to follow NEA's push for centralized control, our schools will increasingly become education factories where student learning happens as a byproduct of a financial plan rather than the goal of an education program.

To a large degree, public education is what it is because a faction within NEA effectively forced change by imposition and preemptively took control away from citizens. Their commitment and persistence have lasted since the mid-1800s through successive generations of NEA officials; and as long as forced unionism prevails, the radicals within NEA will have the leverage they need to continue their control of public education.

It is ironic that while NEA's self-declared "educational trust" has unilaterally imposed changes on parents, teachers, and taxpayers, union bosses now demand that today's parents, teachers, and taxpayers who want to change education do so only by working within the existing system, and only with NEA's involvement and approval.

SOLUTIONS BECOME PROBLEMS

Prior to and just after the turn of the century, NEA bosses' dissatisfaction with existing rules led them to impose a new set of rules. As earlier described, their strategy was to impose centralization and professionalization. These new rules increasingly prevented local people from voting on or otherwise deciding issues affecting their schools. NEA's new rules were its solution to what it believed to be a problem. This solution—a misdirected solution gained through undemocratic processes—has stayed essentially unchanged even as world events, social conditions, and economic realities have changed significantly.

It is natural to resolve problems by developing solutions. But while solutions tend to be static, problems tend to be dynamic. Today's problems will change and evolve into something very different. Static solutions—and the norms, structures, and procedures that grow up around them and serve to institutionalize them—tend, after time, to become problems in themselves.

David Boaz, executive vice president of the Cato Institute, is clear about what he thinks of educators' efforts to centralize and professionalize public education. Answering his own question "Why don't the schools work?" Boaz explained, "The story begins in the Progressive Era. The Progressive reformers came up with what they called the One Best System, or the One Best School. Obviously, the application of scientific, rational, professional principles to education would produce the one best school for everybody. It was essentially a socialist system—one system for the whole society, centrally directed and bureaucratically managed, with no place for competition or market incentives."[19]

Writing in *The Irony of Early School Reform* about public educators' penchant during the 1850s to reject constructive criticism, historian Michael Katz observed, "Educators' paranoiac response, their categoric denial of what had really happened, set the tone for the future. Educators were developing their own world. They had associations and training schools to impart their own version of the truth."[20] This much has not changed. In 1993 scholar and educational researcher Myron Lieberman wrote, "As matters stand now, the schools of education train teachers and administrators to function in the existing system. Their focus is on performance within the system, not on critical analysis of that system."[21] Unfortunately, in this case, the past was prologue.

As pointed out in the 1988 Rand study *Teacher Unions and Educational Reform*, state and local teacher unions are not actively involved in educational change and have became "reactors and accommodators, rather than innovators."[22] In this report, Lorraine McDonnell and Anthony Pascal concluded that teachers expect NEA to gain them material benefits. They do not expect, or even want, NEA to work to enhance teaching as a profession. (Both the study and its conclusion seem to have overlooked the fact that teachers are coerced or forced to join NEA as a condition of employment—join/pay dues or be fired. And, given this reality, rank-and-file teachers must respond to a narrow range of options within a coercive environment.)

NEA militants have supported both NEA's policies and the dominant organizational culture that depends on a union-versus-management mind-set to keep teachers loyal. Many of these militants cannot, in all likelihood, be resocialized into a student-oriented, reform-minded culture.

McDonnell and Pascal's research did not, however, suggest that most teachers were not interested in bringing change to education. The research showed only that rank-and-file teachers did not want their union to become involved in such efforts.

This distinction is important for at least two reasons: First, on the strength of this study and based on my twenty years' experience, it is clear that teachers have not said they are not interested in helping to change and improve education. But second, it may be that many teachers do not view their union as the proper vehicle for change. This is good news if it means that teachers believe NEA should only be a labor union and not a controller of education, usurping the rights of boards of education.

What to conclude from McDonnell and Pascal's research findings? On the one hand, many teachers—who are, in the first place, forced to pay union dues—expect their union to be vigilant in its efforts to gain them increased "material benefits." On the other, teachers do not expect a union to "professionalize" teaching. Once again ignoring teachers wishes, NEA-national is intent on controlling the whole of public education.

But is it logical to expect a labor union to help change public education in ways that benefit students but lessen its control over its members?

NEA is a labor union. Claims that NEA is a professional association whose first interest is the welfare of children may play well with union activists and with some media. In truth, the two roles are mutually exclusive on economic grounds, on day-to-day operational grounds, and on ethical grounds.

Teachers who wish to bring productive change to education must take up their part of the challenge to set things right; they must also decide which hat to wear as they take up this challenge—a union-member hat or a teacher hat. The two interests are different and often at odds. The two interests must be separated; if they are not, every educational issue becomes an opportunity for union officials to advance what NEA calls "teacher rights" at the expense of student needs.

INSTITUTIONAL RESISTANCE TO CHANGE

NEA's rabid resistance to school choice is not born of concern for student learning or a desire to ensure the effective use of taxpayer money. NEA resistance has two sources: (1) NEA's concern for its own survival, and (2) NEA's lack of faith in teachers' ability to adjust to and do well in a market-driven system.

For these reasons, NEA militants are busy blocking efforts to introduce competition to public education—when almost every enterprise in every other sector of society draws strength from competition. A quick glance at the surrounding landscapes shows that corporations compete, hospitals compete, radio stations compete, the Blue Birds and Brownie Scouts compete, Republicans and Democrats compete, and even religious organizations compete for market share.

Myron Lieberman, a scholar interested in introducing market forces to education, wrote about problems that would affect education's transition from a monopolistic system to a market system. After examining the transition from both a cost perspective and a human-resistance perspective, Lieberman concluded we have not moved to a market system of K-12 education because its supporters have not been able to overcome objections to the cost of transition.

One problem in changing to an educational market system is that some groups would absorb more of the cost of transition while others would reap more of the benefits. So far, the groups that would suffer during a transition, or believe they would suffer, have been able to block it. "The transition problem," Lieberman wrote, "is how to redistribute the cost and benefits to make the change possible."[23] Lieberman's analysis suggested a systemwide transition to a market system of education in all fifty states. Would "the transition problem" be more easily accomplished if individual states, individual communities, or individual school systems implemented their own brand of market system education? You would think so.

But employees resist when they believe the economic realities of change may eliminate their jobs (as in the case of some district-level administrators, program directors, and teachers of federally mandated programs that local communities may not support) or when employees have to learn new ways and abandon familiar practices. Educational employees, in these cases, do not think first of benefits to students and taxpayers, but of their working conditions and their families' security.

NEA strategists, however, do not seem to realize that parents' desire for educational choice comes from the same source as voters' desire for term limits. Both are affirmations of the belief that our government institutions are supposed to serve us, not the other way around. Both are intended to return control of government institutions to the people. The point is that local teachers, parents, and taxpayers must be able to determine and then act on what they feel is best for students and their communities. Teacher concerns will be recognized, but public education must begin to take its direction from what is best for the learner.

Lieberman's work suggested that "formidable obstacles" to change may more effectively block those who work within the existing system than those who work outside. Changes in the American automotive industry provide an example of the powerful effects of competitive outside forces. Similar to today's NEA-dominated schools, the American automobile industry once held a strong monopoly in the American market. Perhaps because of an "unholy alliance" between automobile manufacturers and the United Auto Workers union, neither of these major players felt a need to deliver a better product at a more reasonable price. They had it made. When labor union bosses demanded more money and concessions, management obliged and passed the cost on to consumers. Under these conditions, what was the incentive to build and market a better product at a more reasonable cost?

In the 1960s and 1970s, aggressive, outside-the-system competitors—Volkswagen and Honda—entered the producer-controlled American automobile market. The competitors focused on customers, and the established order could not control them. At first, automobile manufacturers and unions asked for government subsidies and lobbied for protective tariffs. Like today's NEA, they went to their legislative friends for favors to protect them from outside-the-system threats. Eventually, however, the forces of a competitive market system and the pent-up demands of unsatisfied consumers took effect.

Only after near collapse, critical self-assessment, and reorganization of everything from attitudes and values to technology and training did the American automobile industry respond appropriately to a competitive market system; the results have been beneficial to both consumers and producers.

In the same way the American automobile alliance resisted change, NEA will continue to resist efforts to bring school choice and other variants of a market system to public education. Understandably, some educators will resist the move to new ways of educating. Change can be threatening. But if it is to be successful, change will, of necessity, depend on teachers. Herein lies both a strength and a weakness.

Teachers have tremendous talent and deep knowledge of how to teach. As earlier noted, teachers are one-half of the magical student/teacher equation. Because of their unquestioned central role in education and because of parents' warm regard for teachers, there is a tendency to protect teachers. But until longtime teachers and/or those new to teaching take up the challenge to bring productive change to schools, attempts at change will remain entombed in a pedagogic graveyard.

THE SCOPE OF CHANGE

David Crandall, Jeffrey Eiseman, and Karen Seashore Louis wrote about an apparent paradox in the process of bringing change to education. In their research, they observed that when involving teachers in change

> the larger the scope of personal "demandingness" of change... the greater the chance of success.... [T]he essential finding appears to be in conflict with earlier findings outside the field of education that the more complex the innovation, the less likely it will be adopted. But these earlier studies are of *adoption*—that is, of *the user's decision* to use—as opposed to the implementation of the change *after* an adoption decision has been made. Apparent complexity may initially deter a potential adoptee who has to master the innovation alone (emphasis added).
>
> A more meaningful way of framing these findings is that the greater the teacher effort and energy expended in implementing a new practice, the greater the potential outcome.[24]

This again suggests a situation similar to that of the American automobile monopoly before market forces threatened its survival. Only when competition forced members of the industry's unholy alliance to face their own economic mortality did they step out of the old, familiar, and limited box to invent new ways to do business and develop better ways to give the American consumer an improved product at a competitive price.

The lesson may be this: As unaccustomed as educators are to having their continued employment depend on their performance, the introduction of a produce-or-perish element would give them an incentive to do a good job not only in each educator's own estimation but also in the judgment of the education consumer. The employment-security-tied-to-market-performance idea is, in large part, what school choice is about.

Under forced unionism and with NEA telling them what they must do, teachers have little incentive—or opportunity—to bring substantive change to education. Since NEA typically resists student-centered change, systemic change will most likely not come from inside the system. Ellwood P. Cubberly, one of the powers within the education establishment in 1909, noted this tendency. He wrote, "Advances in organization and in the enrichment of curriculum have nearly all been forced upon the school by practical men from without."[25]

So it is today. Government institutions have a life of their own, and they do not often change of their own volition, even when the need is obvious.

NEA militants have created a niche in which they are comfortable; they will certainly resist change. Consumers of educational services, on the other hand, may be impatient and want measurably better results, without loss of service, almost immediately after effecting a change. This gives union activists who do not want change a grand opportunity to sabotage almost any effort to change. And because this sabotage is not visible to those outside the system, it is all but impossible to stop. Often it takes the form of simply ignoring the mandated change. Since education is presently almost entirely process-oriented (rather than product-oriented), who is to know if legitimate and reasonable efforts were made to incorporate a change into the daily workings of schools and classrooms?

To a large extent, the sabotage of change is possible because school districts and schools are loosely coupled organizations whose members perform in subunits operating semi-independently within the larger organization—under the right circumstances, this can be good. But in public-sector, monopoly-protected institutions, it is possible for individual subunits not to align themselves with or commit to the larger organization's goals or reasons for existing—this is often bad.

Because public education is a monopoly, the forces that drive education are those of bureaucracy, not those of market-driven organizations. In the case of public education, the bureaucracy is all but immune to outside pressures and, therefore, takes its cues from forces within. Since each member of the Unholy Alliance knows the limits of its ability to bring change to its own and the other members' behavior, the range of possible change that can come from within is narrow in scope, limited in duration, and muted in effect.

Competition must break the education monopoly in the same way it broke the pre-1960 American automobile cartel. Market forces must require the education cartel to deliver quality services at reasonable costs.

THE CASE AGAINST MONOPOLY

According to Bert Schundler, mayor of Jersey City, New Jersey, "Getting the union to change its work rules, is sort of like having the American Revolution and then settling for lifting all the oppressive taxes, but allowing King George to remain in power. You've spent all your energy, but the corrupt system is still in place and the union can win it all back from the next politician who comes along."[26]

As if to make his point, Mayor Schundler tried to implement tax-funded scholarships to help poor students in some of the city's worst public schools. After the state blocked this effort, he went to a local PepsiCo™ distributor who offered to pay for some of the scholarships. But when the New Jersey NEA threatened to boycott Pepsi products, the distributor backed down.[27]

Monopolies may bend with the political winds, but they are always monopolies. And as long as they exist, they can unilaterally decide what services they will deliver, who will deliver them, and how much the services will cost.

Even Albert Shanker, former president of the American Federation of Teachers (the nation's second-largest teachers' union and benefactor of forced unionism's coercive control of teachers), agreed. Shanker conceded, "It's time to admit that public education operates like a planned economy, a bureaucratic system in which everybody's role is spelled out in advance and there are very few incentives for innovation and productivity. It's no surprise that our school system doesn't improve: It more resembles the communist economy than our own market economy."[28]

Unlike market systems, monopolies do not have incentives to respond to the changing needs of consumers—nor to operate more efficiently. In fact, for monopolies the incentives are just the opposite.

Expanding on Thomas Jefferson's statement, Edward H. Crane, president of the Cato Institute, said in a 1986 speech to the San Francisco Press Club, "The natural progress of things *is* for government to grow. Why? Because bureaucrats are like the rest of us. They respond to incentives, and for most of them the incentive is to increase funding, to increase the number of bureaucrats under them, to increase power. Unlike the private sector, which has a bottom line and, therefore, incentives to reduce costs and please consumers, bureaucrats generally find themselves with no such market discipline and often in a monopoly situation."[29]

It is important to differentiate the people who work in a monopoly-bureaucracy from the monopoly-bureaucracy itself. David Boaz cautioned, "The people in the public school system aren't necessarily bad people, they are people who face bad incentives. In fact they have good incentives not to change anything."[30]

The difference between a market system and a monopoly is clearly spelled out in comments made by a Portland, Oregon, school board member who attempted to explain why a 1990 statewide tax credit initiative was not a good idea. The member argued, "Public education is not like the free marketplace. In a free marketplace you change the mix if the product is not selling, but public schools serve everyone. We can't change our mix, and that's the big difference."[31] What's that again? Did the school board member say that public education cannot adjust what it is doing to better meet the needs of its changing clientele? Why not?

This bizarre thinking helps explain why parents in a Washington, D.C., suburb waited in line three and four days to enroll their children in an alternative school that emphasizes reading, writing, and arithmetic. Without getting into the intriguing fact that it is an *alternative* school that emphasizes the 3-Rs, the point here is that the educational establishment will not even adjust to market forces and create two, three, or more such schools to meet parent demands and student needs.

The education establishment charges that taxpayers are shirking their duty to fund schools sufficiently to meet today's social challenges and students' ever-increasing needs. In 1960 the cost per pupil was $2,481 in adjusted dollars.[32] In 1992 the American taxpayer spent an estimated $6,993 per pupil for elementary and secondary school students.[33] Where has the money gone? According to Boaz of the Cato Institute, "The public schools are one of the most bureaucratic systems in our society. Between 1960 and 1984 the number of students in public schools was stable. The number of teachers rose 57 percent, which doesn't say much for productivity, but could mean better education. The number of principals and supervisors grew by 79 percent—and the number of other staffers grew by *500 percent*."[34]

In the early 1960s President Kennedy granted collective bargaining privileges to public-sector unions. In doing so, he also gave monopoly power over teachers to public-sector unions. In 1960 NEA changed from a teachers' association into a full-fledged labor union. And 1960 marks the beginning of a downward spiral in student standardized test scores.

The funding of education plays a central part in maintaining the education monopoly and supporting its bureaucracy. In 1991 Joseph Sobran, syndicated columnist, observed, "Private businesses have to produce what people want. Governments only have to want what people produce."[35] In a report entitled *The "Acanemia" Deception*, Lewis Perelman of the Hudson Institute charged, "The 'lag' in U.S. education is not in spending but in productivity: American schools actually are 'shortchanging' the nation by wasting some $100 billion a year through sprawling bureaucracy and outmoded technology."[36]

In public education, bureaucracy and monopoly are almost synonymous, because the bureaucracy that is so much a part of public education is directly dependent on public education's monopoly status for its continuation. Monopolies that exist under law and receive funding through the taxing authority of governments—without regard to productivity—are breeding grounds for sprawling bureaucracies.

The Economic Policy Institute, a Washington D.C.-based liberal think tank, recently made an "explicit pitch to add $20 billion per year to U.S. K-12 spending."[37] In response, a Hudson Institute report countered with the truth about educational funding:

■ U.S. spending on education, as a whole and on K-12, is virtually "unsurpassed"; no major nation spends more per pupil— the only meaningful measure for such comparisons.

- This is not good news. Even if other nations were outspending the United States in schooling, this is a contest we should endeavor to lose—since "winners" are racing toward bankruptcy.
- Poor productivity, not inadequate spending, is the central failure of national education and training systems.
- Technology exists that can at least double the productivity of teaching; adequate investment to develop better teaching and learning technology could achieve even greater efficiency.... [S]ome $100 billion of U.S. education spending is lost annually to wasteful bureaucracy and archaic technology.[38]

In a biting statement on what is wrong with the education monopoly, the Cato Institute's Boaz charged:

> The government schools have failed. Like Soviet factories, they are technologically backward, over-staffed, inflexible, unresponsive to consumer demand, and operated for the convenience of top-level bureaucrats. Like Soviet factories, they cannot keep up with the information age and the global economy. What we need in both areas, if we are going to get progress, is competition that will keep businesses on their toes, that will allow consumers to vote every minute of every day on what kinds of products they are looking for.[39]

This assessment is frightening because of the importance of the system Boaz criticizes. But, at the same time, it is encouraging because Boaz points to a better way to conduct education. This better way places a great deal of importance on competitive systems that may have a difficult time even getting started because of the strength and entrenched nature of the existing education monopoly.

The Hudson Institute report *Looking Back, Thinking Ahead* warned, "Private-sector providers of educational services, while full of long-term potential, face immense challenges in cracking one of the world's largest and toughest monopolies. Present suppliers, those who comprise the existing educational cartel, have enormous advantage, and the inertia-cum-complacency among consumers is such that effective competition is hard to mount. New ideas take time to gain hold; results are slow to arrive; doomsday prophets and nay-sayers are always ready to criticize; suppliers may not respond to new methods of organization; and profits may be thin."[40]

EQUITY OVER FREEDOM

The concepts of freedom and liberty are fundamental to the American people. Among the ideals on which our ancestors founded our nation and based our Constitution was the goal to "secure the Blessings of Liberty to ourselves and our Posterity." We cherish our freedom. We also hold strong beliefs about equality.

Freedom and equality are first-order principles from which school boards develop district policy. The strength of a board's commitment to the concept of freedom or equality affects how the board envisions the district's mission and to what ends it develops policies, administrative regulations, and curricula. A school board's leaning toward one or the other ideal is fundamentally and vitally important.

But freedom and equality, as equality is commonly defined today, are mutually exclusive.

Freedom implies a condition of being unfettered by external control and offers opportunity to succeed, or fail. Freedom is the chance for each individual, as the slogan says, to "be all that you can be." Freedom offers latitude to exercise choice and realize individual capabilities. Freedom allows individuals to choose voluntarily and directly to serve one another. Freedom results from individual action. Through freedom, one person may realize a dream, another may lose a dream, and still another may have no dream—freedom results in inequality. Yet, just as a rising tide lifts all boats, freedom offers every individual opportunity to better himself or herself and, in the process, offers opportunity to better humankind.

As the term is used today, equality is a goal that holds as its aim the condition in which all persons ultimately become equal. Equality speaks to sameness and evenness. Since people are not inherently equal in ability or initiative, attainment of equality needs a mechanism to bring about parity through control. Unlike freedom, equality is achieved through regulation and leveling brought about by agencies and forces external to the individual. Equality does not allow rising to the level of dreams; it levels to someone else's definition of the average human condition. Equality limits individual achievement. Equality limits and constricts freedom.

Since freedom means unfettered opportunity for individual achievement and equality means limiting individual achievement through external regulation, then these two American ideals are at odds. The debate over freedom and equality—in essence, the ongoing battle between the fulfillment of individual potential and the enforcement of social goals—is the origin of much of the turmoil in American society and in our schools. The questions, then, become which path to choose and how to follow that path.

NEA has chosen—for itself and for our public schools. It has chosen equality, almost. Its concept of equality is social activism with preferential treatment. The subject index to *Handbook 1994–1995* contains eight entries that refer to equality. Under "Equal Access to Public Education" NEA declared it "will actively support efforts to defeat the California initiative that would deny any individuals equal access to a public education and other public services regardless of their legal residency status."[41]

In another resolution, "Equity for Incarcerated Persons," NEA announced that it "believes that incarcerated persons, regardless of gender, are entitled to equal access to educational, recreational, and rehabilitative programs within all correctional systems."[42]

In other resolutions, NEA presented its goals for "Equal Opportunities for Women," the "Equal Rights Amendment," and "Equity for Women and Girls." NEA is not interested in individual freedom; NEA is committed to equity for select groups.

Just as NEA has subverted the concept of academic freedom to suit its headlong plunge into unaccountable teacher performance, so too has NEA misused and distorted the principle of equality to support achievement of its social agenda.

School boards must choose which principle—freedom or equality—will guide their local schools. So, too, must individuals choose. Without guiding principles, we are more likely to allow the pressures of the moment to overcome our beliefs. Acting in isolation from our principles, we can more easily be persuaded to follow another's path and abandon or violate our own convictions. To help them decide in what direction they want their schools to move, individuals and school boards must identify the principles that will guide their decisions.

Clearly, NEA has chosen its own hybrid principle of equity under which to lobby for legislation, fund political campaigns, and influence the actions of its 2.2 million members. Judging from the trend in federal legislation over the past thirty years and the evolving nature of many school curricula, NEA activists have been successful in moving public education toward NEA-defined equity.

What of the fifteen thousand school boards in the fifty states? Are they deciding which first-order principle to follow? Not to choose allows ever-changing political and social winds to determine a district's actions. Not to choose subjects students, parents, teachers, administrators, and other staff to an environment where knee-jerk changes and conflicting messages rob people of energy, opportunity, and integrity.

The skeptic might charge that this concern about first-order principles of freedom and equality is just so much esoteric hooey. Yet the same skeptic might consider why some school districts no longer allow students to enter projects in science fairs or compete in spelling bees. These are visible results of choosing equality over freedom.

Ideas do have consequences, and nowhere is it more evident than in the schools and classrooms that emphasize social mission to the detriment of individual achievement.*

---

*This is not to deny the importance of students learning to work cooperatively in groups. On the contrary, many companies cite communication skills and ability to work effectively in groups as major attributes for success in today's work environment. But this reality of the workplace does not justify completely eliminating competition and individual achievement from our schools. Too often, advocates of popular instructional strategies, like cooperative learning, misuse those ideas as tools to accomplish their agenda. These teaching strategies are hijacked, diverted into something innovators never intended, and become the latest educational fad. Cooperation is important; so are competition and individual achievement.

Clearly individual freedom must be tempered with compassion and balanced with responsibility. We must live together as a caring and responsible people. If, however, parents and taxpayers are not content with NEA's persistent move toward equity at the price of losing individual freedom to compete and excel, then strong actions are necessary. The issue is anything but esoteric; it is real, it is pragmatic, and it affects every child, every day in every public school classroom.

NEA's CONTROL OF PRIVATE SCHOOLS

NEA seeks to control the guiding philosophies of public schools, and it seeks to control the very existence and operation of private schools.

As a public high school principal, I was pleased when parents and students had private school alternatives that allowed them to select the best education to meet a student's goals and needs.

Not NEA. NEA is a labor union. Its first priority is the security of union officials and, in the case of this particular labor union, its second priority is the advancement of its ultraliberal social agenda. The welfare of students and the wishes of parents are seldom of interest to NEA, unless these wishes happen to coincide with NEA's interests.

The public education establishment is trying to impose on private schools the same regulations it has fashioned for itself. Members of this establishment refer to this as "a level playing field" or "the same rules for everyone." They emphasize "the need for fairness" if public schools are to compete with private schools for students and dollars.

The battle for control of private schools, however, is not about fairness to the educational cartel. It is about results for students, responsiveness to parents' questions and requests, professional freedom for educators, return on investment for taxpayers, and benefits to communities.

To the extent NEA and its allies are successful in hobbling private schools with the same self-imposed regulations that drag down public education, NEA militants will control private schools and deny students and parents real educational options. If teachers were free to join or not join NEA, and NEA had confidence in its own ability to attract and keep members, it would be fighting for charter schools, vouchers, and other opportunities for teachers to step out from under nineteenth-century rules to compete in the twenty-first-century educational arena. NEA is afraid of competition, so it seeks to control and limit.

CHANGING DIRECTIONS

Unfortunately, flawless logic and eloquent rhetoric will not carry the day. Those who would bring productive change to public education must anticipate that NEA bosses and their allies in the Unholy Alliance will employ any necessary tactic in defense of the world NEA has taken 140 years to construct. NEA is close to accomplishing its goals of creating and controlling one national system of education, and NEA will not easily let local teachers, parents, and taxpayers regain control of their local schools. It has everything to lose; for NEA, it is a battle for life.

Winning this war requires personal involvement and coloring outside the lines.

10

Coloring Outside the Lines

"When Edison invented electric illumination, he didn't tinker with candles to make them burn better. Instead, he created something brilliantly new: the light bulb. In the same fashion, American education needs a fundamental breakthrough, a new dynamic that will light the way to a transformed educational system."[1]

—*Chris Whittle,* The Edison Project

THIS BOOK IS NOT ABOUT EDUCATIONAL REFORM, at least not in the conventional sense of prescribed structural changes, funding formulas, teacher-training programs, cultural renewals, or program revisions. **This book is about clearing the way so educational reform can take root and grow.**

The interviews, information, and data in the preceding chapters describe NEA's character and illustrate the devastating effects of the union's lust for power on students, parents, teachers, taxpayers, and public education. They show that public education must change. More to the point, they demonstrate that before substantive change can come to education, NEA must be deposed from its seat of power. This chapter and the next are about how to do that.

WHAT WE KNOW

I have criticized NEA for making, pressuring, and buying decisions at the national, state, and local levels. Citizens and their representatives should be making those decisions in children's best interests and in the best interests of their communities. I have also criticized the existence of a centralized and controlling education monopoly and its ever-increasing expansion.

It is contrary to our Constitution for the federal government to create and control a nationwide education program or be involved as it is in educational policy formulation. Further, it is contrary to our democratic beliefs for one person or agency to prescribe specific ways to meet the educational needs of all communities—or even one community. The solutions to current education problems do not lie in replacing the present monolithic system with another, albeit different, monolithic system. Any one-right-way, one-size-fits-all system is a major contributor to current and future problems. To learn from cutting-edge organizations and from organization research is to understand that one solution lies in seeking out and developing a variety of solutions.

Chris Whittle's clear challenge in the quotation that introduces this chapter reminds us of Thomas Edison's leap into new realms of thinking. Whittle encourages us to risk thinking outside the known box to find solutions that are different in kind rather than only in degree—as has been typical of work-within-the-system educational efforts at change.

I greatly admire Whittle's vision, courage, and commitment. He, with the Edison Project, is doing exactly what is necessary—working outside the existing NEA-controlled system to bring substantive change to education. We can, I think, assume that Whittle must have had concerns about launching a project of the scope and with the political and economic exposure of the Edison Project while NEA bosses are still the preeminent and controlling power in public education and a strong force in American politics. In retrospect, we can see that NEA chieftains, with their arrogance and power, have clearly targeted the Edison Project for destruction and Whittle for economic ruin.

At first it appeared that NEA would simply badger and boycott Whittle and the Edison Project out of existence. In a July 1994 edition of *Advertising Age*, an article entitled "Whittle Suffers New Woes as NEA Targets Sponsors" told the all-too-familiar story.[2] The fate of the nationwide, for-profit education venture seemed doomed.

But Whittle has quietly persisted, and he may yet triumph in spite of NEA's efforts. Recent accounts of the Edison Project tell a story different from the one NEA had in mind. An article in the June 2, 1997, edition of the Minneapolis *Star and Tribune* told of the Edison Project's continuing life. Entitled "Edison Project's For-Profit Schools Come Back in Size and Test Scores," the article reported that the once all-but-dead project was back and that it "will double its size next year, to 25 schools in eight states with about $70 million in revenue."[3]

Also encouraging is a quote from Denis Doyle, a senior fellow at the Hudson Institute. "I think," said Doyle, "there is every reason to believe we are witnessing a fundamental transformation of American education in which Edison is playing a big part, at least symbolically. They're certainly a significant entering wedge in the way of thinking about schools."[4] Given that standardized test scores for fifth-graders in the Dodge-Edison Elementary School in Wichita went from the 46th to the 59th percentile in reading and from the 35th to the 64th percentile in math, one can guess that parents and teachers will also believe that a "fundamental transformation" is taking place.[5]

If we have learned anything from NEA's long history, especially since 1960, it is that a teachers' organization cannot be both a professional association and a labor union—not if the welfare of students and the interests of a democratic people are to be paramount. If these concerns are paramount, then consumers and taxpayers can no longer support the Unholy Alliance by allowing business as usual. We must step outside the known box, color outside the lines, and find new ways to educate our children.

It would not be particularly productive for parents and taxpayers to storm the education Bastille by attacking school boards and superintendents. This is precisely the kind of attack the current system so effectively repels or contains. Further, such actions work within the system and ask for the system's permission to change the system. Rather, we must change the laws, regulations, funding mechanisms, and practices used to generate the bulwarks that support and protect the existing education cartel.

In a world of limitless options and endless possibilities, one indisputable truth about educational change is that no substantive, student-centered, parent-responsive, teacher-enabling, taxpayer-sensitive change can happen until we remove NEA from power. The public has a right to neighborhood schools where students' needs are the first and most important priority. To achieve this end, we must no longer allow NEA to be the privileged, powerful agent of social engineering that it is now.

As noted earlier, one action necessary to accomplish this is to reverse NEA's compulsory union privileges by rescinding the union bosses' power to: (1) force "representation" onto teachers, (2) force teachers to pay union dues as a condition of employment, and (3) force school boards into mandatory collective bargaining.

In the private sector, in general and to varying degrees, market forces drive producer decisions. In the private sector, successful enterprises use resources efficiently, meet or exceed market demands, and strive to serve consumers better. Emphasis on creative, competitive success breeds resistance to centralized government control. For NEA's high command, the first premise is that centralized control and uniformity are necessary. But it is foolish to believe the NEA union bosses will easily give up the income, control, and power they have amassed. How then to dismantle this unwanted giant?

How to Get from Here to There

There seem to be but three choices—four given the possibility that unknown concepts or technologies may arise to change our whole notion of what education is and how it gets done. Until then, the likely options are: (1) confront NEA head-on and work within the existing system to bring about systemic changes that will allow local changes to develop and survive, (2) work outside the existing system to create better ways to educate, better ways to learn, and better ways to teach, and (3) combine these two by working within the existing system to bring needed changes, and outside the system to invent new definitions, new roles, and new goals for teaching, learning, and education.

The third option is potentially the most effective. While some mount large-scale, outside-the-system attacks on Fortress NEA, others will labor inside the system on small and large scales. To work at the outer limits of NEA's reach we need to employ a variety of approaches—big and small, public and private, nonprofit and for-profit. Creating better systems of education outside the existing monolithic system will force NEA and the other members of the Unholy Alliance to compete for students, good teachers, and resources. They will either respond to market pressures, or languish and eventually perish.

THE UNDOING OF NEA

The fall of NEA will not come through traditional career politicians; many have been accomplices in NEA's rise to power. The fall of NEA will not come through the routine efforts of school boards, superintendents, and principals; they are ensnared in the NEA world that exists in large measure because of their cooperation and acquiescence. And the fall of NEA will not come because NEA suddenly sees the error of its ways and vows to become a better citizen. No, if NEA is to fall, it will fall because of the combined efforts of individual parents, taxpayers, teachers, administrators, professors of education, public policymakers, and elected public officials who no longer can tolerate the Unholy Alliance's self-serving ways.

NEA'S VULNERABILITY

NEA is vulnerable for two reasons: (1) its policies, practices, and goals are unacceptable to a growing number of people (as noted in the Kamber report) and (2) it is a huge empire open to incursion on many fronts.

NEA's aggressive antichild, antiteacher, antiparent, and antitaxpayer policies and practices have become increasingly apparent and have even drawn negative attention from some in the media. NEA policies are also beginning to alienate those whom public education serves and who support public education. Its size makes it vulnerable to citizen attacks in fifty states, fifteen thousand school districts, and eighty thousand public schools. NEA will aggressively resist such movements, but it does not have the control over parents and taxpayers that it has over members of the education cartel who depend on it.

NEA's new boss knows that the union is in serious trouble. In the words of the Kamber report, "NEA now faces a crisis."[6] In large part this is because it is widely viewed as the number-one obstacle to better public schools.[7] It is possible that NEA may openly continue its blatant and confrontational practices. More likely, as recent post-Kamber-report actions testify, NEA will become more public-relations conscious. But whatever its public strategy, NEA will continue to ply its time-tested, behind-the-scenes tactics.

Those of us who send our children to public schools or work under the stifling control of the Unholy Alliance have been servants of NEA. It is time to end this servitude. Freedom can be a hard road. Will history record that we did not respond to our challenge? We are not asked to risk our lives or even our material possessions. We have only to regain control of public education.

Power must move from NEA union bosses back to parents and taxpayers. Power must be met with power. And, while responsibility can be delegated, power must be taken. A successful rebellion against this massive, deeply entrenched education cabal must act on and strengthen the principle that We the People jealously control the public agencies we create to serve us.*

Because the undoing of NEA can best come about through many small-scale and large-scale efforts, no one game plan can or should guide campaigns to regain control of schools and free teachers. What

---

*As a reminder of how it should be, 42.17.251 of the Revised Code of Washington reads, "The people of this state do not yield their sovereignty to the agencies that serve them. The people, in delegating authority, do not give their public servants the right to decide what is good for the people to know and what is not good for them to know. The people insist on remaining informed so that they may maintain control over the instruments they have created."

follows is an incomplete discussion of what needs to be undone and what needs to be done to undo it.[8] It is only a start. The ingenuity and unique needs of people in their local circumstances will generate a host of actions.

MULTIPLE CHOICE—THE UNDOING OF NEA

In his book, *The Structure of Scientific Revolutions*, Thomas Kuhn wrote about the relationship between rules and values. As earlier discussed, Kuhn believed, "The points at which values must be applied are invariably also those at which risks must be taken."[9]

A departure from rule-bound decisions in favor of values-driven decisions brings with it a level of risk. We have, however, come to manage our school districts and our schools by ever-increasing numbers of rules. Certainly some rules are necessary to the orderly operation of schools and school districts. Yet, in many school districts, rules have become more important than values, and big-system rules tend to keep people from acting on their values.

In her article "Restore Public Schools to the People," Joanne Hatton paraphrased Andrew Nikiforuk, a Canadian columnist. She wrote, "The central failure, leading to many others, was the severing of community influence and authority over what schools teach, how they teach it, and why."[10]

As it stands, the current proliferation of rules serves NEA more than it serves the community. According to David Cohen, who studied the politics of education, "The reality of power in education is becoming incongruent with the formal structure; increasingly the political forces that determine local school decisions are neither locally nor democratically controlled."[11] Our challenge is to ensure that those who work in the school respond to the will of the local people rather than to the dictates of distant union bosses.

A vital first step is to understand what you believe and why you believe it—and then to act on those beliefs. Some may conclude that NEA's goals for public education are proper. If so, you need do nothing. If, however, you conclude otherwise, you will want to think about what needs to be done to remove NEA from its unelected seat of power.

THE TWO EDGES OF LEGISLATIVE CHANGE

Laws govern a goodly portion of our lives, and professional law-makers write and enact the majority of our laws. This is our system of representative democracy. If the people elected do as the voters wish, they are returned to office. If they do not, they are booted out. This is the theory. But since NEA coffers fund and support so many politicians and union bosses control many state legislators and legislatures, it is unrealistic to think that the legislative process will serve as a ready vehicle through which to do battle against NEA. It is, after all, through state-level legislatures that NEA got and now keeps so much of its privilege and power.

Changing laws can be tricky, because using the legislative process means entering NEA's home court; it can result in unintended consequences. Writing about bringing vouchers and parental choice into law, David Boaz of the Cato Institute cautioned, "One of the biggest concerns about the voucher plan, of course, is that it might lead to further state regulations of private schools."[12] Once a bill enters the political process, NEA's lobbyists, puppet politicians, and power brokers use NEA's money and its huge voting block to manipulate legislation to achieve its goals.

Nonetheless, laws must be changed to end NEA's control over education, and we tend to think that only elected legislators can effect these changes. This is not true. In over half the states, voter initiatives or citizen petitions allow citizens to work outside the usual legislative process to directly create, change, or abolish laws.[13]

Boaz advised, "One way to solve the regulation problem is to implement educational choice through the initiative process—to avoid legislative politics."[14] Once the initiative is put on the ballot, however, NEA can use its wealth and political power to move the vote on the initiative to an off-year election when fewer people vote. It then has an easier time using its influence to sway this smaller block of voters. Even with this weakness, the initiative process may stand a better chance of beating NEA.

With all its shortcomings, some argue that working through elected representatives is still the best way to effect needed laws. In some states, the political climate has changed, and legislators are actually taking a lead in the fight for citizens to regain control of government institutions. In Portland, Representative Chuck Carpenter (R-Ore.) introduced state Senate Bill 750 as a way of "taking power back from the cynical labor elite and returning it to the people."[15] Carpenter's bill encouraged "stricter limits on who may be represented by unions, limits on what issues may be negotiated during bargaining sessions, elimination of so-called 'fact-finding' hearings as a way to resolve contract disputes and a 90-day limit on negotiations."[16] According to an article in the Eugene, Oregon, *Register-Guard*, this resurgence of public control of public institutions is taking place because "public-sector managers believe unions—particularly teacher unions—have gained too much control over the workplace."[17]

Public-sector unions, of course, are outraged. But so are the Oregon state legislators who listed some of the issues these unions currently bargain for: "restrooms, grooming standards and the right to listen to the radio."[18] To avoid what often amounts to harassment of administrators and gross misuse of public resources, Senate Bill 750 "would limit bargaining subjects to wages, hours, health insurance premiums, holiday pay, grievance procedures, disciplinary actions, sick leave and some safety issues."[19]

LEGISLATION IN DEFENSE OF HOME SCHOOLING

At the national level, at least one politician jumped into the fray to assist parents battling NEA over who controls their children's education. In this case, home schooling was the issue and Representative Dick Armey (R-Tex.) the political champion. This is a most instructive case study.

NEA's *Handbook 1994–1995* states, "The National Education Association believes that home schooling programs cannot provide the student with a comprehensive education experience."[20] To protect its empire, NEA demands that home-school "[i]nstruction should be by persons who are licensed by the appropriate state education licensure agency, and a curriculum approved by the state department of education should be used."[21] NEA bosses also believe no state or federal money should support the estimated 700,000 to

1,000,000[22] young people now educated through home schooling. Because home schooling is a major threat, NEA union bosses are deadly earnest about stopping its further spread.

In an effort to defeat NEA, Representative Armey worked closely with Mike Farris of the Home School Legal Defense Association (HSLDA) and with representatives of the National Center for Home Education to pass an amendment to proposed legislation "that not only exempts home-schoolers from teacher certification, but also exempts home-schoolers and all private schools from the entire thousand-page H.R. 6 (the reauthorization of the Elementary and Secondary Education Act). It further protects home-schoolers by rewriting the federal definition of school to exclude them."[23] The victory did not come easily to the home-school community, and an aggressive, well-timed, and well-coordinated effort was necessary to gain desired ends.

Learning that NEA was about to push through federal-level legislation that would require teacher certification for parents who wish to educate their children at home, Representative Armey joined forces with home-schoolers in February 1994 to stop the union.[24] Excerpts quoted from Grover Norquist's (president of Americans for Tax Relief) account of the ordeal described what happened:

- **Monday, February 14, 1994** Within an hour of discovering the threat to home schooling, Dick Armey offers an amendment in committee to exempt home-schoolers and private schools from the teacher-certification requirement. George Miller leads the entire Democrat side of the committee in voting down the Armey language. Miller's vote makes clear in retrospect that the *intent* of the school bill has from the beginning been to regulate home-schoolers.

    Farris hires several local printers to print 38,000 copies of a letter outlining home-schoolers' fears, which are out the door to all HSLDA members within fifty-six hours. Copies are delivered to Congress, and a "national fax alert" begins.
- **Wednesday, February 16** Farris tapes an interview with Pat Robertson's *700 Club*. An hour later, he gives a two-hour

interview to Marlin Maddoux, host of *Point of View*, a syndicated radio show that reaches four million listeners. By four that afternoon, congressional staffers begin calling HSLDA, promising that their bosses will vote for a "Home School/Private School Freedom Amendment" and asking for an end to the calls from their districts.

- **Thursday, February 17** The wave of calls into Washington builds. At [1:00 PM], Farris tapes an interview with James Dobson, whose radio show will reach 1,500 stations on Monday, February 21. One Democrat congressman's chief of staff tells home schooling leader Doug Phillips he has already received six hundred calls today, and begs Phillips to ask for the calls to stop....

- **Friday, February 18** Armey announces that he will lead the fight for the Home School/Private School Freedom Amendment, which has the support of several congressmen by nightfall. Two problems arise: anti-home-school congressional offices misinform callers, telling them that their concerns have been taken care of. The waters are further muddied by the efforts of a fringe coalition of small moderate and liberal homeschoolers to negotiate compromise language—independent of Farris and Armey....

- **Monday, February 21** Armey's language is updated and a national fax alert goes out to home-schoolers with the most recent language.

  Rush Limbaugh discusses the home-school blitz of Congress.... At 10:00 PM a thousand people gather in Dallas at a home-school rally.

- **Tuesday, February 22** The phone blitz continues. A number of congressmen instruct staff to stop answering all calls....

- **Wednesday, February 23** The phone calls continue. Homeschoolers arrive on Capital Hill from Georgia, Missouri, Virginia, Pennsylvania, and West Virginia, as an ice storm hits Washington.... Mike Farris spends an hour on Pat Buchanan's radio show....

- **Thursday, February 24** Dick Armey sends out a "Dear Colleague" letter explaining that a compromise amendment by Education and Labor Committee Chairman William Ford will not protect home-schoolers.

At 9:00 AM, Democrats on the Rules Committee introduce a wrong version of the Armey amendment for the day's votes....

At 2:00 PM, debate begins on the final language of Armey's Home School/Private School Freedom Amendment....

At 3:38 PM, the Armey amendment passes, 374 to 53.[25]

According to Norquist, parents "knew the Clinton administration would make a move against home-schoolers on behalf of the NEA."[26] But they were ready to act. Home-schoolers not only stopped NEA's clandestine attack but also took the initiative and passed legislation that gave them more protection than they had prior to NEA's political chicanery. Home-schoolers taught a valuable five-part lesson to those who would fight NEA and win:

1. They picked the right champion—in this case, Dick Armey.
2. They went for total victory—not simply protecting themselves from attack but rolling back other threats and protecting private schools.
3. They did not fall for the Democrats' ploy of "get them to stop calling and then I'll vote for you." The pressure was unrelenting.
4. Within ten days, Farris had sent out five faxes to his network, and his message went out repeatedly to all supportive radio stations so that home-schoolers knew, hour by hour, the exact state of play.
5. They knew that procedural votes are important and didn't allow Congress to fool voters with meaningless votes that were canceled out by procedural motions.[27]

DEMOCRACY AND AUTONOMY

When writing *Politics, Markets, and America's Schools*, policy researchers Chubb and Moe found "three major causes of student achievement—student ability, school organization, and family background—roughly in that order."[28]

In relation to "school organization," Chubb and Moe discovered that "institutions of direct democratic control promote ineffective school organizations."[29]

Yes, you read that correctly—direct democratic control promotes ineffective schools. The two authors established that democratically controlled schools were "[d]riven by politics, [and that] these institutions encouraged the bureaucratization and centralization of school control and discouraged the emergence of coherent, strongly led, academically ambitious, professionally grounded, teamlike organizations. Institutions of market control encourage pretty much the opposite."[30]

Comparing forms of organization common to public schools with those common to private schools, Chubb and Moe concluded that in public schools the governance mechanism is democratic control and the locus of control is society at large. Thus, in public schools, ever-changing political powers whipsaw schools across political battlegrounds without regard for the effect on schools, teachers, or students.

Asserting that "existing institutions cannot solve the problem, because they *are* the problem," Chubb and Moe concluded:

> There is nothing in the concept of democracy to require that schools be subject to direct control by school boards, superintendents, central offices, departments of education, and other arms of government. Nor is there anything in the concept of public education to require that schools be governed in this way. There are many paths to democracy and public education. The path America has been treading for the past half-century is exacting a heavy price—one the nation and its children can ill afford to bear, and need not. It is time, we think, to get to the root of the problem.[31]

A main point of their findings is that administrators and teachers within schools must be free to build their own teams, design curricula, and choose appropriate methods of instruction to meet the goals set by the parents and those who govern local schools.[32]

Equally important is the commitment parents and community make to those hired to lead the change and administer the schools. If a school community hires a principal or similar leader expecting that person to lead a school through such a change, that person must have parental and community support throughout the five to seven years it will take to transform schools from politics-driven to market-driven schools.

David Boaz, executive vice president of Cato Institute, believes, "One of the things that is essential to excellence in schools is autonomy for the school itself, particularly for the principal—who should be the CEO of the school but usually doesn't have that authority."[33] As it stands now, people who work to bring real change in public schools frequently become targets of NEA and suffer professionally and personally for their efforts. Publicly punishing these leaders reinforces NEA's power and discourages others who would lead change efforts.

NEA's ARGUMENTS AGAINST CHOICE*

"Choice," wrote Chubb and Moe, "*is* a panacea.... Choice is a self-contained reform with its own rationale and justification. It has the

---

*The vocabulary of "choice" can be confusing. To deflect parents' demands for choice, NEA fought for and got "pubic school choice" in some states and school districts. Public school choice allows parents to send their children to *public* schools of the parents' choice. Because public school choice only moves students around within the same system, it is essentially anticompetitive and will not have the effect on public education that a truly market-driven approach would have. Public school choice protects NEA by keeping real parental choice and market forces out of public education. Real school choice gives parents the freedom to send their children to the public or private school of the parents' choosing (or to keep them home to be home-schooled) and the ability to pay for all or part of the tuition with a tax credit, voucher, or some other tax-supported vehicle.

capacity *all by itself* to bring about the kind of transformation that, for years, reformers have been seeking to engineer in myriad other ways."[34]

To emphasize their belief that the existing system cannot change of itself, Chubb and Moe advised, "If choice is to work to greatest advantage, it must be adopted *without* these other [traditional, work-within-the-system] reforms, since the latter are predicated on democratic control and are implemented by bureaucratic means.... Taken seriously, choice is not a system-preserving reform. It is a revolutionary reform that introduces a new system of public education."[35]

In response to productive public discussions about school choice, NEA bosses throw up the same unproductive augments. School choice, NEA people shrilly charge, would use public money to pay tuition for students to attend private sectarian and nonsectarian schools.

There are at least two arguments in NEA's anti–school-choice smokescreen. First, NEA representatives claim such distribution of tax funds would be an improper use of public money; and second, they contend school choice is a violation of the principles of separation of church and state.

In their strident insistence that tax monies should be "resources that rightfully belong to public education,"[36] NEA union bosses argue that public money in the form of tax credits or vouchers should not in any way support a private entity—in this case, a private school. This thinking is of course inconsistent with the way NEA, a private entity, gets tax money to support its own operations.

If government agencies transfer public funds to private citizens through tax credits and vouchers and these citizens choose to use this money to pay tuition at private schools, how is this different from the tax money paid to teachers who are *required* to give a percent[37] of their salaries as dues to NEA—a private, nongovernmental, public-sector labor union? If it is permissible for NEA members to transfer tax money to a private labor union, then it should be permissible for parents and students to transfer tax money to private schools. Moreover, under a voucher plan, parents have an opportunity to choose where they enroll their children. Many teachers have no similar freedom of choice—they are required to join NEA and/or to pay dues if they want to teach. The logical response to NEA's argument is to give both parents and teachers a choice.

The second NEA argument against school choice centers on NEA's concern for using tax money to pay tuition at private religious schools. Consider this precedent. In 1944 Uncle Sam created the GI Bill to, among other purposes, help returning veterans attend the post-secondary school of their choice. Over the years, veterans by the hundreds of thousands used this money to attend colleges and universities across the nation. Some chose to attend small state colleges, some attended land-grant universities, and some attended Notre Dame and other private religious schools.

The GI Bill worked for generations of veterans, and it worked for our nation. Through the GI Bill, the government returned tax money to private citizens who decided within the free market of educational choice where they would spend their money. The federal government also provides Pell Grants to numerous students who attend private, religiously affiliated colleges.[38]

The point is that the GI-Bill-national-voucher system has worked in America for decades. NEA's arguments against the same principle being applied to K-12 school choice do not hold water either educationally or economically.

With respect to tax money being used to "support" religion, U.S. military services have for decades commissioned and paid for chaplains to give religious guidance and spiritual support to our troops stationed all over the globe. Presumably tax money pays these chaplains' salaries, and no harm has come to our service people or our nation because of this practice.

It seems likely that tax credits and vouchers can work. Why then is school choice an issue at all, and why has it as taken so long to create a tax credit or voucher mechanism to support real choice for parents and students? The answer, of course, is that NEA knows school choice will unravel its empire.

Those who wish to clear paths to substantive educational reform will need first to dethrone NEA. Chapter 11 offers ideas on how to accomplish this goal.

11

....

Final Test:
How to Regain Control

"As the Progressive movement demonstrated many years ago, attempts to transform political institutions are not doomed to fail. They may succeed when they have widespread support and when the resources of powerful social groups can be mobilized behind change. Something of the sort could happen in the next decade."[1]

—*John E. Chubb and Terry Moe*, Politics, Markets, and America's Schools

A TIME FOR ACTION

A GOVERNING PREMISE OF THIS BOOK is that no significant reform can come to American education until NEA is first deposed from its ill-gotten position of power and control. We must also realize that NEA and the Unholy Alliance will attempt to deflect and co-opt any efforts to bring change. The distinction between *confronting NEA* and *reforming education* is important. A necessary beginning to educational reform is for parents, taxpayers, teachers, and communities to recognize this distinction and start by disempowering NEA. As parents and taxpayers take back control of public education, they can begin to determine the ends public education is to serve in their communities and states.

As explained in the Prologue, the two teachers' unions, NEA and AFT (American Federation of Teachers), are essentially the same in strategies and tactics and may soon officially join to become one giant superunion. The following recommendations, therefore, also apply to AFT.

RECOMMENDED ACTIONS

The people to whom I offer these recommendations include political and community leaders, public policymakers, business executives, journalists, and educators. But, because parents and taxpayers must move the existing system off center, the focus is on them.

The trick is to think about what must be done from the frontline vantage point of parents and taxpayers; doing so will make the issues clearer and the necessary actions more effective.

Institutions seldom change themselves. Time and again, recognition of the need for change and the impetus for change have come from forces outside established institutions. We cannot expect the education bureaucracy to be different.

It was difficult in previous pages not to write about the many promising ideas for education reform. Certain reforms will disempower NEA, and a disempowered NEA will allow certain reforms to take root and prosper. One reform idea we have touched on is choice. Choice is the perfect example of a reform that will weaken NEA's control of public education and, at the same time, make education stronger. Still, until NEA loses its control of teachers and public education, choice will be impossible to implement.

The most promising way to improve education is to work outside the web of NEA's regulations and laws. Yet a majority of current efforts address changes within the system, as do a number I recommend. Actions to bring changes from outside the system are fewer and more direct—the main one being to write new laws and regulations to allow private nonprofit and for-profit educational enterprises to emerge. While this simple statement is tantamount to

Roosevelt telling Eisenhower to win the war in Europe, it is, nonetheless, exactly what must be done.

Taken together, changes inside and outside the system will reduce or eliminate institutionalized hurdles and allow educational entrepreneurial spirit and market forces, guided by minimal state-level regulations, to do the rest.

A word of caution: Those who act on these and their own ideas should expect NEA militants, UniServ operatives, and local union activists to attack them personally and economically. Since NEA's people cannot win the battle of ideas, they attack the people who advance ideas. Killing the messenger is an ugly fact of contemporary life.

NATIONAL-LEVEL ACTIONS

National-level NEA powers and privileges were born through a political process and should die through a political process. Tell your senators and representatives that you and your group want these and other actions taken to return public education to the control of parents and taxpayers. Then follow up with requests for status reports about the actions they have taken.

- **Stop Forced Unionism and Monopoly Bargaining** If no other action were taken but to rescind NEA's power of forced unionism and its privilege of monopoly bargaining, this alone would go a long way toward achieving the goals outlined in previous chapters. This two-part action cuts across national-, state-, and local-level actions—which testifies to its fundamental importance. (This issue is addressed again under state-level actions.)
- **Eliminate the U.S. Department of Education** The Department of Education is big-government intrusion into the rights and obligations of the states to provide education to their citizens. The cabinet-level Department of Education was born of a political union between NEA's union bosses and President Carter. It is a political comrade of NEA and a threat to public education. As such, it has little relationship to what happens in schools and classrooms, except to bring NEA's goal for a

nationally centralized and controlled system of education closer.

The department's 1998 estimated appropriation of $39,470,231,000 is 34 percent larger than its 1997 appropriation of $29,366,057,000.[2] What will it be in five and ten years?

One division within the Department of Education, the National Center for Education Statistics, has a legitimate function—to collect and distribute data. Parents, taxpayers, educators, and policymakers can use these data to monitor states' efforts to provide educational services, and the states can use the data to manage state educational programs. In the future, a confederation of the fifty states could determine the center's mission and fund its operations. Whatever the course of action, the Center for Educational Statistics should continue.

It is important to clarify that the elimination of the Department of Education should bring about the elimination of the many federal programs that now litter the educational landscape. If some programs are to survive, the states should fund and run them.

Eliminating federal programs will be more threatening to the many thousands whose jobs depend on those programs than eliminating the department. Some of these people may continue in similar jobs when federal programs are transferred to the states. The states may or may not continue the programs or may alter them in response to state-level needs. This, of course, is precisely the point: states will provide the programs their citizens deem necessary. Welcome to a rebirth of the states as laboratories of democracy. Welcome also—we can hope—to decreased federal taxation.

■ **Expand "Public Education"** NEA insists that "public money" should be spent only on "public education." NEA uses public money as the major source of its ability to play power politics. Its control of public money, therefore, is absolutely essential. Distribution of public money other than to NEA-controlled schools would severely weaken its financial and power bases.

NEA has created an artificial distinction between "public school students" and those who do not attend educational programs that fit NEA's self-serving definition of public schools. Unlike NEA, however, many parents and taxpayers view schools from a student-first perspective. Tax money, they reason, should support any good school, be it a private school, charter school, or voucher-supported school.

Earlier chapters discussed the use of public money to support student attendance at nonpublic postsecondary schools. A debate over how best to use public resources to educate the public's children in broadly defined "public" elementary and secondary education is long overdue.

NEA's self-centered thinking controls the current debate. We need to expand the debate and the definition of "public education" to allow public money to support a wider array of K-12 educational endeavors. In so doing, however, we must be careful not to change the definition of public education in ways that would allow NEA to attack the private schools that are so important to our traditions of American education.

One goal is for states to create ways for public money to support educating children in a variety of schools. Through expanded definition, elementary and secondary education would be financed and controlled through local market forces.

Denver is finding a way to accomplish this. In its July 6, 1998, edition, the *Denver Post* observed, "Charter schools frequently operate on an abundance of enthusiasm but a shortage of capital. To help overcome that obstacle, lawmakers approved tax-exempt bonds for charters—a big money-saving device with financing options previously out of reach. The Colorado Educational and Cultural Facilities Authority has two bond sales headed to market—$3.2 million for the new Wyatt-Edison Center School in Denver and $3.6 million for the 1-year-old Liberty Community Charter School in Fort Collins...."[3]

■ **Beef-Up the Hatch Act** President Franklin Roosevelt signed the Hatch Act in 1939 to limit inappropriate political activities by government workers. The act also protected government workers from extortion by political parties to gain "campaign contributions" and "volunteer campaign labor" in exchange for job security and promotions. In 1989 only 32 percent of federal employees wanted the Hatch Act weakened, but senators voted 68 to 30 to gut the act.[4] Because NEA is not subject to curbs such as the Hatch Act, it has been able to build political clout that is the envy of other government unions. It is past time to limit NEA's political activities. NEA should be subject to the rules, the restrictions, and the full force of the Hatch Act.

- **End ETI** According to Brimelow and Spencer, NEA's Executive Director Don Cameron "invented the latest fashionable idea on picking the public pocket; economically targeted investing (ETI)—the use by pension funds of their members' money for politically targeted subsidies to various liberal-favored enterprises—and their indemnification by taxpayers for their inevitable losses."[5] This NEA ruse has all the indicators of becoming an educational S&L debacle and should be stopped before taxpayers forfeit more of their tax money to support NEA and its political partners.

- **Amend the Hobbs Act to Close the Enmons Loophole** In 1946 Congress passed the Hobbs Act to give the federal government authority to investigate and prosecute cases of union violence. In the 1973 Supreme Court decision on *U.S. v. Enmons*, the Court "held that union violence, if carried out in furtherance of a legitimate collective bargaining objective such as higher wages, does not, *regardless of the methods employed or the harm done*, violate the extortion and robbery provisions of the federal Anti-Racketeering Act of 1934 (48 Stat. 979) as amended in 1946 by the Hobbs Act (60 Stat. 420)"[6] (emphasis added).

  As it now stands, wrote Frank and Joseph Andritzky in *Government Union Review*, "the federal government has lost its authority to prosecute cases of [public- and private-sector] union violence involving robbery and extortion affecting interstate commerce under the Hobbs Act if the violence committed was perpetrated to meet an end loosely defined as 'legitimate.'"[7]

John F. Kennedy and the Supreme Court gutted the Hobbs Act to checkmate congressional efforts to close the loophole that allows union violence, extortion, and robbery.[8] It is past time for Congress to take steps to protect taxpayers and people who are the targets of public-sector union violence. Congress must strengthen the Hobbs Act.

- **Balance the Budget** What does a balanced federal budget have to do with what happens in local schools? To a significant degree, the education cartel exists on money that many state and local taxpayers would not choose to spend in support of a bureaucracy that scorns their wishes and their values. When money is plentiful (as it is for a government with unlimited ability to tax and borrow), it is easy to continue paying for existing programs and initiate new ones without regard for effective and efficient program operation, or for the justification of the program in the first place. Not so when money is less plentiful. Decision makers must then weigh needs, establish priorities, and make decisions about what should and can be done within a limited budget. A plentiful money supply dulls thinking and encourages sloppy decision making. When money is tight, people act on their values. A balanced federal budget is one more way for taxpayers to regain control over what happens in their schools.

- **License Teachers Only at State or Local Levels** NEA is pushing hard for national teacher standards and national teacher certification—all the better for it to control who gains admission into the teaching corps and who teaches what subjects and values in local schools. Whoever controls the portals into a profession to a large degree controls the profession. If NEA can achieve national teacher licensure and if it can succeed in imposing curriculum standards and funding standards at the national level, it is only a matter of time until NEA union bosses control public education across the fifty states.

Chubb and Moe wrote, "[I]ndividuals should be certified to teach if they have a bachelor's degree and if their personal history reveals no obvious problems. The question of whether they are truly good teachers will be determined in practice, as schools determine whom to hire, observe their own teachers in action over an extended period of time, and make decisions about merit, promotion, and dismissal.... The state will hold the schools accountable for meeting procedural requirements. It will ensure that schools continue to meet the criteria presumed by their charters."[9]

This recommendation directly challenges NEA's efforts to nationalize, centralize, and control public education. New York State, in its recent discontinuation of life-long teacher certification, is moving toward Chubb and Moe's recommendation.

We must confront and stop all efforts to impose national teaching certification. States and communities should jealously guard their prerogatives in this area.

■ **Read the NEA Manifesto** The *NEA Handbook* is an annual publication that tells a great deal about NEA's values and goals. Parents, teachers, and taxpayers should know what NEA believes and plans to accomplish so they can better talk with policymakers, school board members, superintendents, and others about NEA's goals for public education.

How many teachers have read the *Handbook*? Do teachers at your local school support NEA's resolutions and legislative program agendas? This would be a good topic for discussion at PTA meetings and for guest editorial columns in local papers. The address for ordering a copy of the current *National Education Association Handbook* is:

NEA Professional Library
P.O. Box 509
West Haven, CT 06516

1-800-229-4200
FAX: 1-203-933-5276

For NEA members $ 5.00
For nonmembers $15.00

■ **Know the NEA Network** Research the voting records on educational issues of your local politicians and find out what relationships your national, state, and local politicians have with NEA. According to NEA, anyone who votes for its favored legislation is a friend of education. Don't believe it. Also, check the national and local organizations you support and to which you belong to learn how they relate to NEA. If you find an organization that supports NEA's legislative and political action programs, consider dropping your contribution to or membership in the organization. Be certain to tell the organization's leaders the reasons for your actions, and let other people know what you did and why.

■ **Stop National Education Standards** For those who have grown up believing standards come only from the federal government, the fact that our federal government is now working to establish national education standards seems unremarkable—something to be accepted. Yet this assault on the Constitution is anything but acceptable. The central problem is that the Constitution does not put the federal government in control of public education. National educational standards—even voluntary national standards—are in conflict with the Constitution's provision reserving the powers of education to the states.

Who, then, should develop education standards? According to the Tenth Amendment, the individual states or the people of each state. If multistate standards are desirable, they should come about through a voluntary confederation of states. Standards thus derived will be less likely to reflect the political might and long arm of NEA. Additionally, state-consortium standards should be standards that individual states can decide to use as they see best. We must resist any move to nationalize, centralize, and standardize public education.

■ **Monitor Money Spent on Education** Public education is a huge enterprise requiring a constant infusion of tax funds to support it. But what level of funding is necessary to achieve desired results? For NEA, the answer is simple: The taxpayer must provide more and more money. NEA equates increased funding with better education, or at least this is the frequently heard justification of NEA's unending demands for more money from all levels of government.

The federal government should not be spending money on public K-12 education. The reality, however, is that Uncle Sam spends huge sums on public education, as do states and communities. The amount of money spent on a per-pupil basis is one indicator of a school's fiscal efficiency. Data are available (or should be) from your local schools and school district regarding per-pupil costs, from your state regarding both state average per-pupil costs and comparative data for all the school districts in your state, and from the National Center for Education Statistics for all fifty states. Parents and taxpayers can use these data to monitor a school's efficiency, a school district's efficiency, and a state's efficiency.

Some educators consider their mission to be above this kind of measuring. NEA has conditioned them to believe that the economic limitations that are realities for everyone else in society should not be their reality. This strange notion contributes to some educators' belief that money, money, and more money is the answer to public education's problems.

Monitoring money is not an end in itself. One reason for monitoring the money spent on education is to gain information to help you help others to understand that resources are limited. Because resources are limited, educators must use them well to achieve the educational goals local communities wish to achieve. Another purpose is to help parents, taxpayers, and educators learn that more money by itself does not guarantee improved results. Finally, this information will help you confront and refute NEA's deceitful claims that schools always need more money to serve children's needs. NEA uses children as hostages to capture more money from taxpayers and to convert that money into increased NEA dues and political clout.

This is not an argument for reducing educational funding or for compensating teachers poorly. Rather, it is an argument for funding education as close to the point of delivery as possible and for monitoring the efficient use of the money. Education is not an exact science, but we can get better at funding what parents and taxpayers want and at finding better ways to get more for the money spent.

- **End Administrative Associations' Support of NEA** Rank-and-file members of the National Association of School Boards, American Association of School Administrators, National Association of Secondary School Principals, and National Association of Elementary School Principals should demand that their associations take aggressive national- and state-level actions to confront, make public, and defeat those NEA programs, strategies, and tactics that hobble administrators and prevent them from being the leaders their schools and communities deserve.

  The strategy of these organizations has been to coexist peacefully with NEA and to establish a coalition that organization leaders can call on when a piece of legislation they desire needs NEA's support. Meanwhile, NEA's UniServ agents and tactics bombard principals. It is time administrative associations take action to help and support working principals and other district-level and building-level administrators.

  The elected officers and hired staff of national administrative associations should work each year with their memberships to determine which NEA programs and practices hinder administrators from doing their jobs. The leadership of each association should then develop a plan to confront and eliminate these NEA programs and practices. At the end of the year, the associations' leadership should report to the membership and explain what they accomplished, what was left undone, what needs to be done next, and who should do it. The same holds true for state-level administrative associations.

  If there are no significant differences between NEA's programs and practices and those of an administrative association, then one is unnecessary. Parents and taxpayers should be aware of the actions of all these associations and communicate their desire that the associations help bring public education back under local control.

STATE-LEVEL ACTIONS

- **Eliminate Compulsory Public-Sector Collective Bargaining** As we have seen, compulsory public-sector collective bargaining is unconstitutional and actively works against the principles and practices of representative government.[10] Compulsory public-sector collective bargaining should not be modified, adjusted, or otherwise "fixed."

Beyond the unconstitutionality of compulsory public-sector collective bargaining, the premise that it can efficiently manage personnel issues in the workplace is wrong. And derivatives of a wrong premise can only be wrong. Compulsory public-sector collective bargaining should be stricken from state statutes and made illegal, as in North Carolina and Virginia where the practice has been found to violate each state's constitution.

Collective bargaining and forced unionism are NEA's lifeblood. NEA will unleash all its fury and resources to stop efforts to roll back compulsory public-sector collective bargaining. That it has been used for decades is irrelevant. That it is a preferred tool of public-sector labor unions is irrelevant. That it is convenient for NEA and other members of the Unholy Alliance is irrelevant. What is relevant is that it is unconstitutional and all laws and regulations that compel its use should be (1) rescinded and (2) rewritten to forbid its use.

What will replace compulsory public-sector collective bargaining? How will school districts determine teachers' compensation? Boldly departing from the current NEA-controlled system, school districts will find that the systems used in countless corporations and businesses work quite well. Without getting too much into the philosophies and mechanics of commonly used compensation systems, it would be simple enough to establish ranges of compensation for different jobs and then use individual or group achievement and/or performance to determine merit pay within the range. It is done every day in the private sector and in other public-sector agencies.

Compulsory bargaining is one of the principal roadblocks to instituting results-driven compensation systems. As long as compulsory bargaining remains, there will be no real way to reward anyone for achieving the educational goals of local and state school boards. For, as Upton Sinclair wrote, "It is difficult to get a man to understand something when his salary depends upon his not understanding it."

As it exists today, collective bargaining has grown to include anything and everything UniServ operatives and union negotiators can force onto the bargaining table. NEA uses monopoly collective bargaining to hobble and control teachers, to bludgeon communities until they give in to its demands, and to create public policy during closed negotiations sessions.

In his book, *To Break and Control the Violence of Faction: The Challenge to Representative Government from Compulsory Public-Sector Collective Bargaining*, Harvard-educated Edwin Vieira, Jr., Ph.D. and J.D., wrote that in the ongoing interplay between public-sector unions' goals and the public's interests, harm comes to the public "from the complicity of state legislators and administrators who, through compulsory-collective-bargaining laws and regulations, aid and abet the unions in their designs to compel society to accept political dictation."[11]

NEA did not just divine laws and regulation into existence. It did so with the active assistance of politicians and government officials—who in return got something from NEA. Efforts to change the status quo will be difficult, but not impossible. Those efforts, however, will have to be well thought out. The public-policy arena is littered with the corpses of campaigns launched on the belief that a just cause in itself was enough to win the day.

■ **Roll Back Compulsory Unionism** Chubb and Moe strongly recommended that "[t]he legally prescribed bargaining unit [should] be the individual school.... If teachers in a given school want to join a union or, having done so, want to exact financial or structural concessions [from that school's governing body], that is up to them. But they [should] not be allowed to commit other schools or teachers to the same things, and they must suffer the consequences if their victories put them at a competitive disadvantage in supplying quality education."[12] NEA will fight this idea and its enactment to its dying breath.

We must repeal state laws and regulations that require or support so-called "union shop" or "agency shop" mandates requiring teachers to join NEA. This is America; if teachers want to form a union voluntarily, this is their right—but forced unionism is wrong. Currently, twenty-one states have some form of right-to-work laws that variously prohibit discriminating against teachers for payment or nonpayment of union dues or for membership or nonmembership in a labor union. In the remaining states, NEA still has the power to require teachers to join the union and/or pay dues.

In the same way that public education's near monopoly permits the system to ignore the wishes and needs of its consumers, NEA's near monopoly of public education's teachers permits union bosses to live a life separate from the realities of classroom teachers and other school-based personnel. Since teachers cannot choose not to join the union when the union does not represent their wishes, the union's bosses can do whatever they want.

Compulsory unionism is the hot-button issue for NEA. Whether parents and taxpayers work to roll back compulsory unionism through traditional legislative processes or through the initiative process, NEA will pull out the stops, call in its political favors, and vigorously attack.

- **Stop Automatic Dues Payments to NEA-PAC** Currently, many NEA members regularly and automatically pay, along with their mandated union dues, a sum of money into NEA's political action committees. Compulsory dues-paying teachers often do not realize that NEA uses a portion of their money to support causes and candidates that they find repugnant. We need to change automatic "dues payment procedures" so deductions do not include money for NEA-PAC. Individual NEA members who wish to donate money to NEA-PAC or to specific political causes can do so.

- **Plug NEA's Tax-Money Funnel** NEA requires its members to pay dues. But why do school districts pay tax-supported staff to operate computerized payroll programs that collect membership dues for NEA and then, at each payroll, spend more tax money to transfer these collected dues to NEA? Some districts argue that dues deductions and money transfers take place inexpensively via computer operations—an expected response from members of the Unholy Alliance.

"Expensive" is a matter of opinion, but the simple fact is that public employee time and public tax money are supporting and funding a private union. This practice, common as it is, must end. NEA must find its own way to collect dues from teachers. School districts have no business acting as union enforcers and NEA collection agencies—even for a fee.

■ **Implement School Choice** As earlier discussed, this is not a book about educational reform, *per se*. Yet implementing various forms of school choice is, perhaps, the fastest way to regain control of local schools. In public discussion of school choice, NEA consistently—and predictably—tells tales of gloom and doom, warning about elitists abandoning public education and the certain failure of all school choice efforts.

While some "choice" schools will inevitably fail and go out of business—unlike some public schools that fail but stay in business—the truth is that choice schools are making a difference for students, parents, taxpayers, and teachers.

In a July 1997 article, "School Choice is Working," the *Washington Times* reported that choice schools in Milwaukee, Cleveland, New York, Chicago, and Minnesota are working well. A Harvard University study documents the performance of a voucher program in Milwaukee. The study found that "youngsters in kindergarten through third grade scored 5.5 percentile points higher on standardized tests and 15 percentile points higher in math concepts."[13] And this remarkable success is in central city schools.

Sol Stern, contributing editor for the Manhattan Institute's *City Journal*, more recently visited four publicly funded voucher schools in Milwaukee and Cleveland. In the winter 1999 *Journal* Stern wrote, "What I saw was exhilarating. No one who has spent any time at these schools could fail to be impressed by their orderly, energetic atmosphere and solid academic achievement—all the more impressive when compared with the violent, dysfunctional inner city public schools that were the alternative for these children."[14] Stern believes that "[t]he schools succeed because they are accountable to parents and dedicated to making sure every child learns the fundamentals of civility, hard work and basic education."[15] "I can see," Stern added, "why the education establishment is frightened."[16]

School choice—voucher programs and true charter schools—is showing that NEA's control of schools is bad for everyone involved. The winds of change are blowing, and NEA's house of cards is beginning to tumble.

- **Fund School Students, Not School Districts** Reconceptualize the way education is financed. Change the rules at their core by tightly tying education funding to students and allow parents to choose which school their children attend and which schools thereby receive student-based funding.

  This one change would require restructuring the financial foundations on which contemporary public education is based. It would force significant changes in a state's school districts, office of public education, and legislature. Because this change could force a rethinking of education, it will be targeted by NEA and its many allies. For this reason, a state's voters might need to bypass the legislative process and take the issue directly to the people in the form of an initiative.

- **Keep NEA Out of Private Schools** We can expect NEA to test the waters and look for ways to force into membership the 503,000 teachers and staff[17] that work in private schools. If teachers in private schools wish to unionize, that is their decision. But we should not allow NEA to force them to inherit its old-world mentality, self-serving values, and knack for ruining schools. Of course, one of the best ways private schools can prevent NEA from organizing their teachers is to treat their teachers well, give them clear attainable goals, and help them to accomplish these goals. Schools that treat teachers well will attract and hold the best. Schools that treat teachers poorly will soon lose the teachers they most need. Market forces cut both ways.

(**A Note to Teachers:** Some teachers are not NEA members or are members but no longer wish to tolerate NEA's policies and practices. For teachers who seek the professional association of other teachers and such protections as liability insurance (which can also be individually purchased), Appendix A provides a directory of alternate teacher associations.

As you investigate alternatives or start your own, be careful not to advocate one-best-way solutions to educational, organizational, and political problems—thus becoming another NEA. Additionally, do not begin new teacher associations with the aim of creating one huge association to replace NEA. Perhaps several associations within each state or region would be better. These associations could meet individually whenever they wish and *en masse* annually under the auspices of a confederation of teachers' associations. Such meetings would provide the benefits of intergroup exchange while supporting the growth and development of smaller associations that better match individual interests, needs, and beliefs.)

- ■ **Promote Educational Enterprise Zones** In her 1984 book, *NEA: Propaganda Front of the Radical Left*, Sally D. Reed presented the concept of an Educational Enterprise Zone (EEZ) and described it as an "innovative, bold new concept... intended to reduce centralized bureaucratic control of local schools, [and] remove union restrictions and burdensome state regulations in a designated school district or zone, thereby promoting parental and community involvement. The prime objective of the EEZ is to return control of the school to parents and community members."[18]

  Some state reform plans encourage teachers to set up and operate their own publicly funded schools; in Minnesota and elsewhere, such schools are called charter schools. Teachers ask permission of the local school board to establish and operate public schools of a specified design. Most districts require that certified teachers provide the instruction, and some teachers have started such charter schools.

Why not extend the offer to parents who wish to hire teachers to start and operate a locally controlled public or private school taught by certified or uncertified teachers?

Where tuition tax credit, vouchers, and other choices are not available, this option would allow parents to petition state departments of education or state school boards for funding to support a unique educational program. Departments of education or state school boards might grant the parent group funds to hire a core of people to help bring their concept to life. Some states allow educators to petition the department of education for a variance from state rules and regulations; parents could also request such variances. These would include an exemption from requirements to join and/or support a teachers' union and follow the terms and conditions of local negotiated agreements.

Once parents obtain variances, they could hire teachers and a principal who support their concept for a school and agree to work under the variances. In this way, EEZ schools would be more responsive to parents and their ideas of good schooling. EEZ schools could be completely independent from local school boards, or local boards could assume some responsibility but share the direction and operational oversight with EEZ neighborhood parent groups.

■ **Research the Research** Research is fundamentally important to finding and developing better ways to learn, teach, and organize education. While not all research is worth what taxpayers pay for it, many potentially good ideas and questions go unresearched because they would challenge the status quo of the education establishment. Each state's citizens should know or be able to find out what their tax-supported universities and colleges are researching.

Like university research, university-level education programs play a major part in public education's status-quo. Few of today's education courses challenge the existing order. They do not search for new ways to learn and teach and govern. Programs in education administration abound with courses on teachers' rights, and the university's message to future administrators is that they had better abide by the rules NEA has woven into statute law, case law, state regulations, school board policy, and negotiated agreements.

Maybe those universities should offer some different courses. One might be entitled *Administrator Duty: The Responsibility of Administrators to Lead Schools by Demanding and Supporting Good Teaching*. Another course might be *Lead, Follow, Or Get Out Of The Way: A Primer for Principals, Superintendents, and School Board Members*. A third could be *The Educational Entrepreneur: How to Start and Operate Your Own School*. And still another might be *The Educational Revolutionist's Cookbook: One-Hundred-and-One Formulas for Changing an Adults-First System to a Students-First System*.

The existing system functions to support and perpetuate itself. Few education researchers and university professors of education administration step outside the known box to search for different and better ways. The wave-makers are people like Chris Whittle, John Chubb, Terry Moe, and others who live and function outside the education cartel.

Universities should accomplish and publish research that allows those concerned about American education to lobby state legislatures for relief from archaic laws, regulations, and practices. Universities should form partnerships with school districts to pioneer more effective approaches to K-12 education. Some of this is happening, but not enough.

Higher education has long traditions of autonomy and independence. These traditions are important to academic freedom—so that those in power do not inappropriately limit or direct research. Universities are also tuition- and tax-supported and are responsible to the people they directly serve and to the greater community from which they draw support. Taxpayers might ask state legislators to require colleges of education to report annually what they are doing to bring about more effective and efficient K-12 public education.

Something akin to this is happening in South Carolina. In its article, "Earning Appropriations: States Link Spending on

Colleges to Progress in Meeting Specific Goals," *The Chronicle of Higher Education* described how South Carolina has changed the funding procedures for its colleges. The South Carolina General Assembly voted overwhelmingly to stipulate that "the amount of money each public college gets from the state will depend entirely on its progress in meeting a list of goals."[19] This funding is tied directly to the achievement of pre-identified goals.

■ **Stop Strikes** Like falling leaves, teacher strikes are a predictable occurrence each September. Too often, striking teachers are acting illegally. Why, students must wonder, do their teachers break the law? My teacher breaks the law because: (1) laws are not really important to a free, democratic people, (2) teachers are above the law, (3) teacher unions have special privileges others don't have, or (4) those in authority are afraid to enforce the laws because this might upset powerful teacher union bosses?

We should either enforce state laws that preclude teacher strikes or change the laws. To have laws against teacher strikes but not enforce them makes us accomplices to teacher unions' unlawful behavior.

Whatever the legal, ethical, and moral issues, union officials can easily call strikes because members risk nothing by walking out on their jobs. NEA power brokers have gotten state laws that require a minimum number of school days each year, so striking teachers know they will eventually work their full contract and receive their full salary; they may have to work a few Saturdays, but they will get all their money. Even during illegal strikes, teachers' benefits, seniority, and tenure apply throughout the strike. Laws and practices must change so school calendars stay intact and striking union members are not paid for the time they do not perform their duties.

NEA, in response, will argue that teacher unions are different and that teachers strike only when school boards are unreasonable and insensitive to their needs. Ironically, in the spring of 1971 NEA's own employees' organization called a strike against it just as NEA was preparing for the annual Representative Assembly meeting. NEA spokesman Allan West explained that the strike occurred "when agreement could not be reached within the limits set by the [NEA] Executive Committee."[20]

NEA's Executive Committee apparently understands that responsible leadership requires setting limits beyond which an organization will not go. Even NEA has labored under financial constraints akin to those of school board members.

In his effort to explain how difficult this situation had been for NEA management, West confided:

> Living through a strike is always difficult. For the NEA, it was especially hard, even traumatic, for some of the management personnel. They had been leaders in winning the right to bargain for teachers, had walked the picket lines and encouraged members to take the risks involved in aggressive action to achieve better school conditions.
>
> But striking against an employee organization was different. That organization had demonstrated publicly its sensitivity to the needs of employees. Why didn't the employees trust them? Why did they fail to recognize that there were reasonable limits beyond which we could not go?[21]

So, "striking against an employee organization was different." All this time I thought schools were different. I thought because of the children they teach, because of the faith they must keep with parents, and because of the central and fundamental role they hold in our communities, that schools were special, even noble institutions. Evidently NEA does not think so. Schools are struck, students abandoned, laws violated, contracts broken, and trusts traded. NEA is not a professional association interested in the well-being of children; NEA is a labor union.

In Michigan, the long-standing ban on teacher strikes has finally been enforced. Governor John Engler signed into law— effective April 1, 1995—sweeping changes in the way teacher unions and school boards do business. To enforce the ban on teacher strikes, "[a] fine of $5,000 per day will be levied on striking unions, and teachers will be docked one day's pay for every day they walk. The district will be fined $5,000 a day and board members will be docked $250 a day. Neither unions nor school boards will be permitted to compensate themselves for strike fines in any bargaining agreement."[22]

But as this book was going to press, NEA members were illegally striking[23] school districts across the length and breadth of Washington State. Unlike their counterparts in Michigan, Washington State authorities—governor, superintendent of public instruction, school board members, and school district superintendents—are apparently not concerned about the illegality of the teacher strikes or how best to serve students' needs and taxpayers' interests. They are instead considering whether teachers should be able to claim and receive sick-leave pay for the time they walk picket lines and lobby the public and state legislature. In Washington State, it would seem that taxpayers are obligated to subsidize aggressive union activities and students are expected to ignore union teachers' breaking state law, breaching contracts, and boosting public money to support illegal strikes.

- **Repeal State Tenure Laws** Tenure, touted as a form of academic freedom,[24] is a product of another time and another place. If it is applicable at all, it is applicable only to higher education.

    At the K-12 level, tenure is just another teacher-union strategy to gain life-long salaries for its members—and, therefore, cash flow for NEA—regardless of a teacher's effectiveness. Coupled with state department of education regulations and negotiated agreements, state tenure laws restrict how principals assign teachers and make it all but impossible to change the structure of schools. Tenure unnecessarily complicates staffing decisions and works against the flexibility needed to meet new demands and circumstances.

    In a competitive market eager for good teachers, an individual school wishing to grant tenure as a condition of its employment contract with a specific teacher can do so—that is the school's business. Tenure awarded for individual merit is one thing; tenure granted to all teachers as a reward for coming to work for two or three years is ridiculous. We must repeal state tenure laws.

■ **Give Teachers Choice** The present teacher retirement system requires teachers to work in one district or one state in order to build and protect retirement benefits. This makes it difficult for teachers to move in order to try something new or work with different people on an interesting project. Instead, teachers stay year after year in the same district and, often, even in the same school, if not the same classroom.

Many teachers in higher education, however, are able to move from state to state while still contributing to a non-state-specific retirement program. K-12 teachers would benefit from a choice of retirement programs provided by a confederation of states or by privately managed companies. Under the current state-provided systems, NEA's union bosses usually have a good deal of influence over the boards that direct teacher retirement programs. Any move away from this established order diminishes NEA's control of money and teachers, and would provide teachers more control over their own career paths and retirement plans.

Such programs would also begin to move one element of public education out of the public and into the private sector. Now state governments collect taxes—take your money—to raise the funds needed to manage investment and retirement programs. In the private sector, people who manage such programs make money, pay salaries from profits or fees, and contribute to a community's or state's economic strength.

LOCAL-LEVEL ACTIONS

■ **Eliminate Compulsory Public-Sector Collective Bargaining** Similar to actions taken at the state level to eliminate compulsory public-sector collective bargaining, actions at the local level can accomplish what may not immediately change at the state level.

Of course, any local effort to rescind NEA's most powerful tool of intimidation and control will attract state UniServ operatives and even national NEA bosses. This issue, nonetheless, is at the heart of efforts to return control of schools to parents and communities.

■ **Form a Citizens Information Group** In Philadelphia in 1996 the Philadelphia Campaign for Public Education was formed to intervene and lend some sanity to a bitter battle between David Hornbeck—a reform-minded superintendent—and a local chapter of the American Federation of Teachers. The group's mission was to disseminate accurate information about the teachers' union and the positions union activists were taking in their personalized attack on Hornbeck. In response to the union's massive advertising campaign against the superintendent—a union strategy that stems from Saul Alinsky's advice to personalize issues and target individuals—the Philadelphia Campaign published color newsletters using charts and graphs to show how the union's position on issues was not in the best interests of children or taxpayers. One newsletter, for example, published a union contract's work rule that blatantly declared "open positions in schools are filled according to a pecking order that favors [seniority] over all other factors."[25]

Sol Stern, author of "How Teachers Unions Handcuff Schools," studied this case and observed that the union was initially outraged but later began to negotiate with Hornbeck. In the end, the union signed a new contract that included one of Hornbeck's goals: "[T]eachers who receive an unsatisfactory [performance] rating lose their automatic pay increase—a provision," according to Stern, "that seems utterly unexceptional to a normal person but is revolutionary in the context of teacher unionism."[26]

How did the group tackle the issues? It made available to the public, in easily understandable text and graphics, what most people do not know or take time to examine:

■ data and graphs showing the length of Philadelphia's school day in relation to other districts' school days;

- provisions in the contract that show clearly how unions control schools in their best interests and not in the interests of students;
- rules that prevent dismissal of incompetent teachers; and
- rules that force principals to hire teachers based on seniority.[27]

The creation of groups such as this, groups that refuse to be intimidated by NEA or AFT and that intervene in the nasty personal campaigns that unions throw up, is a powerful local-level action. It provides a base for all the recommended actions that follow.

- **Get Involved** Run for a school board, sit on a site-based management team, join the PTA, attend meetings, and talk individually or in small groups with the principal to ask questions about the current condition and future direction of the school program. Come to your own conclusions about what is happening in your district as a result of NEA's policies and practices. In doing so, you will begin to learn what NEA is doing in your schools and what effects it has on children and teachers.

Remember that NEA members are not inhibited by laws or codes of professional behavior—they can and do publicly criticize school administrators. NEA plays both the public media and the private rumor mill with an effectiveness that comes from years of practice. But laws do preclude school principals from discussing many personnel issues, and a code of professional ethics strictly prevents them from engaging in the rumor mill. These restrictions often put principals at a disadvantage with NEA. This, therefore, is an excellent opportunity for a citizen information group to help put clear issues and real facts before the public.

When involved in meetings and discussions, you might ask in reference to particular issues and proposals: "How will this contribute to student learning and student welfare?"

It is a simple question, but one that is not asked often enough. The first response elicited is often a rebuke for having dared to asked such an "inappropriate" question. Do not be put off by hostile responses, and do not allow unclear responses to go unclarified.

- **Read the Negotiated Agreement** Obtain and read a copy of the negotiated agreement between your district and teacher union and ask: "How will this contribute to student learning and student welfare?" NEA has moved well past bread-and-butter union issues and is deeply involved in educational and public policy issues.

  As you examine the negotiated agreement, you are likely to see numerous provisions and school board concessions that only protect the union and its activist members. You will also see provisions that prevent good teachers from doing the jobs they want to do. If you see something you find objectionable, work with other parents and taxpayers to communicate with the school board what should or should not be allowed into the next negotiated agreement. Open the closed process, and bring it into the public's view.

- **Open Negotiations** Best, of course, would be to rid communities, school districts, and teachers of NEA-style compulsory public-sector collective bargaining. What follows is offered only until this is achieved.

  Under protection of closed negotiations meetings, NEA demands and often gets benefits and concessions it would find difficult if not impossible to request in full view of the public. To help keep the process student-focused, parents and taxpayers should insist that school boards and state legislatures make negotiations sessions and materials, including NEA's initial demand package, available for public review.

  Moving negotiations into the open may be the easy part. Because contract negotiations frequently take months and meetings are generally laborious and detailed, consistent attendance at meetings will require the efforts of more than one or two people.

  Anticipate this by forming a negotiations observation tag-team, the members of which can spell one another at the meetings. And remember: NEA negotiators will try to co-opt your group into "understanding" or even supporting their contract demands. This can be OK; *teachers* have legitimate needs. But union take-over of the principles and mechanisms of local control is not among them.

Attendance at negotiations meetings, as important as it is, will not be enough to keep NEA reasonable. Your tag-team should develop a way to report regularly to parents and the community; this might be something a Philadelphia-style citizens information group could do.

- **Tighten the Contract** The following actions are stop-gaps that you can take until needed fundamental changes are achieved.
    1. **Limit What Can Be Bargained** Like Representative Chuck Carpenter and his colleagues in the Oregon legislature (Chapter 10), to limit the subjects the union can bargain to wages, benefits, and working conditions.
    2. **Limit What Can Be Grieved** (A grievance is the filing of a complaint based on an alleged violation of some article of the master contract.) Do not allow the union to use grievances as tools to expand the contract beyond what was negotiated or to create "rights" outside the subjects of wages, benefits, and working conditions.
- **Eliminate Master Contracts and Lock-Step Salary Schedules** NEA negotiates a master contract that binds all the teachers of a district. The ultimate goal is to change laws so that teachers can individually negotiate their own employment contracts—as is done every day in private-sector hiring and performance review meetings.
- **Eliminate Binding Arbitration** It is essential that individual teachers have some means for resolving disputes with administrators; it is also essential that NEA not continue to convert this legitimate need into one more tactic for gaining control of schools. Myriad laws and regulations exist to support employees—including teachers—who wish to resolve a dispute with an immediate supervisor. Effective models are used in the private sector every day.

In districts where binding arbitration cannot be eliminated outright, and since it is unresolved grievances that lead to binding arbitration, it is important that you read the grievance provisions of the local contract. Then talk with experienced administrators to learn if, in the process of providing teachers a means to resolve disputes, grievance provisions cause undue administrative constraint. If they do, communicate your concern to the board of education and to the public at large. If, for example, grievance procedures insulate union members from responsibility for their actions, the board must take steps to connect staff performance to staff accountability.

■ **End Maintenance of Standards** Inspect your local negotiated agreement, and talk with the district administrator who is responsible for contract negotiations and with building principals—who must implement negotiated agreements—to learn if school administrators work under the constraints of a maintenance-of-standards agreement. If they do, tell the school board of your dissatisfaction with this tool of union control. The sooner school administrators are free to do what is best for students without first considering if their every action will paint their school into a maintenance-of-standards corner, the sooner students will begin to get the kind of education parents and taxpayers want.

■ **Use "Out-Sourcing"** Demand that your local school board both protect and appropriately use its ability to contract for services. Because out-sourcing undermines its monopolistic control of a school district's labor force, NEA is adamantly opposed to it. Out-sourcing often provides districts the same or better services and increased control at lower costs. As the Hudson Institute put it, "Rather than attempting to bring about reform by forcing schools to comply with rules and procedures, out-sourcing uses results for quality control. Private firms are contractually bound to reach specific goals. If a private manager does not produce the agreed-upon results, its contract can be canceled."[28] Try that with NEA. Performance-based compensation is what accountability is about, and this is one reason why NEA fights any attempt to use out-sourcing.

■ **Volunteer Your Services** Many private schools require parents to assist in the school a minimum number of hours each school year. Parent or not, you might volunteer your services to your local school. Listen to teachers to learn their concerns and needs.

Most teachers teach well. Most teachers are professional and committed. Yet, the core of "union" teachers seems too often to be the group that speaks for the faculty and controls the school. If it were otherwise, if the professional and committed teachers spoke for the faculty and controlled the teacher-politics of the school, the world of public education would be different and much better.

- **Undo NEA's Web of Financial Support** To avoid the Mafia-like control many Michigan NEA locals have over school boards (e.g., being able to choose which vendors provide health insurance coverage to school districts), investigate the connections between providers of such services and NEA organizations. Inform your school board members about Michigan's MESSA mess so they know what to look for, and support them in resisting NEA's efforts to import or maintain similar scams in your school district. In this and like issues, you can work with objective local reporters to investigate and publish information. Or, as in Philadelphia, start your own citizens information group.

- **Burn the Ships (Sell the Schools)** Like Hernando Cortez, who burned his ships to commit his crew to the enterprise of discovery, communities should investigate the benefits of selling school buildings, land, support facilities, bus fleets, and other assets. If your community does decide to sell some assets, it can then contract out education services and provide choice and voucher options to private-sector education enterprises. This would liberate taxpayers and educational entrepreneurs from the confining effects of outdated buildings and outdated ways of structuring education.

The sale of assets may produce a single, lump-sum payment or, depending upon how sales are structured, a cash stream. Even if no revenue came from such sales, some communities would be ahead of the game just to get out from under the stifling confinement of factory-style buildings and the burden of paying for artifacts of bygone eras.

Through this method, parents and taxpayers could effect "change by imposition" on an NEA-driven system that has historically imposed its wants on parents and taxpayers. Some of the benefits gained from selling publicly-owned education assets might include:

- forcing the innovation of more productive forms of education;
- encouraging smaller and more intimate "schools" and similar education enterprises;
- allowing education enterprises to locate closer to student homes and neighborhoods;
- requiring less pupil transportation;
- encouraging flexibility in the location and design of physical plants;
- relieving taxpayers from supporting, students from attending, and teachers from teaching in factory-style schools;
- providing ways for parents to be more directly involved in the formation and oversight of schools;
- testing the idea that schools boards as they are defined today are not necessary to the creation and operation of education enterprises—market forces responding to parents and communities would support the good and abandon the bad;
- testing the idea that superintendents as they are defined today and large district office staffs are not necessary to the creation and operation of educational enterprises (This would allow moving more resources to the schools.);
- inviting private enterprise to convert schools into retirement homes to house the baby boomers whose numbers originally required their construction; and
- allowing privatization proponents and the dynamics of the market to create options and develop solutions that could never exist under the present system.

■ **Change Superintendents into Education Services Brokers**
Instead of rewarding superintendents for building buildings, hiring staff, and otherwise extending an old paradigm, redefine the job to that of an educational services broker (ESB) who contracts with public and private entrepreneurs for specified educational services. Under this arrangement, the ESB would identify educational needs, write performance specifi-

cations, and contract for services. Once services are contracted, the ESB would monitor compliance and student performance. Approaches that meet and exceed performance specifications are rewarded. Approaches that do not are revised or discontinued.

This would require innovation and flexibility. From it might come a variety of independent public and private partnerships and joint ventures with, for example, libraries or community colleges.

Of course, state laws and funding mechanisms would eventually need to change to support this approach. Initially, demonstration projects could secure waivers from existing laws and regulations.

- **Help School Boards and Superintendents** Help your school board and superintendent stand against union demands and NEA's attempts to control public education. Do not let the Unholy Alliance be your board and superintendent's only or best refuge. At the same time, if you detect that the Unholy Alliance has a firm grip on your board and superintendent, do your utmost to bring the facts to light and break up the Unholy Alliance.

- **Question Class-Size Limits** NEA uses this issue to camouflage its real goal, which is gaining more dues-paying union members. If parents and taxpayers want smaller classes, they might consider shifting resources to hire more elementary classroom teachers or paying more taxes.

- **Question Elementary School Specialists** Hiring specialists would make elementary schools much like high schools— where teachers have, by comparison, passing relationships with their students.

Ask school boards and administrators why they are considering hiring elementary specialists, and be ready to debate the issue on educational and economic levels. If the existing negotiated agreement mandates elementary specialists or class-size limits, you will need to convince the board to negotiate an end to NEA's control of issues that are—or should be—the school board's to control. Encourage your district to investigate the use of less expensive ways to accomplish desired results—team teaching, for example. If all else fails, remember that voters control who sits on school boards and whether operation and maintenance levies pass or fail.

■ **Join the PTA** Join your PTA and help it work for all parents, teachers, and students rather than for NEA. You might serve as a national or state officer and work to move the PTA from under NEA's control. If necessary, consider starting a different parent group to work with and support your school. Remember the Philadelphia Campaign for Public Education.

■ **Question School Levies and Bonds** If you decide to support a building project, make certain the language of the bond issue and the fund-transfer practices of the school district do not allow bond money to go to support operational costs; this may be a state-level accounting code issue. Bond money should not supplant some other budget fund that can legally—if not deceptively—be transferred and then used to support NEA's habits. When a community wishes to pay its teachers more, the ways and means to increase salaries and benefits should be openly discussed.

■ **Stop NEA's Misuse of Children** NEA activists use children to carry their message and advance their causes. This can be seen, for example, when these activists encourage "a concerned student" to speak against something NEA dislikes.

Sometimes NEA members blatantly insist that students and parents support their demands and threaten reprisals if students or parents refuse. In at least one instance, NEA members held students and parents hostage by "refusing to write college recommendations unless the students and their families supported aspects of the union's agenda."[29] One way to stop this is to expose every instance when NEA activists turn your concerns about NEA into punishment of your children. Inform your school principal should reprisals be threatened or taken. And then demand action.

The Need for New Ways of Thinking

Albert Einstein warned, "Everything has changed but our ways of thinking, and if these do not change we will drift toward unparalleled catastrophe." Clearly NEA is mired in wrong ways of thinking. Its principal aims—(1) the control of public education through centralization and standardization, and (2) the control of teachers through compulsory public-sector collective bargaining and forced dues payment—will continue to push public education toward unparalleled catastrophe. We need new ways of thinking and new ways of acting.

The recommendations in this chapter suggest countermeasures to problems discussed throughout the book. These recommendations cannot exhaustively sum up all that must be done. Rather, they are like water used to prime a pump that, once primed, flows productively. You and others will develop and act on ideas that will depose NEA and return control of neighborhood schools to parents, taxpayers, and communities. In this lies the importance of this book.

Which Path to Which Future?

The future is uncertain and cannot be known. Yet we have to make decisions, and our decisions influence the future. Sometimes we discover that one or more of our decisions put us on a wrong path. In the case of public education, a series of decisions has led to loss of local control over neighborhood schools.

We must move away from the stifling system of public education that NEA controls. The one-best-way strategy has not worked, and we must take great care not to replace the existing bureaucracy with another dysfunctional, one-size-fits-all bureaucracy.

The solution lies in many solutions.

With expulsion of the federal government from public education, American ingenuity and the many ideas that will come from the states will provide the best possible education for students, produce answers to our questions, and provide solutions to our challenges. A greatly redesigned system of public schools may be the outcome.

In addition, we might also have an assortment of private nonprofit and for-profit educational enterprises and continuing growth of home schooling.

The soft conspiracy of self-inflicted sameness and compliance has been deadly to individual initiative and to the effectiveness of public education. This soft conspiracy has allowed the hard conspiracy perpetrated by the largest labor union in our nation to create and control one system of public education.

In truth, today's public schools are not students', parents', and taxpayers' schools. They are not even teachers' schools. Public schools belong to NEA. The Unholy Alliance that binds NEA, school boards, and superintendents continues to protect itself against internal or external forces that threaten its survival. To a large degree, NEA is in control of public education because we have allowed NEA to be in control. If we continue to play NEA's game by NEA's rules, NEA will continue to spend our money, control our schools, and decide our children's values.

Parents, taxpayers, and educators who wish to regain control of their neighborhood schools should follow two paths: (1) work within the existing system to take public schools from NEA's control, to break up and realign the Unholy Alliance, and to reconfigure the existing system of public schooling into many smaller, locally controlled schools, and (2) work outside the system to foster and support private nonprofit and for-profit educational enterprises constituted and conducted outside NEA's influence. These two paths will give parents choices. They may choose to send their children to a new generation of public schools or to a variety of private-sector options—including home schools. For now, NEA has effectively stopped market forces and parent choice in the majority of our schools.

We are at a crossroads. Either parents and taxpayers topple NEA's hidden hierarchies and bring an end to NEA's grab for power, or NEA will continue to run and ruin our schools. There are no other choices.

Appendix A

....

ALTERNATE TEACHER ORGANIZATIONS
AND
TEACHER ASSISTANCE ORGANIZATIONS

Information about the majority of these organizations is from the Concerned Educators Against Forced Unionism's list of alternate teacher organizations. Since some might also be interested in learning about Concerned Educators Against Forced Unionism, I have included its address and the address of the National Right to Work Legal Defense Foundation, Incorporated—both are listed on the last page under Teacher Assistance Organizations.

ALTERNATIVE TEACHER ORGANIZATIONS

Mr. Jim Parsons
Executive Director
Arkansas Christian Educators
　Association
707 Turtle Creek Drive
Rogers, AR 72756
501 631-7347

Mr. David Smith
Arizona State Professional
　Educators
1412 East Broadway
Mesa, AZ 85204
602 834-5182

Mr. David Smith
President
Mesa Independent Professional
    Educators
1401 E. Broadway, Suite C
Mesa, AZ 85204
602 834-5182

Ms. Dianne Foster, President
Professional Educators Group
    of California (PEG)
PO Box 375
Livermore, CA 94550

Mr. Gary Beckner, Executive
    Director
Association of American
    Educators
26012 Marguerite Parkway,
    #333
Mission Viejo, CA 92692-3263

Mr. William Crockett, President
National Association of
    Professional Educators
412 First Street, SE
Washington, DC 20003
202 484-8969

Dr. Barbara Christmas
Professional Association of
    Georgia Educators
3700 B Market St.
Clarkston, GA 30021

Highland Professional
    Educators
1330 Old Trenton Road
Highland, IL 62249

Ms. Jane Ping, President
Indiana Professional Educators
    (IPE)
6919 E. 10th St., Suite B4
Indianapolis, IN 46219
317 356-2878

Mr. Dennis Norman
Alliance of Professional
    Educators (APE)
795 Fox River Road
Valparaiso, IN 46383

Mr. Jeff Fritz
Clay Community Organization
    of Professional Educators
RR2, Box 120-A
Clay City, IN 47841

Mr. Don Georg
Professional Educators of Iowa
    (PEI)
PO Box 564
Oskaloosa, IA 52577
515 255-2859

Professional Educators
    Association of Kansas
    (PEAK)
Route 3, Box 236
Baldwin, KS 66006

Ms. Ruth Greene, Executive
 Director
Kentucky Association of
 Professional Educators
 (KAPE)
PO Box 24506
Lexington, KY 40524-4566

Mr. Jim McDavitt, Director
Kansas Education Watch NET
PO Box 483
Wichita, KS 67201

Mr. William II. Matthews
Associated Professional
 Educators of Louisiana
 (APEL)
PO Box 14265
Baton Rouge, LA 70898-4005

Mr. Lon Anderson
A+Plus
17700 Lafayette Drive
Box 143
Olney, MD 20830
301 924-4472

Mrs. Teresa Bryant
Mississippi Professional
 Educators
629 N. Jefferson St.
Jackson, MS 39202-3102

Kent King, Executive Director
Missouri State Teachers
 Association (MSTA)
407 S. 6th St.
Columbia, MO 65201

Professional Educators of North
 Carolina
1212 S. Blvd., Suite 101-A
Charlotte, NC 28203
704 355-0089

Ms. Mary Kosinski
Teachers Opposed to Forced
 Unionism
Box 2122
Plainesville, OH 44077
216 352-4624

Ms. Connie Bancroft
Teachers Saving Children
PO Box 125
Damascus, OH 44619
216 537-2546

Mr. Richard Wingerter
Ohio Professional Teachers
 Independently Organized
 Non-
 Coercively
6969 Stonecreek, NE
North Canton, OH 44721

Mr. Randy Hoffman
Keystone State Teachers
 Association
640 Billet Drive
Mechanicsburg, PA 17055
717 432-5185 or 697-0509

Ms. Ann Monteith
BEST for PA
RD2, Box 132
Annville, PA 17003

Dr. Elizabeth Gressette
Palmetto State Teachers
   Association
2010 Gadsen Street
Columbia, SC 29201

Bradley County Association of
   Professional Educators
PO Box 1443
Cleveland, TN 37364-1443

Mr. Doug Rogers, Executive
   Director
Association of Texas
   Professional Educators
505 E. Huntland Dr., #250
Austin, TX 78752
512 467-0071

Mr. Richard Miller
Congress of Houston Teachers
2103 Chantilly Lane
Houston, TX 77018

Ms. Elizabeth Mow
West VA Professional Educators
36 Central Avenue
Buckhannon, WV 26201

Ms. Megan Lott
National TARS
PO Box 1896
Manassas, VA 22110-1896

Mr. Dave Stuller, Chairman
Vermont Educators for
   Professional Free Choice
PO Box 275
Burlington, VT 05402
802 862-4275

Ms. Beth Graham, Chairman
Coalition of Independent
   Education Associations
505 E. Huntland Dr., #250
Austin, TX 78752
512 467-0071

Ms. Cindy Omlin
WEA (Washington Education
   Association) Challenger
   Network
4815 E. Pineglen Lane
Mead, WA 99021

TEACHER ASSISTANCE ORGANIZATION AND CONSULTANTS

Concerned Educators Against
 Forced Unionism
8001 Braddock Road
Springfield, Virginia 22160
703 321-8519

National Right to Work Legal
 Defense Foundation
8001 Braddock Road
Springfield, Virginia 22160
703 321-8510

Mrs. Jo Seker (former CEAUF
 Director)
Educational Consultant
47 S West Avenue
Shiremanstown, PA 17011

Appendix B

....

COMPULSORY UNIONISM
AND
RIGHT-TO-WORK STATES

Taken from pages 23–28 of "Government Union Review: A Quarterly Journal on Public Sector Labor Relations" by Milton Chappell, Esq. © 1996 by the Public Service Research Foundation, Vienna, Virginia

TEACHER COLLECTIVE BARGAINING
& UNION SECURITY TABLE

State Name	Bargaining Statute	Mandatory Subjects of Bargaining	Compulsory Unionism/ Agency Shop	Collective Bargaining Tolerated
Alabama (model 1)	No[1]	N/A	No-RTW Ala. §25-7-30	Yes
Alaska (model 1	Alaska Stat. §§ 14.20.550, 23.40.070	Employment & fulfillment of professional duties[2]	Yes— §§23.40.110(b) & 23.40.225	N/A

[1] However, school employers must meet & confer on school management, but not pay or benefits.
[2] Additionally, school employers and unions may meet & confer on educational policy.

TEACHER COLLECTIVE BARGAINING
& UNION SECURITY TABLE *(continued)*

State Name	Bargaining Statute	Mandatory Subjects of Bargaining	Compulsory Unionism/ Agency Shop	Collective Bargaining Tolerated
Arizona (Model 4)	No[3]	N/A	No—RTW Ariz. Rev. Stat. Ann § 23-1301	No[4]
Arkansas (Model 3)	No[5]	N/A	No—RTW Ark. Code § 11-3-301	Yes[6]
California (Model 1)	Cal. Gov't § 3540	Matters within the scope of representation[7]	Yes—§§ 3540.1(i), 3546, 3564.3	N/A
Colorado (Model 3)	No	N/A	No[8]	Yes—In 1/3 of the districts
Connecticut (Model 1)	Conn. Gen. § 10-153a	Salaries, hours, empl. terms/conditions	Yes—§ 10-153a(c)	N/A

[3] Any agreement cannot preclude other negotiations or agreements between employer and individual employees or other representatives, nor can agreement be with any exclusive representative. Atty. Gen. Op. No. 74-11 (R-24) (May 20, 1974). However, school board and union may meet & confer on wages, terms & working conditions.

[4] A few districts meet & confer, but no exclusive representation.

[5] However, a written grievance procedure is required.

[6] Public employer may, but does not have to, engage in collective bargaining with an exclusive representative on conditions of employment, grievance procedures, work rules, disciplinary standards and other nonmonetary conditions. Atty. Gen. Op. No. 77-99 (June 10, 1977).

[7] The scope of representation shall include matters relating to wages, hours of employment, and other terms and conditions of employment, which include health and welfare benefits, leave, transfer and reassignment policies, safety conditions, class size, procedure for employee evaluation, union security, grievance procedures and layoffs, § 3543.2. However, § 3547 requires all initial bargaining proposals of the union and the school employer, which become public documents, to be presented at a public meeting of the school board. Moreover, negotiations cannot begin until after the public has had the opportunity to become informed and express itself at another public school board meeting. Additionally, the cost to the school district of the collective bargaining agreement must also be disclosed at a public school board meeting, § 3547.5. Finally, school districts must consult on definition of educational objectives, the determination of the content of courses and curriculum and the selection of textbooks and may consult on the others.

[8] Some school districts provide each teacher a "professional fee" fringe benefit in the amount of the union's dues; while other districts require fee payments, with a "reverse check-off" method to opt out of paying any fees.

TEACHER COLLECTIVE BARGAINING
& UNION SECURITY TABLE *(continued)*

State Name	Bargaining Statute	Mandatory Subjects of Bargaining	Compulsory Unionism/ Agency Shop	Collective Bargaining Tolerated
Delaware (Model 1)	Del. Code Ann. tit. 14, § 4001	Employment terms/conditions[9]	Yes—§§ 4002(s), 4019	N/A
District of Columbia (Model 1)	D.C. Code Ann. § 1-602.1	Wages, hours, union security employment terms/conditions	Yes—§§ 1-618.7 1-618.11	N/A
Florida (Model 2)	Fla. Stat. Ann. § 447.201	Wages, hours, empl. terms/conditions; except pensions[10]	No—RTW Fla. Const. art. 1, § 6	N/A
Georgia (Model 4)	No	N/A	No—RTW Ga. Code Ann. § 34-6 20	No
Hawaii (Model 1)	Haw. Rev. Stat. § 89-1	Wages, salary steps, hours, health fund contributions, employment terms/ conditions[11]	Yes—§§ 89-3.5, 89-4	N/A
Idaho (Model 2)	Idaho Code § 33-1271	Any matter & condition to which the parties agree[12]	No—RTW Idaho Code § 44-2001	N/A
Illinois (Model 1)	115 Ill. Comp. Stat. 5/1	Wages, hours, grievance procedures, employment terms/ conditions	Yes—§ 5/11	N/A

[9] Means matters concerning or related to wages, salaries, hours, grievance procedures and working conditions, § 4002(r). However, matters of inherent managerial policy, such as the functions and programs of the public school employer, its standards of services, overall budget, utilization of technology, the organizational structure, curriculum, discipline and the selection and direction of personnel, are not mandatory subjects of bargaining.

[10] Moreover, negotiations must be open to the public.

[11] School employer must consult over all matters affecting employee relations.

[12] Records of the negotiation are public documents and any contract must be jointly ratified at a public meeting.

TEACHER COLLECTIVE BARGAINING
& UNION SECURITY TABLE *(continued)*

State Name	Bargaining Statute	Mandatory Subjects of Bargaining	Compulsory Unionism/ Agency Shop	Collective Bargaining Tolerated
Indiana (Models 1 & 2)	Ind. Code § 20-7.5-1-1	Salary, wages, hours wage-related fringe benefits, grievance procedures[13]	Yes—contracts entered into before 6/30/95 No—contracts entered into after 6/30/95	N/A
Iowa (Model 2)	Iowa Code § 20.1	Wages, hours, other terms/conditions[14]	No—RTW Iowa Code § 731.1	N/A
Kansas (Model 2)	Kan. Stat. Ann. § 72-5411	Professional service terms/conditions[15]	No—RTW Kan. Stat. Ann. § 44-831	N/A
Kentucky (Model 3)	No	N/A	No	Yes—A few districts
Louisiana (Model 3)	No[16]	N/A	No—RTW La. Rev. Stat. Ann. Rev. 23:981	Yes— § 17:100.4
Maine (Model 2)	Me. Rev. Stat. Stat. Ann. tit. 26, § 961	Wages, hours, working conditions, grievance procedures[17]	No—*Churchill v. Teachers Ass'n*, 97 LRRM 2162 (1977)	N/A
Maryland (Models 1 &2)	Md. Code Ann. Educ. § 6-401	Wages, salaries, hours, working cond., ex. tenure	Yes—in 5 districts;[18] No—in all others	N/A

[13] Must discuss working conditions, curriculum development and revision, textbook selection, teacher methods, student discipline, expulsion or supervision of students, pupil-teacher ratio, class size, budget appropriations, and hiring, promotion, demotion, transfer, assignment and retention of employees, § 20-7.5-1-5.

[14] Vacations, insurance, holidays, leave, shift differential, overtime, supplemental pay, seniority, transfer procedures, job classifications, health & safety, evaluation, staff reduction, in-service training, dues checkoff, grievance procedures, other mutually agreed upon matters, except merit system & retirement. In addition, the initial bargaining proposals must be presented at a public meeting.

[15] The duration of the school term & school hours are excluded from mandatory bargaining subjects. Also, all negotiations are subject to the open meeting law.

[16] School employer must consult & adopt a grievance procedure.

[17] School employer must meet & consult on educational policies.

[18] Baltimore City, Allegheny, Garrett (only to new employees), Montgomery & Washington counties, § 6-407.

TEACHER COLLECTIVE BARGAINING
& UNION SECURITY TABLE *(continued)*

State Name	Bargaining Statute	Mandatory Subjects of Bargaining	Compulsory Unionism/ Agency Shop	Collective Bargaining Tolerated
Massachusetts (Model 1)	Mass. Gen. L. ch. 150E, § 1	wages, hours, productivity & performance standards, class size, workload, empl. terms/conditions	Yes—§ 12	N/A
Michigan (Model 1)	Mich. Comp. Laws § 423.201	Wages, hours, empl. terms/conditions	Yes—§ 433.210	N/A
Minnesota (Model 1)	Minn. Stat. § 179A.01	Grievance procedures, empl. terms/ condition[19]	Yes—§ 179A.06.3	N/A
Mississippi (Model 4)	No	N/A	No—**RTW** Miss. Code Ann. § 71-147	No—CB illegal Atty. Gen. Op.
Missouri (Model 3)	No	N/A	No[20]	Yes[21]
Montana (Model 1)	Mont. Code Ann. § 39-31-010	Wages, hours, fringes, grievance procedures, employment conditions	Yes—§§ 39-31-204, 39-31-401(3)	N/A
Nebraska (Model 2)	Neb. Rev. Stat. § 48-801	Wages, employment terms/conditions	No—**RTW** Neb. Rev. Stat. § 48-217	N/A

[19] School board must meet & confer on policies & other matters, but only with exclusive bargaining representative.

[20] However, one court of appeals has upheld agency fees for teachers.

[21] Teachers may join in groups, including unions, to make proposals to school boards, but boards cannot enter into any agreements or contracts involving more than one teacher. However, boards may consider teacher groups' proposals and are not precluded from adopting the proposals. Atty. Gen. Op. No 275 (Dec. 12, 1968). Nevertheless, courts have allowed collective bargaining agreements, although there are limitations upon what may be enforceable.

[22] *See also* § 288.150 for a long and detailed list of specific subjects of mandatory bargaining and subjects reserved to the employer to discuss with the bargaining agent. Furthermore, school employers must discuss all other subjects.

TEACHER COLLECTIVE BARGAINING
& UNION SECURITY TABLE *(continued)*

State Name	Bargaining Statute	Mandatory Subjects of Bargaining	Compulsory Unionism/ Agency Shop	Collective Bargaining Tolerated
Nevada (Model 2)	Nev. Rev. Stat. § 288.010	Wages, hours, grievance procedures, employment terms/ conditions[23]	No—RTW Nev. Rev. Stat. § 613.230	N/A
New Hampshire (Model 2)	N.H. Rev. Stat. Ann. § 273-A:1	Wages, hours, employment conditions, except merit system	No—Statute prohibits discrimination to encourage union membership[23]	N/A
New Jersey (Model 1)	N.J. Rev. Stat. § 34:13A-1	Disciplinary disputes, employment terms/ conditions	Yes—§ 34:13A-5.5	N/A
*New Mexico (Model 2)	N.M. Stat. Ann. § 10-7D-1	Wages, hours, grievance procedures, employment terms/ conditions, except retirement[24]	Dues deduction a mandatory subject of bargaining, § 10-7D-17.B	N/A
New York (Model 1)	N.W. Civ Serv. § 200	Salaries, wages, hours grievance procedures, empl. terms/conditions	Yes[25]—§§ 201.2(b), 208.3	N/A
North Carolina (Model 4)	No	N/A	No—RTW N.C. Gen. Stat. § 95-78	No[26]—Illegal § 95-98

* In mid-1999, Governor Gary Johnson vetoed reauthorization of New Mexico's monopoly bargaining statute. (Gleason, Stefan and Mark Mix, telephone conversation with author, 10 June 1999.)

[23] This position is currently being litigated. Moreover, the New Hampshire Department of Labor ruled on June 6, 1995, that automatic deduction of agency fees violates the Wage & Hour statute, which requires written authorization by the employee for any deduction from wages. *Ober v. SAU 27—Hudson School Dist.*

[24] This is the latest state to require collective bargaining (1992). Additionally, school employer and union may bargain on any issue.

[25] Agency fee deductions are mandatory and automatic, not negotiable, upon certification of the exclusive bargaining representative.

[26] Joining affiliated union is also illegal, § 95-97.

TEACHER COLLECTIVE BARGAINING
& UNION SECURITY TABLE *(continued)*

State Name	Bargaining Statute	Mandatory Subjects of Bargaining	Compulsory Unionism/ Agency Shop	Collective Bargaining Tolerated
North Dakota (Model 2)	Code§ 15-38.1-01	Employer-employee relations, salaries, wages, empl. terms/ conditions	No—RTW N.D. Cent Code. § 34-01-14[27]	N/A
Ohio (Model 1)	Ohio Rev. Code Ann. § 4117.01	Wages, hours, grievance procedures, employment terms/ conditions[28]	Yes—§ 4117.09(C)	N/A
Oklahoma (Model 2)	Okla. Stat. tit. 70, § 509.1[29]	Wages, hours,fringe benefits, employment terms/conditions	No—Statute silent	N/A
Oregon (Model 1)	Or. Rev. Stat. § 243.650	Employment relations[30]	Yes—§§ 243.666, §§ 243.650(10), 243.672(1)(c)	N/A
Pennsylvania (Model 1)	Pa. Cons. Stat. § 1101.101	Wages, hours, empl. terms/conditions	Yes—§ 1102.1[31]	N/A
Rhode Island (Model 1)	R.E. Gen Laws § 28-9.3-1	Hours, salary, working conditions, professional empl. terms/conditions	Yes[32]— § 28-9.3-7(e)	N/A
South Carolina (Model 4)	No	N/A	No—RTW S.C. Code Ann. § 41-7-10	No

[27] Notwithstanding the Right to Work Law, any nonmember may be charged "actual representation expenses" when the nonmember has specifically requested in writing to use union grievance representation. "Actual representation expenses," cannot include the union's general contract negotiations or collective bargaining expenses, § 34-01-14.1.

[28] Also includes the continuation, modification or deletion of any CBA provision.

[29] However, any person may elect in writing not to be represented by any organization, § 509.2. Also, collective bargaining agreements may not exceed one year.

[30] This includes, but is not limited to, direct or indirect monetary benefits, hours, vacations, sick leave, grievance procedures, employment conditions.

[31] Maintenance of membership is also permitted, § 1101.301(18).

[32] Agency fee deductions are mandatory and automatic, not negotiable, upon certification of the exclusive bargaining representative.

TEACHER COLLECTIVE BARGAINING
& UNION SECURITY TABLE *(continued)*

State Name	Bargaining Statute	Mandatory Subjects of Bargaining	Compulsory Unionism/ Agency Shop	Collective Bargaining Tolerated
South Dakota (Model 2)	S.D. Codified Laws Ann. § 3-18-1	Grievance procedures, employment conditions	No—RTW S.D. Codified Laws Ann. § 60-8.3	N/A
Tennessee (Model 2)	Tenn. Code Ann. § 49-5-601	Grievance procedures, salaries, wages, hours, employment conditions[33]	No—RTW Tenn. Code Ann. § 50-1-201	N/A
Texas (Model 4)	No	N/A	No—RTW Tex. Code Ann. § 101.051	No—Illegal § 101.004[34]
Utah (Model 3)	No	N/A	No—RTW Utah Code Ann. § 34-34-1	Yes
Vermont (Model 2)	Vt. Stat. Ann. tit. 16, § 1981	Salary, related economic conditions, grievance & complaint procedures, mutually agreed matters	No—*Weissenstein v. Burlington Educ. Ass'n*, 128 LRRM 2220 (1988)	N/A
Virginia (Model 4)	No	N/A	No—RTW Va. Code Ann. § 40.1-58	No—Illegal § 40.1-57.2, *Virginia v. Arlington Co. Bd.*, 94 LRRM 2291 (19971)
Washington (Model 1)	Wash. Rev. § 41.59.010	Wages, hours, empl. terms/conditions	Yes— §§ 41.59.060(2) 41.59.100	N/A

[33] Other working conditions include insurance, fringe benefits (excluding State pensions or retirement), leave, student discipline procedures, payroll deductions. School employer and union may discuss other terms and conditions. Negotiations must be open tot the public, § 8-44-201(a).

[34] *Cf. Moreau v. Klevenhagen*, 113 S. Ct. 1905 (1993) (Texas prohibits public sector collective bargaining).

Teacher Collective Bargaining
& Union Security Table *(continued)*

State Name	Bargaining Statute	Mandatory Subjects of Bargaining	Compulsory Unionism/ Agency Shop	Collective Bargaining Tolerated
West Virginia (Model 3)	No	N/A	No	Yes[35]
Wisconsin (Model 1)	Wisc. Stat. § 111.70	Wages, hours, employment conditions	Yes— §§ 111.70(1)(f), (2), (3)(a)3	N/A
Wyoming (Model 3)	No	N/A	No—RTW Wyo. Stat. § 27-7-108	Yes

Model 1   Mandatory, monopoly and compulsory exclusive bargaining—20 states and the District of Columbia.

Model 2   Mandatory monopoly exclusive bargaining without compulsory unionism—14 states

Model 3   No Mandatory bargaining statute, but bargaining is not illegal and does occur at the will of the local school board— 9 states

Model 4   Collective bargaining illegal or not accepted—7 states

[35] County school boards may officially recognize labor unions and negotiate and enter into a collective bargaining agreement with them, but they may not agree to binding arbitration. Atty. Gen. Op., June 26, 1974.

Notes

·····················

PROLOGUE

1. *NEA Journal*, December 1967, 34.
2. Fredrich A. Von Hayek, *The Constitution of Liberty* (Chicago: The University of Chicago, 1980), 269.
3. Peter Brimelow and Leslie Spencer, "The National Extortion Association," *Forbes*, 7 June 1993, 80.
4. Peter Brimelow and Leslie Spencer, "Comeuppance," *Forbes*, 13 February 1995, 121.
5. Ibid., Peter Brimelow and Leslie Spencer, "The National Extortion Association," *Forbes*, 7 June 1993, 79.
6. Allan M. West, *The National Education Association: The Power Base for Education* (New York, New York: The Free Press, 1980), 16.
7. National Education Association, NEA Handbook 1993–1994. (Washington, D.C.: National Education Association, 1993), 244.
8. Charleen Haar, Myron Lieberman, and Leo Troy, *The NEA and AFT: Teacher Unions In Power and Politics* (Rockport, Massachusetts: Pro>Active Publishing, 1994), 66–75.
9. The Kamber Group, "An Institution at Risk: An External Communications Review of the National Education Association," 14 February 1997, ii.
10. Ibid.
11. Ibid
12. Ibid.

13. Ibid., iii.
14. "The Appearance of Reform at the NEA," *The Washington Times*, 16 January 1997.
15. National Education Association, *NEA Handbook 1996–1997.* (Washington, D.C.: National Education Association, 1996), 7.
16. Ibid., 7–8.
17. Albert Shanker, "State of the Union Address," 2 August 1996, Cincinnati, Ohio, available from http://www/aft.org.
18. Mary Crystal Cage, "A Merger Misfires," *The Chronicle of Higher Education*, 17 February 1995, sec. A, 17.
19. National Education Association, *NEA Handbook 1996–1997.* (Washington, D.C.: National Education Association, 1996), 387.
20. Sol Stern, "How Teachers' Unions Handcuff Schools," *City Journal* (Spring 1997): 36.
21. David Tyack and Elisabeth Hansot, *Managers of Virtue*, (New York: Basic Books, Inc., 1982), 140.
22. Ibid.
23. George S. Counts, *Dare the School Build a New Social Order?* (Carbondale, Ill: Southern Illinois University Press, 1978), 26.

CHAPTER ONE

1. Allan M. West, *The National Education Association: The Power Base for Education* (New York: The Free Press, 1980), 1.
2. Ibid., 2.
3. Samuel L. Blumenfeld, *NEA: Trojan Horse in American Education* (Boise: The Paradigm Company, 1993), 19-20.
4. Edgar B. Wesley, *NEA: The First Hundred Years* (New York: Harper, 1957), 24.
5. West, 5.
6. Ibid.
7. Sol Cohen, ed., *Education in the United States, a Documentary History* (New York: Random House, 1974), 1935.
8. Ibid., 1947.
9. Ibid., 1951.
10. Ibid., 2278.
11. Ibid., 2279.

12. Ibid., 2289.
13. West, 9.
14. Ibid., 9–10.
15. Ibid., 41.
16. National Education Association, *NEA Handbook 1993–1994* (Washington, D.C.: National Education Association), 167.
17. Ibid.
18. West, 15.
19. Ibid.
20. Ibid., 16.
21. "Democrats Love Bureaucrats," *Wall Street Journal*, 22 July 1993, sec. A. 14.
22. Ibid.
23. Ibid.
24. Ibid.
25. William P. Hoar, "Monopolizing Teachers," *The New American*, 8 August 1994, 27–28.
26. Ibid.
27. West, 17.
28. Ibid.
29. *NEA Handbook 1993–1994,* 167.
30. West, 18.
31. Ibid., 18-19.
32. James Herndon, *Notes from a Schoolteacher* (New York: Simon and Schuster, 1985), 151.
33. West, 41.
34. Timothy M. McConville, Vice President, National Right to Work Legal Defense Foundation, Inc., Memorandum to author on 29 April 1997.
35. Dan C. Alexander, *Who's Ruining Our Schools? The Case Against the NEA Teacher Union* (Boise: Save Our Schools Research and Education Foundation, 1988), 91.
36. Ibid., 91–92
37. Jeff Archer, "NEA Agrees To Abandon Property-Tax Break," *Education Week,* 1 October 1997.
38. Peter Brimelow and Leslie Spencer, "The National Extortion Association," *Forbes*, 7 June 1993, 81.

39. Dawn Kopecki, "A Behind-The-Scenes Reason for the NEA's Tax Generosity?," *The Washington Times,* 6 October 1997.

40. "National Education Association Pledges $1 Million To D.C. Treasury," 23 September 1997 press release, http://www.nea.org/nr/nr970923.html.

41. Frank W. Andritzky and Joseph G. Andritzky, "The *Enmons* Loophole: A Need to Amend the Hobbs Act," *Government Union Review* (Fall 1986), 37.

42. Blumenfeld, 89.

43. Ibid., 89–90.

44. Sally H. Christensen, Deputy Assistant Secretary for Budget, Department of Education, Letter to author, 11 May 1995. Documents included with this letter are: *The Fiscal Year 1996 Budget: Summary and Background Information prepared by the Department on 6 February 1995; Table 31, "Total expenditures of educational institutions related to the gross domestic product, by level of institution: 1959–60 to 1993–94" from the Department's publication "Digest of Educational Statistics 1994"; the Department's budget from 1980 through 1996 "Education Department Budget by Level, 1980–1996"; and a table pertaining to the full-time equivalent positions in the Department of Education for 1980, 1988, and 1994.*

45. "*Department of Education Fiscal Year 2000 Budget Request,*" The Department of Education, United States of America, 1 February 1999, n.p.

46. Blumenfeld, 170.

47. "Budget Targeted by Lobbyists," *Associated Press News Service,* 27 July 1994.

48. Brimelow, 81.

49. "The NEA Comes to Town," *Washington Post,* 8 July 1992, 28.

50. Ibid.

51. Brimelow, 74.

52. Eugene H. Methvin, "Guess Who Spells Disaster for Education?" *Readers Digest,* May 1984, 91.

53 ."Overwhelming Choice," *Wall Street Journal,* 8 April 1993, sec. A. 14.

54. Brimelow, 74.

55. "A Fierce Fight South of the Border," *Alberta Report,* 15 November 1993.

56. Dave Farrell, "Political Hardball Is MEA's Game," *Detroit News,* 12 December 1993, 1A.

57. "NEA Opposes Immigrant Plan," *The Associated Press News Service,* 4 July 1994.

CHAPTER TWO

1. National Education Association, *NEA Handbook 1993–1994* (Washington, D.C.: National Education Association, 1993), 167.

2. Peter Brimelow and Leslie Spencer, "The National Extortion Association," *Forbes,* 7 June 1993, 79.

3. Peter Brimelow and Leslie Spencer, "Comeuppance," *Forbes,* 13 February 1995, 121.

4. Ibid., 72.

5. Thomas D. Snyder, Charleen M. Hoffman, and Claire M. Geddes, Digest of Educational Statistics 1996 (Washington, D.C.: U.S. Government Printing Office, 1996), 85.

6. *NEA Handbook 1996–1997,* stated, "Dues of active members engaged in or on limited leave of absence from professional education employment shall be .00225 times the national average salary of classroom teachers in public elementary and secondary schools... plus .00055 of the national average annual salary... to be allocated to UniServe grants according to the policy of the Board of Directors" (p. 191).

7. Ibid., National Education Association, *NEA Handbook 1996–1997,* 63–92.

8. Edgar B. Wesley, *NEA: The First Hundred Years* (New York: Harper & Brothers, 1957), 381.

9. NEA's 1995–1996 LM-2 Organization Annual Report (file number 000-342) as filed with the U.S. Department of Labor, Office of Labor-Management Standards and signed off on 19 December 1996.

10. Victoria Lytle, "New Look for Your National Headquarters," *NEA Today,* October 1991, 29.

11. "Budget Targeted by Lobbyists, Associated Press," 27 July 1994.

12. Ibid., Peter Brimelow and Leslie Spencer, "The National Extortion Association," 80.

13. Unless otherwise noted, all information taken from: *NEA Handbook 1993–1994.*

14. Ibid., Peter Brimelow and Leslie Spencer, "The National Extortion Association," 79.

15. Peter Brimelow and Leslie Spencer, "Comeuppance," *Forbes*, 13 February 1994, 126.

16. Ibid.

17. Ibid.

18. Ibid.

19. Ibid., Peter Brimelow and Leslie Spencer, "The National Extortion Association," 83.

20. Charlene K. Haar, Myron Lieberman, and Leo Troy, *The NEA and AFT: Teacher Unions in Power and Politics* (Rockport, Mass.: Pro>Active Publications, 1994), 31.

21. Ibid., Peter Brimelow and Leslie Spencer, "The National Extortion Association," 83.

22. National Education Association, *NEA Handbook 1994–1995* (Washington, D.C.: National Education Association, 1993), 391.

23. Ibid., National Education Association, *NEA Handbook 1996–1997*, 397.

24. Ibid., *NEA Handbook 1993–1994*, 380.

25. Ibid., West, 19.

26. Ibid.

27. Ibid., *NEA Handbook 1996–1997*, 243.

28. Keith Geiger, interview by George Will, 29 August 1993, interview transcript Federal News Service, ABC "This Week with David Brinkley."

29. Denis P. Doyle, "Where Connoisseurs Send Their Children to School," (Chevy Chase: The Center for Educational Reform, 1995), 4–5.

30. Ibid., 5.

31. Ibid., *NEA Handbook 1996–1997*, 251.

32. Ibid., 247.

33. Ibid., 253.

34. Ibid., 272.

35. Ibid., 257.
36. Ibid., 278.
37. Ibid., 299.
38. Ibid., 330.
39. Ibid., 338.
40. Ibid., *NEA Handbook 1993–1994*, 245.
41. Ibid., *NEA Handbook 1996–1997*, 251-252.
42. Ibid., *NEA Handbook 1993–1994*, 327.
43. Ibid., 327.
44. Ibid., 329.
45. Ibid., *Handbook 1996–1997*, 347.
46. Ibid., 354.
47. Ibid.
48. Ibid., 356.
49. Ibid., 357.
50. Ibid., 359.
51. Ibid.
52. Ibid., 360.
53. *NEA Handbook 1993–1994*, 89.
54. Ibid., 45.
55. Ibid., listed on pages 98 through 153.
56. Ibid., 34.
57. Ibid., 36.
58. Ibid., 37.
59. Ibid., 50.
60. NEA's 1995–1996 LM-2 Labor Organization Annual Report (file number 000-342) as filed with the U.S. Department of Labor, Office of Labor-Management Standards and signed off on 19 December 1996.
61. Charlene K. Haar, Myron Lieberman, and Leo Troy, *The NEA and AFT: Teacher Unions in Power and Politics*, 6.
62. Ibid., 10.
63. Ibid., 6.
64. Sol Stern, "How Teachers' Unions Handcuff Schools," *City Journal NYC* (Spring 1997), 36.
65. Ibid., Haar, Lieberman, and Troy, *The NEA and AFT: Teacher Unions in Power and Politics*, 5.
66. Ibid., 145.

67. Mary Crystal Cage, "A Merger Misfires," *The Chronicle of Higher Education*, 17 February 1995, sec. A, 17.
68. Frank Swoboda, "Teachers' Union Agrees To Merger: San Francisco Locals Enter Pact," *Washington Post*, 11 October 1989, sec. A, 26.
69. Mary Jordan, "For Teachers Union Head, Another Sign of Influence: Merger Abroad Reflects AFT-NEA Cooperation," *Washington Post*, 28 January 1993, sec. A, 3.
70. "Across the USA: News From Every State," *USA Today*, 1 September 1998, p. 8A.
71. Carol Innerst, "Visionary Shanker Still Keeps Focus on Academics: Seeks Impact in Rival NEA," *Washington Times*, 17 July 1994, sec. A, 5.
72. "Q & A: Union Relations," *NEA Today*, April 1994, 33.
73. Edline, 23 August 1990.
74. Maurice R. Berube, "The Powerful Teachers' Unions: Political Clout for the Status Quo," *Commonwealth*, 8 April 1988, 207.
75. Kathy Jones of Concerned Educators Against Forced Unionism in a telephone conversation with the author on 25 July 1995.

Chapter Three

1. Susan P. Choy et al., *Schools and Staffing in the United States: A Statistical Profile, 1990–91* (Washington, D.C.: U.S. Government Printing Office, 1993), v.
2. Ibid., 27.
3. Thomas D. Snyder, Charlene M. Hoffman, and Claire M. Geddes, *Digest of Education Statistics 1996* (Washington, D.C.: U.S. Government Printing Office, 1996), 70.
4. Ibid., 77.
5. Choy et al., *Schools and Staffing in the United States: Statistical Profile*, 27.
6. Snyder, Hoffman, and Geddes, *Digest of Education Statistics 1996*, 1.
7. Ibid., 11.
8. Ibid., 13.
9. Ibid., 74.

10. Thomas D. Snyder, and Charlene M. Hoffman, *Digest of Education Statistics 1993* (Washington, D.C.: U.S. Government Printing Office, 1993), 1.

11. "Education: Benefits and Student Needs Increase the Cost," *Anchorage Daily News,* 27 November 1994, A6.

12. Chester E. Finn, Jr., "The Return of the Dinosaurs," *National Review* (20 September 1993), 3 of Academic Abstracts.

13. Snyder and Hoffman, *Digest of Education Statistics 1993,* 47.

14. Ibid., 74.

15. Ibid., 13.

16. Susan P. Choy et. al., *America's Teachers: Profile of a Profession* (Washington, D.C.: U.S. Government Printing Office, 1993), 8.

17. Snyder, Hoffman, and Geddes, *Digest of Education Statistics 1996,* 79.

18. Ibid., v.

19. U.S. Department of Commerce, Bureau of the Census, *Statistical Abstract of the United States 1994, September 1994,* 18.

20. Susan P. Choy et al., *Schools and Staffing in the United States: A Statistical Profile, 1990–91,* 29.

21. Ibid., v.

22. Charles H. Hammer and Elizabeth Gerald, *Selected Characteristics of Public and Private School Teachers: 1987–88,* 3.

23. Thomas D. Snyder and Charlene M. Hoffman, *Digest of Education Statistics 1993,* 150.

24. Snyder, Hoffman, and Geddes, *Digest of Education Statistics 1996,* 150.

25. Ibid.

26. Ibid.

27. Susan Tifft, Michael Mason, and Janice C. Simpson, "The Lure of the Classroom," *Education,* 13 February 1989, 69.

28. Ibid.

29. Ibid.

30. Ibid.

31. Ibid.

32. Susan P. Choy et al., *Schools and Staffing in the United States: A Statistical Profile, 1990–91,* vi.

33. Ibid., v.

34. Thomas D. Snyder and Charlene M. Hoffman, *Digest of Education Statistics 1993*, 161.

35. Thomas D. Snyder, Charlene M. Hoffman, and Claire M. Geddes, *Digest of Education Statistics 1996* (Washington, D.C.: U.S. Government Printing Office, 1996), 85.

36. Thomas M. Smith et. al., *The Condition of Education 1994*, (Washington, D.C.: U.S. Government Printing Office, 1994), 154.

37. Timothy McConville, letter to the author, 30 April 1997.

38. Susan P. Choy et al., *Schools and Staffing in the United States: A Statistical Profile, 1990–91*, vi.

39. Ibid., 60.

40. Ibid., 61.

41. Ibid., 60.

42. Thomas D. Snyder and Charlene M. Hoffman, *Digest of Education Statistics 1993*, 81.

43. Susan P. Choy et. al., *America's Teachers: Profile of a Profession*, vi.

44. Ibid., 121.

45. Ibid., 120–121.

46. Thomas D. Snyder and Charlene M. Hoffman, *Digest of Education Statistics 1993*, 126.

47. National Education Association, *NEA Handbook 1993–1994*, 341.

48. National Education Association, *NEA Handbook 1993–1994*, 293.

Chapter Four

1. Andrew Bockelman and Joseph P. Overton, *Michigan Education Special Service Association: The MEA's Money Machine* (Midland, Michigan: Mackinac Center of Public Policy, 1993), 10.

2. Myron Lieberman, "NEA-Dominated GOP Teacher Groups Hate Party Principles," *Human Events*, 29 April 1994.

3. Peter Brimelow and Leslie Spencer, "The National Extortion Association," *Forbes* (7 June 1993): 82.

4. Ibid.

5. Ibid.

6. Bockelman and Overton, 10.

7. Ibid.

8. Thomas D. Snyder, Charlene M. Hoffman, and Claire M. Geddes, *Digest of Education Statistics 1996* (Washington, D.C.: U.S. Government Printing Office, 1996), 75.

9. National Education Association, *Handbook 1994–1995* (Washington, D.C.: National Education Association, 1994), 165.

10. Andrew Bockelman and Joseph P. Overton, *Michigan Education Special Services Association: The MEA's Money Machine* (Midland, Michigan: Mackinac Center for Public Policy, 1993), 10.

11. National Education Association, *NEA Handbook 1994–1995*, 251.

12. Glen E. Robinson, "Synthesis of Research on the Effects of Class Size," *Educational Leadership* (April 1990): 81–82.

13. John W. Alspaugh, "The Relationship Between School Size, Student Teacher Ratio and School Efficiency," *Education* (Summer 1994), 600.

14. Ibid., 597–598.

15. "School Promise: Minneapolis Should Bend on Class Size," *Star Tribune*, 9 March 1995, sec. A, 18.

16. National Education Association, *NEA Handbook 1996–1997*, 304.

17. *Collective Bargaining Agreement between Port Angeles School District No. 121 and Port Angeles Education Association*, (Port Angeles, Washington, 1993), 43.

18. Mr. Milton Chappell, telephone conversation with the author on 24 January 1995.

19. Thealan Associates Inc., *Teacher Contract Demands: Analysis and Response for the School Board Negotiator* (Albany, New York: Thealan Associates, 1976), XXVI-D.

20. Ibid., iii.

21. Center for Education Policy and Management, "Contract Administration: Understanding Limitations on Management Rights. A Presenter's Guide. Research Based Training for School Administrators" (National Institute of Education, Washington, D.C., 1983), 12–13.
22. David Tyack and Elisabeth Hansot, *Managers of Virtue: Public School Leadership in America, 1820–1980* (New York: Basic Books, Inc., 1982), 175–176.
23. Nina Bascia, *Unions in Teachers' Professional Lives: Social, Intellectual, and Practical Concerns* (New York: Teachers College, Columbia University, 1994), 31.
24. Ibid., 40.
25. *Agreement by and between the Board of Education Federal Way School District and Federal Way Education Association, effective September 1, 1991 through August 31, 1994 (Federal Way, Washington, 1991)*, 35.
26. "Teachers, Administration Meet Without Progress," *Peninsula Daily News*, 11 October 1995, sec. A, 5.
27. Sam Allis, "Laying Siege to Seniority," *Time*, 23 December 1991, 64.
28. Tyack and Hansot, 96–98.
29. Ibid., 99.
30. National Education Association, *NEA Handbook 1994–1995*, 164.
31. Mary Crystal Cage, "A Merger Misfires," *The Chronicle of Higher Education*, 17 February 1995, sec. A, 17.
32. Ibid., 281.
33. National Education Association, *NEA Handbook 1996–1997*, 292.
34. Ms. Jo Seker, telephone conversation with the author on 25 January 1995.
35. National Education Association, *NEA Handbook 1993–1994*, 307.
36. Ibid., 308.
37. Ibid., 307.
38. Ibid., 308.
39. Ibid.

40. Ibid., 286.

41. Ibid., 246.

42. "Grad Standards: Make Students, Teachers Accountable," *Minneapolis Star Tribune,* 3 January 1995, 8A.

43. Samuel L. Blumenfeld, *NEA: Trojan Horse in American Education* (1984; reprint, Boise, Idaho: The Paradigm Company, 1993), 205.

44. Brimelow and Spencer, "The National Extortion Association?" 80.

45. *Robert Patrick Roesser, Intervenor-Appellant, v. University of Detroit and University of Detroit Professors Union, Defendants-Appellant,* Nos. 89-1084m 89-1226 (United States Court of Appeals, 6th Cir. 1), December 1989.

46. Ibid.

47. Ibid.

48. Dr. Robert Roesser, telephone conversation with the author on 25 January 1995.

49. Mr. James Belhumeur, telephone conversation with the author on 25 January 1995.

50. Ibid.

51. Ibid.

52. Ibid.

53. Ibid.

54. "Union Bosses Sue Teacher for Exercising Freedom of Speech," *Foundation Action* (Springfield, VA.: National Right to Work Legal Defense Foundation, Inc., October 1994), 4.

55. Ibid.

56. Ibid.

57. Dennis Norman , telephone conversation with the author on 13 September 1997.

58. Ibid.

59. Mr. Milton Chappell, telephone conversation with the author on 24 January 1995.

60. Mr. Steve Oban, telephone conversation with the author on 25 January 1995.

61. "Union Dues Settlement Reaches 9,000 Teachers Statewide," *News Release, National Right to Work Legal Defense Foundation, Inc.,* 8 October 1998.

62. Taken from the settlement statement that Stefan Gleason of the National Right to Work Legal Defense Foundation faxed to the author on 8 March 1999, 3.

63. Ibid.

64. *Agreement by and between the Board of Education Federal Way School District and Federal Way Education Association, effective 1 September 1991 through 31 August 1994*, 44.

65. *Collective Bargaining Agreement between Seattle School District No. 1 and SEA Certified Non-Supervisory Employees 1993–1996* (Seattle, 1994), 4.

66. Ibid.

67. Thomas D. Snyder, Charlene M. Hoffman, and Claire M. Geddes, *Digest of Education Statistics 1996* (Washington, D.C.: U.S. Government Printing Office, 1997), 162.

68. NEA's 1995–1996 LM-2 Organization Annual Report (file number 000-342) as filed with the U.S. Department of Labor, Office of Labor-Management Standards as signed off on 19 December 1996, 4.

69. Phyllis Schlafly, "GOP's Task: Cut the Power of the Teacher Unions," *Conservative Chronicle*, 25 January 1995, 6.

70. NEA's 1995–1996 LM-2 Organization Annual Report (file number 000-342) as filed with the U.S. Department of Labor, Office of Labor-Management Standards as signed off on 19 December 1996, 2.

71. Bascia, *Unions in Teachers' Professional Lives: Social, Intellectual, and Practical Concerns*, 29.

72. Ibid.

73. National Institute for Labor Relations Research, *Violence: Organized Labor's Means to an End*, (Springfield, Virginia: National Institute for Labor Relations Research, 1993), 7.

74. Amy Mednick, "Strike Turns Ugly at Area Schools," *News Pilot*, Thursday, 18 May 1989.

75. "Striking Teachers Arrested in Rocking-Throwing Incident," *News Pilot*, 25 May 1989.

76. James Cummings, "Kettering Students Staying Away During Strike," *Dayton Daily News*, 26 January 1991.

77. "Beaver Employee Faces Charge from Strike Violence," *Vindicator*, Youngstown, Ohio, 17 May 1990.
78. Patricia Nugent, "Strike Teachers Trying to Collect on Damages," *Star-Beacon*, 3 February 1988.
79. National Institute for Labor Relations Research, *Violence*, 3.
80. Mr. Michael Antonucci, Director of Education Intelligence Agency, forwarded e-mail on 9 June 1999.
81. "Choice Politics," *Wall Street Journal*, 15 October 1993, sec. A, 10.
82. Mary McGrath, "60% in Poll Back Vouchers for Schools, Jersey City Would Test Program," *The Record*, 4 July 1994, sec. A, 1.
83. "Golden State Opportunity," *National Review*, 1 November 1993, 12.
84. Brimelow and Spencer, "The National Extortion Association," 84.
85. Myron Lieberman, *Public Education: An Autopsy* (Cambridge, Mass.: Harvard University Press, 1993), 303.
86. Jo Seker, telephone conversation with the author on 25 January 1995.
87. Brimelow and Spencer, "The National Extortion Association?," 83.

CHAPTER FIVE

1. Marc Gaswirth and Garry M. Whalen, *Collective Negotiations* (Trenton, New Jersey: New Jersey School Boards Association, 1983), 9–10.
2. Peter Brimelow and Leslie Spencer, "The National Extortion Association," *Forbes*, 7 June 1993, 72.
3. Gaswirth and Whalen, *Collective Negotiations*, 3.
4. Brimelow and Spencer, "The National Extortion Association," 72.
5. Ibid., 74.
6. Peter Baker, "NEA Lauds Fairfax Merit Pay: In Switch, Leader Calls Plan a Model," *The Washington Post*, 28 January 1989, sec. A, 1.

7. Ibid., sec. A, 14.

8. Edward B. Fiske, "Lessons," *The New York Times*, 12 April 1989, sec. B, 6.

9. Ibid.

10. William Raspberry, "Educational Stone Soup?," *The Washington Post*, 15 March 1993, sec. A, 19.

11. DeNeen L. Brown, "Fairfax County School Board Abandons Merit Pay System," *The Washington Post*, 12 March 1993, sec. B, 1.

12. Ibid., Baker, "NEA Lauds Fairfax Merit Pay," sec. A, 1.

13. Peter Baker, "Fairfax Board to Give Top Teachers 9% Bonus," *The Washington Post*, 15 February 1989, sec. A, 1.

14. Peter Baker, "Fairfax Teachers Drop Support of Merit Pay," *The Washington Post*, 16 March 1989, sec. A, 1.

15. Edward B. Fiske, "Lessons: In a Virginia School District, a Bold Experiment in Merit Pay Falters," *The New York Times*, 12 April 1989, sec. B, 6.

16. "Merit Pay Revisited," *The Washington Post*, 26 December 1991, sec. A, 22.

17. DeNeen L. Brown, "Fairfax Teacher Merit Pay Plan May Fall to Budget Ax," *The Washington Post*, 18 February 1992, sec. B, 1.

18. DeNeen L. Brown, "Fairfax Votes to Suspend Merit Pay for Teachers," *The Washington Post*, 19 February 1992, sec. A, 1.

19. Steve Twomey, "There's No Merit in Their Decision," *The Washington Post*, 20 February 1992, sec. B, 1.

20. "An F for Merit in Fairfax Schools?," *The Washington Post*, 15 March 1993, sec. A, 18.

21. Joanna Richardson, "Va. District To Give Bonuses to Top-Rated Teachers," *Education Week*, 25 May 1994, 13.

22. *Looking Back, Thinking Ahead: American School Reform 1993–1995* (Indianapolis: Hudson Institute, 1994), 13–14.

23. Ibid., 14.

24. Ibid.

25. Nancy Bartley, "PE Teachers Key Stumbling Block in Fed. Way School Negotiations," *Seattle Times*, 2 September 1994, sec. B, 1.

26. Ibid.

27. John Gessner, "Dist. 191 Budget Cuts Claim 56 Teachers," *Burnsville This Week*, 26 March 1995, sec. A, 1.

28. Ibid., sec. A, 13.

29. Ibid.

30. Ibid.

31. John Bartlett, *Familiar Quotations* (Boston: Little, Brown and Company, 1980), 609.

32. Caroline Minter Hoxey, "How Teacher Unions Affect Education Production, *Quarterly Journal of Economics* (August 1996), 711.

33. Ibid., 712.

34. "NEA Union Bosses Deny Teacher's Right to Help Students," *Foundation Action* (Springfield, VA: National Right to Work Legal Defense Foundation, 1994), 4.

35. Ibid.

36. *NEA Handbook 1996–1997* (Washington, DC: National Education Association, 1996), 310.

37. Ibid.

38. "Councils, Not Boards, Carry 'Real Authority" in Schools," *The Courier-Journal*, 20 November 1993, p. 1A.

39. Ibid.

40. John E. Chubb and Terry M. Moe, *Politics, Markets, and America's Schools* (Washington, D.C.: The Brookings Institute, 1990), 205.

41. Myron Lieberman, *Public School Choice* (Lancaster, Pennsylvania: Technomic Publishing Company, 1990), 86–87.

42. Bruce Bimber, *School Decentralization* (Santa Monica: Rand, 1993), x, 14–15.

43. Michael E. McGill and John W. Slocum, Jr., *The Smarter Organization* (New York: John Wiley & Sons, Inc., 1994), 16.

44. "How Teachers Erase Boards," *The Wall Street Journal*, 18 April 1994, sec. A, 14.

45. "Far Right Targets School Boards," *NEA Today*, September 1993, 6.

46. Ibid.

47. Ibid.

48. "How Teachers Erase Boards," sec. A, 14.

49 Ibid.

50. Hofstadter, Richard and Walter P. Metzger, *The Development of Academic Freedom in the United States* (New York: Columbia University Press, 1955), 487.

51. *NEA Handbook 1996–1997* (Washington, DC: National Education Association, 1993), 301–302.

52. Ibid.

53. "National Extortion Association—Pro & Con," *Forbes,* 19 July 1993, sec. Aftermath.

54. "Pennsylvania Education Secretary Hickok Criticizes Union President for Urging Teachers to Blast School Choice in Class: 'Union President Gondak is Asking Teachers to Violate Our Trust,'" PRNewswire, Pennsylvania Department of Education Press Release, 8 June 1999, at http://biz.yahoo,com/prnews/990608/pa_hickok_1.html.

55. Charlene K. Haar, *PTA: It's Not "Parents Taking Action"* (Washington, D.C.: Capital Research Center, 1994), 1.

56. Ibid.

57. Ibid.

58. Ibid.

59. Ibid., 3.

60. Ibid.

61. Ibid., 5.

62. Ibid., 5–6.

63. Ibid., 6.

64. Jonathan Riskind and Tim Doulin, "Voucher Backers Eye 1995," *The Columbus Dispatch*, 6 February 1994, sec. A, 1.

CHAPTER SIX

1. Myron Lieberman, *Public Education: An Autopsy* (Cambridge, MA: Harvard University Press, 1993), 62.

2. Jay M. Shafirtz and J. Steven Ott, *Classics of Organization Theory, Second Edition, Revised and Expanded* (Pacific Grove, California: Brooks/Cole Publishing Company, 1987), 305.

3. Ibid., 304–305.
4. David Tyack and Elisabeth Hansot, *Managers of Virtue: Public School Leadership in America, 1820–1980* (New York: Basic Books, 1982), 222.
5. Ibid., 222–223.
6. Steven Goldschmidt, "An Overview of the Evolution of Collective Bargaining and Its Impact on Education." In K. Duckworth and W. DeBevois, eds., *The Effect of Collective Bargaining on School Administrative Leadership*, Eugene, OR: Center for Educational Policy and Management), 3–9.
7. Marc Gaswirth and Garry M. Whalen. *Collective Negotiations.* Trenton, New Jersey: New Jersey School Boards Association, 1983, x.
8. Steven M. Goldschmidt and Leland E. Stuart, "The Extent and Impact of Education Policy Bargaining," *Industrial and Labor Relations Review*, Vol. 39, No. 3, April 1986, 350.
9. Lorraine M. McDonnell, "Political Control and the Power of Organized Teachers," Discussion Draft, RAND Corporation, Santa Monica, California, March 1981, 19.
10. Charles D. King and Mark van de Vall, *Models of Industrial Democracy*, (New York, Mouton Publishers: 1978), Chap. 29, "Roads Toward the Goal," 3–4.
11. Goldschmidt, "An Overview of the Evolution of Collective Bargaining and Its Impact on Education," 5.
12. McDonnell, 15.
13. Harry H. Wellington and Ralph K. Winter, Jr., "The Limits of Collective Bargaining in Public Employment," *Yale Law Journal*, Vol. 78, No. 7, June 1969 1114–1115.
14. Ibid., 1122.
15. Ibid., 1120.
16. Ibid., 1122.
17. Gaswirth and Whalen, 3.
18. Wellington and Winter, Jr., 1116.
19. Ibid., 1122.
20. Ibid., 1124.
21. Ibid., 1111.
22. McDonnell, 31.

23. E. E. Schattschneider, *The Semi-Sovereign People*, Holt, Reinhart, and Winston, New York, 1960, 20, quoted by Lorraine M. McDonnell, "Political Control and the Power of Organized Teachers," Discussion Draft, RAND Corporation, Santa Monica, California, March 1981, 31.

24. Clyde W. Summers, "Public Sector Bargaining: Problems of Governmental Decisionmaking," *University of Cincinnati Law Review*, 44, 1975, 669–670.

25. Wellington and Winter, Jr., 1110.

26. Leo Troy, "The Impact of Public Employee Unionism on the Philosophy and Policies of Organized Labor," *Government Union Review* (Spring 1982), 9.

27. Ibid., 1124.

28. Charlene K. Haar, *PTA: It's Not "Parents Taking Action"* (Washington, D.C.: Capital Research Center, 1994), 5.

29. Kendrick Scott, "The Case Against Collective Bargaining in Public Education," *Government Union Review* (Spring 1982), 19.

30. Edwin Vieira, Jr., *To Break and Control the Violence of Faction: The Challenge to Representative Government from Compulsory Public-Sector Collective Bargaining* (Arlington, VA: Foundation for the Advancement of the Public Trust and Public Service Research Foundation, 1980), 93–94.

31. "Phony 'Arbitrators' Rubber Stamp Union-boss Coercion," *Foundation Action* (Springfield, VA: National Right To Work Legal Defense Foundation, December 1994), 6.

32. Ibid., 6.

33. "The American Arbitration Association: Reserving Big Labor's Forced-Unionism Agenda by Undermining Supreme Court Doctrine," *Issue Briefing Paper* (Springfield, VA: National Right To Work Legal Defense Foundation), 2–3.

34. "School Repair Bill $112 Billion," *Seattle Times*, 1 February 1995, sec. A, 10.

35. Nina Bascia, *Unions in Teachers' Professional Lives* (New York: Teachers College, Columbia University, 1994), 3.

36. Bob Williams, *Washington State's Protected Class III* (Olympia, WA: Evergreen Freedom Foundation, 1995), 1.

37. Ibid., 2.

38. Lieberman, *Public Education: An Autopsy* , 307–308.
39. *Teacher Contract Demands* (Albany, NY: Thealan Associates Inc., 1976), unmarked page.
40. Ibid., unmarked page.
41. Ibid., XIX-D.
42. Keith Ervin, "Unions Hold Key to Educational Reform," *Seattle Times*, 10 August 1994, sec. B, 1.
43. Laurie Blake, "Statewide, School Boards Try to Make Ends Meet," *Star and Tribune*, 6 April 1994, sec. A, 1.
44. Alex Gimarc, "Spending Cuts Can be Made," *Anchorage Daily News*, 16 March 1995, sec. B, 8.
45. William A. Hanbury, "Getting Voters to Say Yes," *The American School Board Journal*, November 1991, 48.
46. Michael Paulson, "Backing May Be Illegal," *Seattle Post-Intelligencer*, 1 March 1995, sec. A, 1.
47. Julie Johnson, "Michigan Teacher to Head Education Union," *New York Times*, 4 July 1989, 30.
48. Allan M. West, *The National Education Association: The Power Base for Education* (New York: The Free Press, 1980), 238.
49. Annual NEA handbooks list, by state and community, the names and locations of UniServ operatives.
50. Myron Lieberman, Charlene Haar, and Leo Troy, *The NEA and AFT: Teacher Unions in Power and Politics* (Rockport, Mass.: Pro>Active Publications, 1994), 31.
51. Information taken from a packet of materials provided by the National Institute for Labor Relations Research: UNISERV, unmarked page.
52. Information taken from a packet of materials provided by the National Institute for Labor Relations Research: UNISERV, III. Statistics.
53. Charlene K. Haar, "Teacher Union Revenues and Political Action," *Government Union Review* (Spring 1994), 24.
54. Ibid., 24–25.
55. Haar, Lieberman, and Troy, 21.
56. Information taken from a packet of materials provided by the National Institute for Labor Relations Research: UNISERV, I. History and Purpose Background Materials.

57. Information taken from a packet of materials provided by the National Institute for Labor Relations Research: UNISERV.

58. *National Education Association Handbook 1994–1995* (Washington, D.C.: National Education Association, 1994), 7.

Chapter Seven

1. William F. Buckley Jr., "What is the NEA All About?," *National Review*, 19 July 1993, 71.

2. Franklin D. Roosevelt's 16 August 1937 letter to L.C. Stewart

3. Ibid.

4. Samuel L. Blumenfeld, *N.E.A. Trojan Horse in American Education* (Boise, Idaho: The Paradigm Company, 1984), 90.

5. "Democrats Love Bureaucrats," *Wall Street Journal*, 22 July 1993, sec. A, 14.

6. Sally D. Reed, *NEA: Propaganda Front of the Radical Left* (Washington, D.C.: National Council for Better Education, 1984), 38.

7. *National Education Association Handbook 1994–1995* (Washington, D.C.: National Education Association, 1994), 294.

8. Sol Stern, "How Teachers' Unions Handcuff Schools," *City Journal NYC* (Spring 1997), 44.

9. "The 1995–96 Resolutions of the National Education Association, *NEA Today*, (September 1995), 43.

10. Ibid., 42.

11. Ibid., 33.

12. Ibid., 32.

13. Ibid., 33.

14. Ibid., 35.

15. Ibid., 42.

16. Ibid.

17. Ibid., 37.

18. *National Education Association Handbook 1994–1995*, 50.

19. Ibid.

20. Ibid.

21. Ibid., 51.

22. Ibid., 50.

23. Ibid., 33.
24. Ibid., 391.
25. Charles R. Babcock, "Contributions to Insiders on Increase," *The Washington Post*, 8 June 1992.
26. Charles R. Babcock, "Both Parties Raise Millions in 'Soft Money,'" *The Washington Post*, 26 July 1992.
27. "The Man from Hope," *NEA Today*, September 1992, 2.
28. Ibid.
29. "Riley's Rally," *Wall Street Journal*, 31 May 1993, sec. A, 14.
30. Ibid.
31. Ibid.
32. Ibid.
33. Ibid.
34. *National Education Association Handbook 1994–1995*, 51.
35. Ibid., 52.
36. Anne Bridgman, "Unions Play Politics," *The American School Board Journal*, November 1991, 43.
37. Ibid., 44.
38. Ibid.
39. Ibid.
40. Ibid.
41. Myron Lieberman, *Public Education: An Autopsy* (Cambridge, Massachusetts: Harvard University Press, 1993), 312.
42. Ibid.
43. Allan M. West, *The National Education Association: The Power Base for Education* (New York: The Free Press, 1980), 201.
44. "Call for the Establishment of a National Bureau of Education," *Education in the United States: A Documentary History, vol. 3 (New York: Random House, 1974)*, 1401.
45. W. Vance Grant, "Statistics in the U.S. Department of Education: Highlights from the Past 120 Years," *120 Years of American Education: A Statistical Portrait*, (Washington D.C., U.S. Department of Education, 1993), 1.
46. David Tyack and Elisabeth Hansot, *Managers of Virtue (New York: Basic Books, 1982)*, 18.
47. W. Vance Grant, 1.
48. Tyack and Hansot, 242.

49. "Fiscal Year 1998 Budget Summary and Background Information," 77.

50. Ibid.

51. Ibid., Appendices, 20.

52. "Call for the Establishment of a National Bureau of Education," 1405.

53. Ibid.

54. Myron Lieberman, Charlene K. Haar, and Leo Troy, *The NEA and AFT: Teacher Unions in Power and Politics* (Rockport, Massachusetts: Pro>Active Publications, 1994), 57.

55. David T. Chester, *Education Department 1990: A Resource Manual for the Federal Education Department* (Washington D.C.: National Center for Education Information, 1990), 7.

56. Ibid., 21.

57. Ibid., 29–32.

58. Ibid., 221–237.

59. Ibid., 167.

60. Ibid.

61. Ibid., 79.

62. Ibid., 61.

63. Ibid., 67.

64. Ibid., 66.

65. Ibid., 138.

66. "Failing to Educate," 10 February 1999, *Online NewsHour* at http://www.pbs.org/newshour/bb/budget/jan-june99/education_2-10.html.

67. Ibid.

68. Ibid.

69. Ibid.

70. "The Nation's Business," 22 February 1999, *Online NewsHour* at http://www.pbs.org/newshour/bb/white_house/jan-june99/clinton_2-22.html.

71. David S. Broder, "School-reform Talk is Easy; Reforming Schools is Hard," *Seattle Times*, 28 February 1999, B6.

72. *Public Schools: Fulfilling the American Dream, Proceedings of the National Education Association, 1993 Representative Assembly* (Washington, D.C.: National Education Association, 1994), 9.

73. Keith Geiger, "The Twin Pillars of Excellence," *NEA Today*, February 1993, 4.

74. Ibid.

75. "Goals 2000: Is This the Most Important Federal Education Legislation in a Generation?," *NEA Today*, May 1994, 3.

76. "Students Model Scientists in GLOBE Program," No. 19 of *Goals 2000: Community Update* (Washington, D.C.: December 1994), 3.

77. "The American People Know Instinctively that Education is the Future," No. 21 of *Goals 2000: Community Update* (Washington, D.C.: February 1995), 1.

78. Ibid.

79. Jeanne Allen and Angela Dale, *The School Reform Handbook: How to Improve Your School* (Washington, D.C.: The Center for Education Reform, 1995), 68.

80. Milton Chappell, memorandum of 27 July 1993 re: Analysis of S.1150 for Compulsory Union Power, to the National Right To Work Legal Defense Foundation, Springfield, Virginia.

81. Ibid.

82. Ibid.

83. Ibid.

84. Jeanne Allen, *Monthly Letter to Friends of the Center for Education Reform*, (Washington, D.C.: The Center for Education Reform), February/March 1995, 6.

85. Stern, 45.

86. Lieberman, 263.

87. Ibid., 261.

88. Lewis J. Perelman, *The "Acanemia" Deception* (Indianapolis: Hudson Institute, 1990), 2.

89. Department of Education, "Fiscal Year 1998 Budget Summary and Background Information," Appendices, 19.

90. Lieberman, 264.

91. Ibid., 264–265.

92. Ibid., 267.

93. Ibid., 303.

94. Ibid., 305.

95. *National Education Association Handbook 1994–1995*, 287.

96. Ibid., 303.

97. Jeanne Allen, *The School Reform Handbook* (Washington, D.C.: The Center for Education Reform, 1995), 67.
98. Ibid., 68.
99. NEA Journal, December 1967, 34.
100. Thomas D. Snyder, Charlene M. Hoffman, and Claire M. Geddes, Digest of Educational Statistics 1996 (Washington, D.C.: National Center for Educational Statistics, 1996), 34.

CHAPTER EIGHT

1. Allan M. West, *The National Education Association: The Power Base for Education* (New York: The Free Press, 1980), 212.
2. Alexander Hamilton, James Madison, and John Jay, *The Federalist* (Franklin Center, Pennsylvania: The Franklin Library, 1977), 335.
3. Phyllis Schlafly, "Controversial History Standards Fight Back," *Conservative Chronicle*, 29 March 1995, 24.
4. W. Edwards Deming, *Out of the Crisis* (Cambridge, Mass: Massachusetts Institute of Technology, 1986), 302.
5. Chester E. Finn, Jr., *We Must Take Charge: Our Schools and Our Future* (New York: The Free Press, 1991), 199.
6. Charles S. Clark, "Education Standards: Will National Standards Improve U.S. Schools?" *Congressional Quarterly*, 11 March 1994, 217.
7. Sol Cohen, ed., *Education in the United States: A Documentary History, Volume 3* (New York: Random House, 1974), 1932.
8. E.D. Hirsch, Jr., *Cultural Literacy: What Every American Needs to Know* (New York: Vantage Books, 1988), 117.
9. Cohen, 2281.
10. Clark, 217.
11. Ibid.
12. Schlafly, 24.
13. Ibid.
14. David Tyack and Elisabeth Hansot, *Managers of Virtue* (New York: Basic Books, 1982), 60.
15. Clark, 217.
16. *National Education Association Handbook 1996–1997* (Washington, D.C.: National Education Association. 1996), 274.

17. Ibid., 299.
18. Carol Innerst, "Little Merit Seen in Process of Setting Teaching Standards," *Washington Times*, 18 May 1994, sec. A, 10.
19. Ibid.
20. Keith Geiger, "President's Viewpoint: Taking Charge of Our Profession," *NEA Today*, April 1993, 2.
21. *National Education Association Handbook 1994–1995*, 7.
22. Innerst, sec. A. 10.
23. Ibid.
24. Ibid.
25. Ibid.
26. Ibid.
27. Ibid.
28. Keith Geiger, "President's Viewpoint: A National Certificate," *NEA Today*, May 1994, 2.
29. Milton Chappell, memorandum of 27 July 1993 re: Analysis of S.1150 for Compulsory Union Power, to the National Right to Work Legal Defense Foundation, Springfield, Virginia.
30. Ibid.
31. John E. Chubb and Terry M. Moe, *Politics, Markets, and America's Schools* (Washington, D.C.: The Brookings Institute, 1990), 205.
32. Ibid., 204.
33. Ibid.
34. *National Education Association Handbook 1993–1994* (Washington, D.C.: National Education Association. 1993), 362.
35. Ibid.
36. Ibid., 363.
37. Ibid.
38. *National Education Association Handbook 1994–1995*, 362.
39. Ibid.
40. *National Education Association Handbook 1996–1997* (Washington, D.C.: National Education Association. 1996), 369.
41. Jay Mathew, "The Entrepreneur's Grade Expectations: Whittle's Mix of Education and Enterprise Faces Tests from Teachers and Financiers," *Washington Post*, 29 July 1994, sec. B, 1.
42. Ibid.
43. Ibid.

44. Ibid.
45. Ibid.
46. Joe Mandese, "Whittle Suffers New Woes as NEA Targets Sponsors," *Advertising Age*, 11 July 1994, 40.
47. Ibid.
48. Carol Innerst, "Teacher Union Lashes Critics," *The Washington Times*, 5 July 1994.
49. Duncan Maxwell Anderson and Michael Warsaw, "Whacked by the Government, the Media, and Educators," *Success*, April 1996, 36.
50. Ibid., 37.
51. Rance Crain, "Whittle, O.J. Tirades Hide NEA Blemishes," *Advertising Age*, 18 July 1994, 16.
52. Shirley D. McCune, *Guide to Strategic Planning for Educators* (Alexandria, VA.: Association for Supervision and Curriculum and Development, 1986), v.

Chapter Nine

1. John E. Chubb and Terry Moe, *Politics, Markets, and America's Schools* (Washington, D.C.: The Brookings Institute, 1990), 3.
2. Kuhn, Thomas S., *The Structure of Scientific Revolutions* (Chicago: The University of Chicago Press, 1970), 68.
3. *The Edison Project* (Knoxville: The Edison Project), 2.
4. Marvin R. Weisbord, *Productive Workplaces* (San Francisco: Jossey-Bass Publishers, 1989), 24–49.
5. Julie Johnson, "Michigan Teacher to Head Education Union," *New York Times*, 4 July 1989, 30.
6. Kuhn, 18.
7. *National Education Association Handbook 1994–1995* (Washington, D.C.: National Education Association, 1994), 166–167.
8. Emily Feistritzer, "Does the NEA Really Speak for Teachers?" *Wall Street Journal*, 30 June 1989, A12.
9. Ibid.
10. Kuhn, 186.
11. Ibid.
12. David Tyack and Elisabeth Hansot, *Managers of Virtue* (New York: Basic Books, Inc., 1982), 3.

13. Ibid., 7.
14. Ibid., 101.
15. Ibid., 117.
16. Thomas D. Snyder, *120 Years of American Education: A Statistical Portrait* (Washington, D.C.: The National Center for Educational Statistics, 1993), 56.
17. Thomas D. Snyder, et al, *Digest of Educational Statistics 1993* (Washington, D.C.: National Center for Educational Statistics, 1993), 12.
18. *National Education Association Handbook 1994–1995*, 167.
19. David Boaz, "The Public School Monopoly," *Vital Speeches of the Day*, 1 June 1992, 508.
20. Michael B. Katz, *The Irony of Early School Reform* (Cambridge, Massachusetts: Harvard University Press, 1968), 159.
21. Myron Lieberman, *Public Education: An Autopsy* (Cambridge, Massachusetts: Harvard University Press, 1993), 285.
22. Lorraine M. McDonnell and Anthony Pascal, *Teacher Unions and Educational Reform* (Washington, D.C.: Rand Corporation, 1988), viii.
23. Lieberman, 279.
24. David P. Crandall, Jeffrey W. Eiseman, and Karen Seashore Louis, "Strategic Planning Issues That Bear on the Success of School Improvement Efforts," *Educational Administrative Quarterly* (Summer 1986), 25.
25. Tyack and Hansot, 206.
26. Joe Klein, "Cities, Heal Thyselves," *Newsweek*, 5 July 1993, 24.
27. Sol Stern, "How Teachers' Unions Handcuff Schools," *City Journal* (Spring 1997): 44.
28. Boaz, 507.
29. Edward H. Crane, "On the Problem of America's Policy Myopia," *Vital Speeches of the Day*, 1 January 1987, 185.
30. Boaz, 508.
31. Ibid.
32. Thomas D. Snyder, Charlene M. Hoffman, and Claire M. Geddes, *Digest of Educational Statistics 1996* (Washington, D.C.: National Center for Educational Statistics, 1996), 166.
33. Ibid.
34. Boaz, 508.

35. Joseph Sobran, "People's Consent Doesn't Matter," *Conservative Chronicle*, 31 July 1991, 1.
36. Lewis J. Perelman, *The "Acanemia" Deception* (Indianapolis: Hudson Institute, 1990), 1.
37. Ibid., 1–2.
38. Ibid., 2.
39. Boaz, 509.
40. *Looking Back, Thinking Ahead* (Indianapolis: Hudson Institute, 1994), 22.
41. *National Education Association Handbook 1994–1995*, 369.
42. Ibid., 256.

Chapter Ten

1. Chris Whittle, *The Edison Project* (Knoxville, Tennessee: The Edison Project), 3.
2. Joe Mandese, "Whittle Suffers New Woes as NEA Targets Sponsors," *Advertising Age*, 11 July 1994, 40.
3. "Edison Project's For-Profit Schools Come Back in Size and Test Scores," *Star Tribune*, 2 June 1997, A7.
4. Ibid.
5. Ibid.
6. *An Institution at Risk: An External Communications Review of the National Education Association* (Washington, D.C.: The Kamber Group, 1997), 3.
7. Ibid., i.
8. Janice A. Moo, taken from the discussion of 29 May 1995.
9. Thomas Kuhn, *The Structure of Scientific Revolutions* (Chicago: The University of Chicago Press, 1970), 186.
10. Joanne Hatton, "Restore Public Schools to the People," *Alberta Report*, 1 November 1993.
11. David Tyack and Elisabeth Hansot, *Managers of Virtue* (New York: Basic Books, Inc., 1982), 248.
12. David Boaz, "The Public School Monopoly," *Vital Speeches of the Day*, 1 June 1992, 509.
13. *The Book of the States*, (Lexington, Kentucky: Council of State Governments, 1990), 267 and 273.

14. Boat, 509.
15. Harry Esteve, "Fractious House Passes Bill Targeting Unions," *The Register-Guard*, 9 May 1995, sec. A, 1.
16. Ibid.
17. Ibid.
18. Ibid., sec. A, 9.
19. Ibid.
20. *National Education Association Handbook 1994–1995* (Washington, D.C.: National Education Association, 1994), 271.
21. Ibid.
22. Grover G. Norquist, "Home Rule," *The American Spectator*, June 1994, 52.
23. Ibid.
24. Ibid.
25. Ibid., 52–53.
26. Ibid., 53.
27. Ibid., 53, 91.
28. John E. Chubb and Terry M. Moe, *Politics, Markets, and America's Schools* (Washington, D.C.: The Brookings Institute, 1990), 140.
29. Ibid., 141.
30. Ibid.
31. Ibid., 229.
32. Ibid., 153.
33. Boaz, 509.
34. Chubb and Moe, 217.
35. Ibid.
36. *National Education Association Handbook 1993–1994*, 8.
37. *National Education Association Handbook 1994–1995*, 188.
38. *The Congressional Quarterly*, 27 April 1991.

CHAPTER ELEVEN

1. John E. Chubb and Terry Moe, *Politics, Markets, and America's Schools* (Washington, D.C.: The Brookings Institution, 1990), 226.
2. Department of Education, "Fiscal Year 1998 Budget summary and Background Information," Appendices, 20.

3. Jeanne Allen, *Monthly Letter to Friends of the Center of Education Reform*, Back-To-School, 1998, The Center for Education Reform, Washington, D.C., ii.

4. "Democrats Love Bureaucrats," *The Wall Street Journal* 22 July 1993, sec. A, 14.

5. Ibid., 74.

6. Frank W. Andritzky and Joseph G. Andritzky, "The *Enmons* Loophole: A Need to Amend the Hobbs Act," *Government Union Review* (Fall 1986), 34.

7. Ibid.

8. Ibid., 34–34.

9. Chubb and Moe, 224.

10. Edwin Vieira, Jr., *To Break and Control the Violence of Faction: The Challenge to Representative Government from Compulsory Public-Sector Collective Bargaining* (Arlington, VA: Foundation for the Advancement of the Public Trust and Public Service Research Foundation, 1980), 76.

11. Ibid., 74.

12. Chubb and Moe, 224.

13. "School Choice is Working," *The Washington Times*, 14 July 1997.

14. Sol Stern, "The Schools That Vouchers Built," *Investor's Business Daily*, Wednesday, 3 March 1999, A24.

15. Ibid.

16. Ibid.

17. Thomas D. Snyder, Charlene M. Hoffman, and Claire M. Gedds, *Digest of Educational Statistics* (Washington, D.C.: U.S. Government Printing Office, 1996), 71.

18. Sally D. Reed, *NEA: Propaganda Front of the Radical Left* (Tacoma, WA: Pacific Lutheran University, 1984), 127.

19. Peter Schmidt, "Earnings Appropriations: States Link Spending on Colleges to Progress in Meeting Specific Goals," *The Chronicle of Higher Education*, 24 May 1996, A23.

20. West, 233.

21. Ibid., 233–234.

22. Lawrence W. Reed, "Michigan's Teacher Bargaining Law: A Model for Illinois," 12 August 1994, *A Heartland Perspective* at http://www.heartland.org.

23. Robert Gavin, "Teacher-pay plan gets Locke's backing," 10 April 1999, Global Seattle Plus Newsline, http://www.seattle-pi.com/pi/local/gary07.shtml.

24. Richard Hofstadter and Walter P. Metzger, *The Development of Academic Freedom in the United States* (New York: Columbia University Press, 1955), 481.

25. Sol Stern, "How Teachers' Unions Handcuff Schools," *City Journal* (Spring 1997), 4t.

26. Ibid.

27. Ibid.

28. *Looking Back, Thinking Ahead* (Indianapolis: Hudson Institute, 1994), 17.

29. Brimelow and Spencer, 81.

Index

....

the Deaf, 170
National Treasury Employees
  Union NTEU, 136
NEA: accountability, 71; centralization, 11, 25, 33, 213-
  215; child and, 51, 102-106,
  115-16, 217; curriculum,
  107-108, 190; Democratic
  party and, 49; extortion techniques, 74, 199-201, 252,
  275; forced membership, 19,
  27, 29, 49, 70, 72-80, 82-83,
  102-106, 260-61; goals of,
  xi, 254-55; incompetence
  desired, 67-68, 70; legal tactics, xv, 31, 76-77; licensure
  authority, 28, 70-72; local
  pressure, 30-33, 94, 232;
  negotiations procedures, 51,
  55, 58, 127, 137-38; political
  purposes of, 9, 33, 49, 164-
  67, 238; self protection, 21,
  61-63, 93, 234; social
  agenda, 13, 15-16, 79, 82,
  160-61, 162-63, 166; socialism and, 11, 15, 127; spending and, 33, 132, 137; strikes
  and, 84-85; structure of, 3, 5,
  20, 21-22, 27-28, 68-69,
  103; taxes and, xiii, 10, 14,
  26, 82, 83, 130, 245, 252,
  261; teachers and, 32, 64-67,
  68, 102-106, 182, 211; universities and, 68-69, 87; violence and, 84
negotiations, 64, 143-44, 146;
  arbitration, 134-36, 273-74;

collective bargaining, 118
  126, 130-31, 138-43, 258-
  59, 269; conflict in, 31, 151-
  53; limits on, 272-73
Nichols, Mary-Jo, 75
Norman, Dennis J., 77
Norquist, Grover, 240

Ohio Education Association,
  119
Oregon, University of, 115

PAC, 165-67
Parent-Teacher Association,
  106, 116-18, 277
Parks, Anne, 74
Pascal, Anthony, 216
Pell Grants, 170
Perelman, Lewis, 224
Philip Morris, 200
physical education, 102-103
political theory, 193
prisons, 227
private schools, 70, 262, 229-
  30
Professional Standards Boards,
  69
Proposition 176, 86, 117
Puerto Rico, 24, 26

race riots, 6
Reed, Sally D.: *NEA:
  Propaganda Front of the
  Radical Left*, 161, 263
religion, state and, 246
research, educational, 181-85
Reuther, Walter, 13